"The Strains of Eloquence"

"The Strains of Eloquence"
EMERSON AND HIS SERMONS

Wesley T. Mott

THE PENNSYLVANIA STATE UNIVERSITY PRESS
University Park and London

Library of Congress Cataloging-in-Publication Data

Mott, Wesley T.
The strains of eloquence : Emerson and his sermons
Wesley T. Mott.
p.   cm.
Bibliography: p.
Includes index.
ISBN 0-271-00660-9
1. Sermons, American—History and criticism.
2. Unitarian Universalist churches—Sermons—History and criticism.
3. Emerson, Ralph Waldo, 1803–1882—Contributions in preaching.
I. Title.
BV4208.U6M68   1989
252'.08—dc19
88–28123
CIP

To my parents,
Theodore W. and Shirley Hanson Mott

my wife, Sandy

and my children,
Nathaniel and Sarah

Contents

Acknowledgments

To the extent that this study escapes the trap of what Emerson called "mere think[ing]," I am indebted to many colleagues and friends who have made scholarship collaborative and fulfilling. Norman Pettit introduced me to Emerson's sermons in a graduate seminar at Boston University and has shaped my understanding of the Puritan context. For indispensable advice and encouragement at several stages along the way, I thank also William R. Bernhagen, Kent Ljungquist, Joel Myerson, David Robinson, Merton M. Sealts, Jr., Ruth L. Smith, Kevin Van Anglen, and Albert J. von Frank. The professional skill of Philip Winsor, Senior Editor at the Penn State Press, and of Cherene Holland, Copyeditor, has been much appreciated.

In slightly different form, chapter 1 originally appeared in *Emerson Centenary Essays*, ed. Joel Myerson (copyright © 1982 by the Board of Trustees, Southern Illinois University–Carbondale. Reprinted by permission of the publishers); chapter 7, in *American Literature* (Duke University Press, 1978); and part of chapter 3 as the introduction to an edition of Emerson's Sermon No. XLIII, a pilot for *The Complete Sermons of Ralph Waldo Emerson*, in *Studies in the American Renaissance 1985*, ed. Joel Myerson (University Press of Virginia, 1985). I thank the editors and publishers for their cooperation.

Emerson's manuscript sermons are quoted by permission of the Ralph Waldo Emerson Memorial Association and of the Houghton Library, Harvard University. Rodney G. Dennis, Curator of Manuscripts, and the Houghton staff always have been gracious and help-ful. A letter from Peter Bulkeley to John Cotton is quoted by permis-sion of the Trustees of the Boston Public Library. Material from the Second Church Records, housed at the Massachusetts Historical Society, is quoted by permission of The First and Second Church in Boston. I thank also the Special Collections Division of Mugar Memorial Library, Boston University, for access to its splendid col-lection of seventeenth-century Puritan sermons; and the State His-torical Society of Wisconsin and the American Antiquarian Society, Worcester, Massachusetts, for generous use of their unmatched hold-ings in nineteenth-century Americana.

Research was assisted by a fellowship from the American Council of Learned Societies under a program funded by the National Endow-ment for the Humanities, and by an NEH Travel to Collections grant. This support is gratefully acknowledged.

My wife, Sandy, has helped with research as well as the manu-script, and my children, Natt and Sarah, busy with their own scholar-ship, have prodded and supported me. They have made it all worth-while.

Abbreviations

The following abbreviations are used throughout this volume:

CW   *The Collected Works of Ralph Waldo Emerson.* Edited by
       Alfred R. Ferguson et al. 4 vols. to date. Cambridge: Harvard
       Univ. Press, 1971– .

EL   *The Early Lectures of Ralph Waldo Emerson.* Edited by
       Stephen E. Whicher, Robert E. Spiller, and Wallace E. Wil-
       liams. 3 vols. Cambridge: Harvard Univ. Press, 1959–71.

J   *Journals of Ralph Waldo Emerson.* Edited by Edward Waldo
       Emerson and Waldo Emerson Forbes. 10 vols. Boston:
       Houghton Mifflin, 1909–14.

JMN   *The Journals and Miscellaneous Notebooks of Ralph Waldo
       Emerson.* Edited by William H. Gilman et al. 16 vols. Cam-
       bridge: Harvard Univ. Press, 1960–82.

L   *The Letters of Ralph Waldo Emerson.* Edited by Ralph L.
       Rusk. 6 vols. New York: Columbia Univ. Press, 1939.

Life *The Life of Ralph Waldo Emerson,* by Ralph L. Rusk. New
       York: Charles Scribner's Sons, 1949.

W   *The Complete Works of Ralph Waldo Emerson.* Edited by Edward Waldo Emerson. 12 vols. Centenary Edition. Boston: Houghton Mifflin, 1903–4.

YES   *Young Emerson Speaks: Unpublished Discourses on Many Subjects.* Edited by Arthur Cushman McGiffert, Jr. Boston: Houghton Mifflin, 1938.

Note: Following Emerson's practice, all but some of the late sermons are identified by Roman numerals. The forthcoming *Complete Sermons of Ralph Waldo Emerson* will uniformly use Roman numerals, since this was not only Emerson's usual habit but also customary in published nineteenth-century sermons.

Emerson kept a Preaching Record detailing the date and place he delivered each sermon. He rarely titled them. Unless otherwise indicated, short titles used in this study are those provided by McGiffert in *YES.*

Quotations from Sermon No. XLIII in chapter 3 are from the text in my "From Natural Religion to Transcendentalism: An Edition of Emerson's Sermon No. 43," *Studies in the American Renaissance 1985,* ed. Joel Myerson (Charlottesville: University Press of Virginia, 1985), 14–26. Unless otherwise noted, sermon quotations are from manuscript.

Most articles and reviews in the *Christian Examiner* and the *North American Review* appeared unsigned. Authors' names, supplied without brackets in the Notes and Bibliography, were identified by William Cushing, whose "Indexes" (1878–79) are reprinted in Kenneth Walter Cameron, *Research Keys to the American Renaissance.*

Introduction

Emerson as Preacher

Lecturing on "Emerson as Preacher" before the Concord School of Philosophy in 1884, Elizabeth Palmer Peabody declared that "Mr. Emerson was always pre-eminently the preacher to his own generation and future ones, but as much—if not more—out of the pulpit as in it; faithful unto the end to his early chosen profession and the vows of his youth."[1] Peabody did not speak simply as one who had felt the moral force of Ralph Waldo Emerson's mature lectures and essays, for she had actually heard him preach from the pulpit (although because she attended William Ellery Channing's church, she did not hear Emerson during his tenure as minister of Boston's Second Church from 11 March 1829 to 28 October 1832). Following Emerson's European trip, she heard his eulogy for his friend and former parishioner George Sampson (3 August 1834), and was so moved that she frequently traveled to East Lexington in the following years when Emerson supplied that pulpit. Moreover, Emerson let her read his sermons in manuscript, and though she came to regard poetry as Emerson's true medium, she pronounced the sermons "all as truly transcendental as any of his later lectures and writings in prose or verse; if a volume of them could be printed to-day in their own form, it would interpret his later revelations, of which they are but a varied expression, and be of great advantage to a certain class of minds."[2]

Over fifty years would pass before twenty-five of Emerson's sermons would be edited by Arthur Cushman McGiffert, Jr., in *Young Emerson Speaks*. But modern scholars, who would consider it irresponsible hyperbole to call the sermons "transcendental," have been slow even to examine whether they do indeed have any meaningful connection with Emerson's "later revelations." Kenneth Walter Cameron renewed the challenge in 1956, announcing that the unpublished sermons are a "rich quarry" of biographical and historical information, and hinting that they offer a remarkable view of Emerson's developing ideas and literary techniques.[3]

Yet while we have had major editions of Emerson's journals, letters, lectures, and essays, only twenty-seven of approximately one hundred and seventy Emerson sermons have been published, and these have received scant attention.[4] "Still greatly needed by Emersonians," according to Merton M. Sealts, Jr., "is a complete edition of Emerson's sermons," a need soon to be met by the four-volume edition forthcoming from the University of Missouri Press.[5]

The present study taps certain veins of this Emerson quarry to examine ways in which his sermons prefigure his great essays, and to explore the integrity of the sermons themselves as touchstones in his personal, vocational, and literary growth.

The past thirty years have seen a thorough revaluation of the Unitarian milieu that nourished Emerson and, in his ultimate turning away from formal religion, contributed to the flowering of Transcendentalism.[6] Though these studies focused on leading Unitarians of the day and resurrected relatively obscure clergymen in charting the course of Unitarianism, they gave little specific attention to the man who, from our perspective, was the key figure in the drama and less to his unpublished sermons. For too long, moreover, Emersonians eager to start with the exuberant addresses and essays of the 1830s have been satisfied with the notion that nothing in Emerson's career as a minister became him like the leaving it.

We have cherished the notion that publication of *Nature* in 1836 signaled a Romantic "emergence" from self-doubt and from confining doctrines and institutions. Emerson's resignation of his only full-time pastorate in October 1832 has been seen as a sloughing off of religious orthodoxy and stifling convention, a gesture sealed by his Ishmael-like departure on a sea voyage to Europe that Christmas. Consequently, the only Emerson sermon until recently considered worthy of serious attention was "The Lord's Supper," delivered on

9 September 1832 to explain his pending resignation of the Second Church pastorate.

The need for closer attention to the sermons is underscored by recent directions in Emerson studies. Owing largely to publication of the early volumes of *The Journals and Miscellaneous Notebooks*, we have discovered that Emerson was not simply a rebel or a sage, but that he had been a brooding, searching young man whose self-conscious gropings toward eloquence are an intriguing prelude to the great Transcendentalist essays. Joel Porte's *Representative Man* is particularly sensitive to the turmoil of young Emerson; and the claim of Gay Wilson Allen's *Waldo Emerson: A Biography* to supersede Ralph L. Rusk's *The Life of Ralph Waldo Emerson* as the standard biography rests largely on Allen's heavy reliance on *JMN*.[7]

Despite growing interest in the private musings of young Emerson, little corresponding attention has been paid to his early public performances. Yukio Irie's *Emerson and Quakerism* was the first critical study to use the sermons extensively, but it makes the rather reductive argument that the sermons prove Emerson to have been a latent Quaker.[8] Sue Kelsey Tester's valuable dissertation is a wide-ranging analysis of the biographical and Unitarian sources of the sermons as well as their impact on Emerson's later writings.[9] A useful calendar of the manuscript sermons has been prepared by William B. Barton, Jr.[10] And David Robinson, in *Apostle of Culture*, has given us the first comprehensive study of Emerson's ministry, demonstrating that Emerson's ongoing concern with self-culture, inherited from his Unitarian background, makes for a previously overlooked continuity in his entire career. The distinct stages postulated by Stephen Whicher (*Freedom and Fate*, 1953) to explain Emerson's intellectual development have tended to obscure the sophistication, vitality, and drama of Emerson's early and late work.[11] Whicher remains one of our most perceptive guides to Emerson, but all future studies of Emerson's ministry, platform style, and evolving ideas will be indebted to Robinson's work.

Claims for the significance and inherent quality of the sermons must, of course, be tempered. Some are limp exercises reflecting the constraints of writing-to-order on a regular basis; some are one-time occasional pieces, curiosities. Some are interesting chiefly for historical reasons, revealing Emerson addressing issues being debated in the contemporary Unitarian pulpit and in the pages of the denomination's "official" periodical, *The Christian Examiner*. Others are stirring, even impassioned, oratory. Some of the sermons account for significant gaps in Emerson's journalizing (*JMN* volume

3); for though many of the early, and some of the late, sermons are derived from the journals, Emerson occasionally neglected his journal as he came to write out his sermons from scratch. And many of the sermons, including several from the first half of his brief ministry, Emerson continued to preach as a supply minister during the late 1830s, the period of the great Transcendentalist essays and addresses. The continuities of vision and technique are often striking. In ways crucial to his later vision and artistic power, the ministry, as no other occupation could have, afforded Emerson the chance to define his values and self-image and to discover his voice.

What needs to be stressed is that Emerson's sermons are more than a repository of historical and autobiographical nuggets, more than merely warmed-over journal stuff. The sermons are a brilliant young mind's dramatic encounter with personal doubt and ambition and with urgent issues of theology, power, and expression, all carried out before a very real audience, an encounter that indelibly stamped the shape of Emerson's mind and career.

"The Strains of Eloquence"

Viewed from the perspective of his ministry, Emerson's "emergence"[12] appears not as a bursting forth of a full-blown Transcendentalist, but as an evolution, an organic outgrowth from a culture that nurtured while it confined. Nothing more dramatically links young Emerson's gathering strength as a thinker and writer with his whole career than his early aspiration to "put on eloquence as a robe" (*JMN* 2:242). His youth marked by self-doubt, Emerson experienced a vocational, intellectual, and personal identity crisis at Harvard Divinity School. But "eloquence," as he came to understand it, embodied the complex personal and public values that fostered his emergence as man and artist.

In the spring of 1824, Emerson revealed his fear of inadequacy in a well-known weighing of vocational options: "I cannot dissemble," he wrote, "that my abilities are below my ambition" (*JMN* 2:238). He lacked the "reasoning faculty" needed for philosophy, but theology, he went on, "is from everlasting to everlasting 'debateable Ground' "—meaning, essentially, that it does not require decisiveness, "outward use . . . or the power to act"; rather, theology seemed to rely on "a sort of moral imagination," a "faculty . . . akin to the higher flights of the fancy." After this remarkable assessment, he noted that law and medicine both demand self-confidence, presence, and "a logical mode of thinking & speaking—which I do not possess, & may not reasonably hope to obtain."

"But in Divinity," he declared, "I hope to thrive." And in a rare reference to his father, he continued: "I inherit from my sire a formality of manner & speech, but I derive from him or his patriotic parent a passionate love for the strains of eloquence." This allusion is often regarded as a backhanded slap at the legacy of his father and his father's generation: Reserve is the trait definitely assigned to William, who died when Waldo was only eight years old, depriving his fourth child of the chance to compete with a real father in the process of coming to manhood, and who is here "punished" by the son in having to share with *his own* Revolutionary father the credit for transmitting genuine fervor through Emerson genes. What is important, however, is Waldo's positive sense of a lineage giving approval, form, and substance to inchoate stirrings in his own heart.

Eloquence is related, in the passage that follows, to an adolescent vision of moral purity, heroism, glorious sacrifice. Emerson fancies himself "the believer (if not the dupe) of brilliant promises, and can respect myself as the possessor of those powers which command the reason & passions of the multitude." This fantasy of power and control suggests that Emerson did *not* approach the ministry with reluctance, or with fear of being smothered by formality and convention. On the contrary, pulpit eloquence seemed to offer flexibility, *freedom* from commitment to elaborate doctrines or from having to try out the rational, social, competitive skills he knew his temperament lacked. Emerson continued for years to fret about his worthiness and about issues of religious belief. But at the outset the ministry seemed to offer a haven for his insecure, ingratiating qualities and promised instead a chance to wield power over others not only through the authority of office but through rhetorical masks and personae that would veil his vulnerable real self. Indeed, Emerson *expected* "that my profession shall be my regeneration of mind, manners, inward & outward estate; or rather my starting point, for I have hoped to put on eloquence as a robe" (*JMN* 2:239).

The image of the robe has led many readers to conclude that young Emerson's sense of rhetoric was one of self-conscious, artificial formalism and display. And indeed his early dreams of eloquence are often characterized by adolescent posing and strutting.[13] But from his first reflections on the subject, he viewed the goal of oratory as moral conversion with millennial stakes. At the age of seventeen, for example, he heard a sermon by Edward Everett—"one of his most (perhaps the most) eloquent efforts" (*JMN* 1:44)—on the importance of charity. The next day Emerson speculated that a "secret of the art of eloquence" was to tap and move unconscious springs of human affections. Yet of "this awakening but ambiguous charm," he declared, "I dare not subjoin an example." In the fashion of a Hawthorne narrator, Emerson's imagined probing of the human heart mingles with a sense of the necessary isolation of a budding artist to engender guilt. In practice, however, the preaching tradition Emerson inherited proved indispensable not so much for specific literary forms and devices as for the larger scope it afforded of a role with legitimate influence, importance, and power.

Emerson's roots in liberal Christianity have been traced most fully to William Ellery Channing (1780–1842). As Lewis Simpson has reminded us, Channing himself "had been in the pulpit almost a decade when Emerson's father died."[14] William Emerson, minister of historic First Church in Boston, was a classic example of the clerical tradition Waldo inherited, and the post-Revolutionary anxieties William sought to reconcile were in many ways internalized by his son.

Believing character, perception, and articulation to be ineluctably linked, liberal theologians of the early republic yoked pulpit oratory to the maintenance of true virtue, civil order, America's providential destiny, and (sometimes almost as an afterthought) the Christian revelation. The newness of the nation combined with lingering memories of French radicalism, the spectre of the Whiskey Rebellion, bitter domestic political debate, and a perceived loss of private and public virtue to make Republicans and Federalists alike wary, in John R. Howe's words, of "the essential frailty and impermanence of republican governments."[15] Waldo's own sermons, reflecting the added tensions of Jacksonian politics, frequently invoke the terms "party" and "sect" as bywords for social evil. A staunch Federalist, William had posited the solution in almost Jeffersonian terms: "It is piety . . . which, by promoting the virtue of individuals, operates the salvation and happiness of the community," leading to proper regulation of wealth, power, charity, education, arts and letters, and everything else William valued as essential to the survival of a vulnerable republic.[16]

Conscious of the connection between content, style, and character, William's generation of Unitarians expected rationality and decorum in the minister as well as in his sermons. In his *Historical Sketch of the First Church in Boston*, for example, he perceived a new version of Antinomianism in the "loose, incoherent" sermons of Whitefield revivalism, which stood in contrast to the "cool and moderate strain of preaching" he favored.[17] Viewing the state of the soul and the soul of the state as inherently linked, contributors to the *Monthly Anthology* tended to conflate political and pulpit eloquence. In repeatedly scoring the irrationality and violence of democratic demagoguery, they were expressing the fear that the republic could be undermined by irresponsible, self-serving rhetoric, much as liberal Christians like William Emerson feared that emotionally heated revivalistic preaching could lead to spiritual confusion and social chaos. John Quincy Adams was typical of William's contemporaries who looked to pulpit oratory for order: "Religion indeed has opened one new avenue to the career of eloquence," he wrote, an avenue opened "by the Founder himself."[18]

William too had a high conception of the Christian minister, a figure whose many roles and duties are reflected in the extraordinary diversity—some say scattering—of William's talents. In an ordination sermon for a colleague, William noted that while a minister's "natural appetites and feelings are the same, as those of mankind in general," he is still responsible for "the dissemination of truth." His burden as a moral guide is to "become all things to all men"; a kind of representative good man, he must cultivate "knowledge . . . piety . . . meekness . . . sobriety . . . heavenlymindedness . . . sympathy . . . industry." The work of a minister is nothing less, he wrote, than "the reformation and felicity of his fellowmen" and the proclamation of the promise of "eternal life."[19] A minister, he wrote in tribute to another colleague, has the prophetic mission of preaching the gospel of Christ crucified; yet, as a paragon of virtue and order, he must also be "a gentleman, [of] benevolent dispositions, integrity of mind, and innocent manners . . . and . . . literary and theological acquisitions."[20]

Though William is generally dismissed as a mediocre mind and a somewhat pompous figure, the great Joseph Stevens Buckminster eulogized him as one whose "faith was always strong enough to render his preaching the expression of his own intimate persuasions, and the cheerful employment of his life." William Emerson was the Christian gentleman even on his deathbed, impressing everyone, wrote Buckminster, with his "collected, intelligent, and strong" expressions of faith, which were "very much to be preferred to the indistinct raptures and ejaculations, which are so often caught from the lips of the dying, where more is supposed to be meant than meets the ear, and more is put into the speech than was originally contained in the thought."[21] Waldo, of course, claimed to be unimpressed by this ultimate model of controlled deportment, writing contemptuously of his father's age as "that early ignorant & transitional *Month-*

of-March, in our New England culture" (*L* 4:179), and in a cold tribute later faulted his father as typical of that transitional generation's fuzziness with regard to the "nature and offices of Jesus."[22] But the epitome of the Christian minister defined and embodied by William Emerson and his ilk remained a potent legacy for young Waldo Emerson.

This study explores how Ralph Waldo Emerson's vocational identity, sermons, and sermonizing are of a piece with the great essays and his later work. This is not a history of Emerson's ministry: David Robinson has demonstrated the ministry's impact on the shape of Emerson's career; and, indeed, because so many of the most interesting sermons were reused for up to a decade, a study emphasizing chronological development among the sermons would be misleading.

In the context of the widespread clerical "identity crisis" that afflicted Emerson's age, we shall focus on the deeply personal way in which Emerson appropriated Jesus in his thinking and career. We then explore the central importance to his theology of an inherently "Transcendentalist" concept of revelation and inspiration, and see him working out in the sermons a highly self-conscious aesthetic theory to describe and convey the experience of the divine. Emerson's theory of language, we shall see, is part and parcel of his formulation of a sophisticated and enduring dialectic of "freedom and fate." Very much his father's son, Waldo insists on the translation of religious conviction into ethics, the cement of a virtuous republic. This synthesis of vision, expression, and social cohesion connects Emerson not only to the "transitional" years of the early republic but also to the larger tradition of New England Puritanism, which he used consciously to empower his rhetoric. Finally, we shall see how the notion of Emerson as Preacher resonated not only in his Transcendental "vocation," but also, for good or ill, in his own denomination's posthumous rehabilitation of his original calling, and in countless subsequent invocations—for all manner of cause—of our American Saint.

Underlying all of these issues is the ideal of eloquence, which for Emerson and his age infused expression with purpose, heroism, and power.

1

"Christ Crucified": Christology, Identity, and Emerson's Sermon No. V

I

In a journal entry in November 1826, Ralph Waldo Emerson wrote: "I would write something worthily on the most affecting of topics[,] upon the personal character & influence & upon the death of Jesus Christ" (*JMN* 3:55). This idea, hardly surprising coming from an earnest Harvard divinity student who had just delivered his first sermon on 15 October, took shape in two subsequent journal entries and culminated in Sermon No. V, "Christ Crucified," first preached on 24 June 1827. This sermon is in one sense a milestone marking the beginning of Emerson's "progress" from orthodoxy to Transcendentalism, from Christ-reliance to self-reliance; in part it is a conventional conservative-Unitarian homily stressing the beauty and perfection of Jesus' personality while berating in stock Calvinistic terms the human propensity to sin. Although Emerson, perhaps embarrassed by the alternately maudlin and militant tone of the piece, shelved Sermon No. V after using it for the twelfth time on 27 July 1828 (*YES* 263), it remains an intriguing expression of his thought and personality during the period from his being licensed to preach (10 October 1826) until several months before his ordination by the Second Church in Boston (11 March 1829).

The months following Emerson's first sermon were a period of profound insecurity, both emotionally and intellectually. His sincere efforts to define his theological beliefs were complicated by deep-seated uncertainty over his vocational choice, an ambivalence tied implicitly to his sense of identity. If, as we now know, the early journals, notebooks, and sermons are the roots of the mature Emerson, Sermon No. V represents a formal resolution of his most urgent fears and aspirations during this critical period. The figure of Jesus became pivotal as Emerson sought not only to come to terms with the tenets of Christianity but, more important, to establish his personal sense of mission. The Jesus of Sermon No. V is the boldest formulation of the values and virtues Emerson was working out for himself prior to his ordination. More than a temporary resolution of Emerson's groping toward self-definition at the start of his ministry, the depiction of Jesus in Sermon No. V points toward concepts of heroism that Emerson would proclaim for years to come.

II

Journal entries of early 1826 show a serious, idealistic young Emerson eager to dedicate himself to some high purpose, but alternately skeptical and hopeful of success. With faith that the meaning of life would be gradually revealed, he wrote: "I wish it were possible for man to imitate . . . the way of his maker. It would be an ascent far above the pitch of ordinary[,] of recorded heroism to dedicate & confine the members of the body & the members of the mind to the exclusive pursuit of good. 'Tis the perfection of moral & intellectual nature when nothing is done in vain" (*JMN* 3:10). Despite this ideal, his skeptical nature prevented him from finding adequate heroes in the annals of history. Bonaparte, Byron, Charles XII—all had shabby sides, convincing young Emerson that "[m]uch of the good of History is no doubt indirect & general" (*JMN* 3:6). He comes a bit closer to defining his true hero when he observes that the "real sovereigns of Britain & France" were not kings but writers and scientists (*JMN* 3:13).

History was a mixed record of tyranny (the emergence of false heroes), of obtuseness in the mass of men (a recurrent motif throughout Emerson's writings), and of sporadic progress among persons of vision, permitting the race to grope forward: "Mere conquerors will be first disregarded as mere units of a crowd and afterwards execrated[,] damned as destroyers of human happiness. It may be said that these opinions will always be confined to philosophers for they always have been; & can never impregnate the inert & sluggish mind of a community which is always slow to recieve [sic] an opinion or dismiss a prejudice. But the very fact that many men have predicted the reformation is the best warrant of its fulfilment" (JMN 3:17). Emerson was developing a melioristic view of history. History comes alive, he believed, when it is morally instructive: "In the error & the rectitude, in the agreeable & distressing events, in the education & degeneracy of so many nations of minds there runs thro' all the same human principle in which our hearts are constrained to find a consanguinity & so to make the registers of history a rule of life" (JMN 3:21). He believed that "our perception of moral truth is instinctive," but that "we need a learned experience" to fulfill our "virtue"; it is for this reason that we crave worthy historical models—to nourish the "growing Godhead within" us (JMN 3:21).[1] History provides, if not examples of perfect greatness, a universal principle of "true greatness," which is "always bottomed on goodness," "on sublime motive" (JMN 3:31).

Significant in this light, Emerson wrote with unflinching honesty that for all its beneficial impact on human progress Christianity enjoys no unique status; truth as found throughout history is universal and knows no sects (JMN 3:15). It is perhaps revealing that Emerson's tribute here to the "Unanimity" of truth is sandwiched between two of his most famous journal entries of despair: "I think that few men ever suffered more genuine misery than I have suffered" (16 March, JMN 3:13); and, "My years are passing away. Infirmities are already stealing on me that may be the deadly enemies that are to dissolve me to dirt and little is yet done to establish my consideration among my contemporaries & less to get a memory when I am gone" (27 March, JMN 3:15). Emerson's sense of history was, in theory, one of progressive unfolding of purpose. But that Christianity enjoyed no special privileges in this scheme withheld absolute consolation from a young man who was making a commitment to the ministry and who aspired himself to be a "great man."[2]

We have long been aware of Emerson's "problem of vocation" after he resigned from the Second Church pulpit in 1832.[3] But he found himself in 1826–28 in a far more vulnerable crisis as he sought to untangle the threads of philosophy, Christian doctrine, vocational choice, and personal identity that were in his own mind indistinguishable. Temperamental and philosophical receptiveness to the idea of original sin and the need for moral growth combined with family tradition to make the ministry a natural career selection for young Waldo. Moreover, the ministry offered an escape from the schoolteaching which from 1822 Emerson had found demeaning, and

it offered an avenue to exercise the "eloquence" he had so long
associated with "greatness" (*Life,* chaps. 7 and 8). However restric-
tive Emerson's ministry appears from the perspective of his later
career, it afforded him time and scope to define values that would
endure long after he resigned from the Second Church. But he remained unconvinced, given his universalist views of history and
truth and his own anxieties about success, that the Christian ministry provided ample range for his talents; and he was unsure whether
the figure of Jesus could satisfy his hunger for a hero to worship and
to emulate. His ambivalence is expressed in a letter to his Aunt Mary
Moody Emerson on 6 April 1826, however self-consciously composed
for effect it may have been (Emerson apparently took it directly from
his journal [*JMN* 3:19–20]). After a moving picture of the "innumera-
ble procession" of mankind, he writes:

> At the last an obscure man in an obscure crowd bro't forward
> a new Scripture of promise & instruction. But the rich & the
> great leaned to their ancient holdings & the wise distrusted
> this teacher for they had been often misled before. But the
> banner inscribed with his Cross has been erected and it has
> been to some a cloud & to some a pillar of fire.
>   We too have taken our places in the immeasurable train &
> must choose our standard & our guide. Is there no venerable
> tradition whose genuineness & authority we can establish, or
> must we too hurry onward inglorious in ignorance & misery
> we know not whence, we know not whither. (*L* 1:167–68)

The figure of Jesus seems at first to be making a dramatic entry
that will change the sad course of human history. Despite Jesus'
"promise," his legacy has been inconclusive. Emerson finds himself
part of the procession of human history; the images of crowds, of
"the immeasurable train," suggest death by smothering throughout
Emerson's writings. For Emerson there is the unpalatable choice of
following an imperfect tradition or risking the same quiet despera-
tion that has marked all history. The dilemma is that Jesus has left
a legacy the validity of which must continually be "established."
Emerson makes no attempt here to define the meaning of Christianity for him, leaving open the possibility that his own heroic efforts
may be doomed. The passage, with its qualifications and confusing
antitheses, frustratingly leaves the dilemma, let alone its articulation, unresolved.

Elsewhere in his journals and letters of the late 1820s, young

Emerson more sharply posed to himself and his relatives the philosophical and personal problems that would define his growth during the period of his ministry, problems that would always color his thought. These tensions included internal debates over such theological issues as the nature of divinity and the nature of one's response to intimations of that divinity, and more broadly existential questions about the nature and meaning of experience.

In his journal for 28 May 1826, Emerson is already expressing the confidence in his powers of intuition that marks the mature Emerson of the great essays: "I *feel* immortal. And the evidence of immortality comes better from consciousness than from reason" (*JMN* 3:25). Yet he is conscious that complete vision is not possible; indeed, "the limits thus set by mind to its daring" offer "an evidence from my instincts of God's existence" (*JMN* 3:26). While Emerson cannot rest easily with the limits of mind, he can accept, in the manner of Jonathan Edwards, the beautiful necessity of God's will: "I willingly hear an oft unwelcome doctrine, harsh & unwelcome in the ear of poverty & complaint that God has administered a real not apparent equality in the fortunes of men" (*JMN* 3:13). This perspective enables Emerson to posit a vantage point from which to allay his obsession with the mutability of human life that haunts the early journals (see, for example, *JMN* 3:50–51).

Emerson's stance of philosophical acceptance did not require a static shelter from the world. In trying further to define a posture that would embrace specific misfortunes within a scheme of cosmic meaning, Emerson proclaimed that human nature was designed to respond to adversity with growth of understanding: Happiness "consists in reliefs not in enjoyments[,] and unhappiness is an uneasiness[,] a useful uneasiness in the body or mind prompting to the attainment of some good agreeable to its nature. That is to say All unhappiness tends to happiness" (*JMN* 3:29). Stasis is neither desirable nor possible, since our experience is ever changing; but the *principle of accepting* flux is an absolute value for Emerson. Emerson's redefinition of happiness resembles the seeds of his concept of "compensation," which begins to appear by that name in the journals in the 1820s. In this context it is clear that Emerson never intended this important concept to be simply a measure of moral reward and punishment, a scale of fixed opposites; rather, "compensation" is a fluid barometer of the state of one's soul. "Compensation" is not simply "conscience," punishing bad acts and rewarding the good. It is a spiritual equilibrium that fosters human improvement, an improvement that needs continual renewal. It moves beyond mere moral approbation to that wisdom in which the mind contemplates its own progress in comprehending and accepting change and adversity.

While Emerson was gradually coming to grips with his sense of self, his relationship to other people posed a problem. His youthful Puritan sense of original sin combined with a constitutional squeamishness about human contact to evoke images of mobs and herds ("screaming" with "unsavoury breath"—*JMN* 3:52) in depicting the mass of humankind. Young Emerson painfully acknowledged his place in the train of history; yet the "mass" represented a threat to the integrity and achievement of the hero/self. This contradiction echoes throughout the years of Waldo's ministry.

In a somewhat softer assessment of the human condition, Emerson was concerned, in reflecting on the ministry, that "men . . . rest satisfied with the weekly or casual expoundings . . . made by ministers & do not feel themselves under any obligation to think for themselves." While this might argue an inherent limitation of the ministry, Emerson maintained democratically that "moral nature is one & not diverse" (*JMN* 3:34). He continued to believe in the potential for spiritual growth in all people. And in the martial terms that signified both conventional Christian phraseology and his own youthful yearnings for active heroism, he desired all to be alert for "private tokens from the world of spirits to a militant mind" (*JMN* 3:35).

For all his reservations about the power of the ministry, Emerson believed religion provided a personal touchstone to measure the attainment of wisdom: "Religion aims to make a man at peace with himself. . . . it [is] impossible to determine the state of the soul without something outside, some fixed idea as that of God" (*JMN* 3:106). Religion provides consolation in the face of flux. "Health, action, happiness. How they ebb from me!" Emerson could lament. Yet he went on to imply the solution, asking, "What is Stoicism? what is Christianity? They are for nothing . . . if they cannot set the soul on an equilibrium when it leans to the earth under the pressure of calamity" (*JMN* 3:45). This pairing of references to Stoicism and Christianity, which was to recur significantly in the Divinity School Address some twelve years later, was frequent in Emerson's writings in the 1820s as he tried to come to grips intellectually and emotionally with the institution of Christianity and its benefits. Long before he commenced preaching, Emerson was attacking historical Christianity, the "testimony of crowds and of ages." "But moral evidence," he declared, "the evidence of final causes when it can be procured is unerring & eternal." Still, the value of Christianity could not be overestimated; it explains "the existence of evil, for if man is immortal, this world is his place of discipline & the value of pain is then disclosed." Indeed, he goes on to argue, in terms that foreshadow his celebration of the *essence* of religion in the 1830s, that the monstrous distortions of historical Christianity do not negate the "nature of Xty" (*JMN* 3:47–49).[4] That Stoicism and Christianity were mingling in his thoughts is suggested in a letter to Aunt Mary on 23 September 1826 that is virtually a blueprint of the Divinity School Address. Identifying with the insistence of "modern philosophy" that "feelings" are superior to the "Bare reason, cold as cucumber," he accepts Christianity as "the expounder of God's moral law" but denies its historical value; he suggests that a minister must speak directly to men, yet he will not rest even in his own newfound convictions: "To grow wise is to grow doubtful" (*L* 1:174–75).

In the midst of his self-doubt Emerson had been concerned principally with the meaning of history, the nature of belief, and the shortcomings of institutional Christianity. But in Cambridge in November 1826 he was wishing, we have seen, to write "upon the personal character & influence & upon the death of Jesus Christ" (*JMN* 3:55). While a sudden concern with the person of Jesus is unexpected, it is significant that the "character" and "influence," even the death, of Jesus lend themselves as much to character study as to doctrinal formulations. Indeed, as Emerson pondered this theme on his trip to the South on which he embarked on 25 November, it was the person of Jesus that continued to have appeal, this at a time when a sense of personal unworthiness was increasingly at war with Emerson's determination to survive and succeed. The southern journey, which intensified both Emerson's fear of failure and his sense of mission, was a turning point enabling him to confront and articulate his dilemma.

At sea en route to Charleston, released from the familiarity of Boston and Cambridge, Emerson felt a momentary surge of confidence, finding as so many nineteenth-century Romantics did "a sovereignty in the mind" that reasserted the centrality of a man amid the turmoil and vastness of nature (*JMN* 3:57). He remained convinced that, within the constraints of human frailty, all "partake" of a "universal beam" that renders us free to travel "the broad or the narrow way"; but for a man who could never claim a single moment of Christian conversion, and for whom even Transcendental "conversion" would later be an ongoing process, the "development of the mind" remained the key to human spiritual potential (*JMN* 3:58).

Into this open-ended view of the spiritual life, Emerson introduced a universalist interpretation of the importance of Jesus. The "real difference between the sentiments" of dogmatists, he argued, is minimal; "hence it happens well that to whatever party names, education or inclination has attached us we sympathize all in the same affecting views of the life & passion of our Lord" (*JMN* 3:59). In declining a neat dogmatic solution to nagging intellectual and personal questions Emerson was perhaps showing courage; but he was also indulging in a sentimentalist evasion of important theological issues, which Lawrence Buell has shown was characteristic of Unitarian ministers of the period.[5] In Charleston on 4 January 1827 Emerson continued his meditation on "the great institution of Jesus Christ, the just religion which embodied all that was known of the human heart & anticipated in its comprehensive revelations all that has since been known." The universality of moral truth did not obscure from Emerson the "prejudice & falsehood" which had marred the history of the search for truth, but he looked hopefully to the time when "the champions of the Cross" will "come at last to the dear & lofty employment of pointing out the secret but affecting passages in the history of the Soul" (*JMN* 3:61–62).

Emerson, however, was far from solving the problem of his own role in removing the old prejudices and pointing out those lofty "passages in the history of the Soul." To his brother William's suggestion that he apply for a pulpit in New York, he replied on 6 January with obvious homesickness, "For myself, I had rather be a doorkeeper at home than bishop to aliens" (*L* 1:185). He clearly needed time before committing himself to great effort far from home and without having found his true voice. On 29 January 1827, he wrote William from Saint Augustine, berating himself for frittering away time and worrying that he might never realize his potential: "Here then in Turkey I enact turkey too. I stroll on the sea beach, & drive a green orange over the sand with a stick. Sometimes I sail in a boat, sometimes I sit in a chair. I read & write a little, moulding sermons & sentences for an hour which may never arrive. For tho' there may be much preaching in the world to come yet as it will hardly be after the written fashion of this pragmatic world, if I go to the grave without finding vent for my gift, the universe I fear will afford it no scope beside" (*L* 1:189). On 2 February 1827 he was lamenting that he was "cold & solitary," unfit to be a "young pilot" to others (*JMN* 3:72). Since arriving in Saint Augustine, Emerson had been worried anew about mutability, alternately accepting the insecurity of the human condition and doubting the very existence of God for lack of evidence (*JMN* 3:68–69).

Yet in a matter of days he was recalling and restating his Stoic/Christian consolation: "I become wise perforce by the progress of life. I strive to be happy but in vain. But every hour and every event fortunate or unfortunate contributes to my wisdom" (*JMN* 3:74). While the trip South initially intensified Emerson's insecurity, he was soon expressing a new self-confidence. "It is a sound doctrine," he declared near the end of his stay in Saint Augustine, "that faith is virtue. If God sent revelations daily none could plead the merit of faith." As if this were begging the question of belief, he went on: "To what was said above of the death of Christ it should be added, Those words & those sufferings are now a part of human history & how deep a dye they have imparted to all the after fortunes of the race" (*JMN* 3:76). While the nature of that "dye" is unspecified, that Emerson clearly felt the sublimity of Christ's heroism is an index of his new enthusiasm and sense of the power latent in his chosen profession.

In this more confident mood, Emerson enjoyed his conversations with the stimulating atheist Achille Murat on the return journey. Far from threatening what seems to have been Emerson's ill-defined, if not shaky, faith, Murat challenged Emerson to redefine his convictions and his goals. Though Emerson liked and admired Murat, he wrote of the tenets of Christianity, "My faith in these points is strong & I trust, as I live, indestructible" (*JMN* 3:77). He felt, moreover, a new sense of purpose by seeing the incompatibility of "greatness in the world & greatness of soul." And he expressed a new trust in his own resourcefulness: "The night is fine; the stars shed down their severe influences upon me and I feel a joy in my solitude that the merriment of vulgar society can never communicate" (*JMN* 3:78). He continued to worry that his "days" "have no honour among men" nor "grandeur" before God (*JMN* 3:78–79). But he was learning to find strength (or refuge) from his weaknesses by simply inverting society's values. If he lacked strength and purpose, that was no matter, for the soul was superior to the world and would make its greatness known in time.

Homeward bound, he continued to be fascinated by Jesus ("God the sun, Christ the light") and to associate perception and insight with the private soul: "Nothing can become known to the human mind but thro' the medium of itself—& this the use of revelation" (*JMN* 3:79). Surprisingly, his imagery now became militant. Speculating on a world in which all had realized their moral potential, he proclaimed, "The young & the old[,] the ardent & the firm would move forward truly & honorably in a Holy War, in the Chivalry of Virtue." The terminology is conventional in Christianity, and certainly Emerson's brand of militancy is based on spiritual, not spatial conquests. But the imagery is important as a sign both of Emerson's confidence in winning his internal debate and of his determination ultimately to translate a passive heroism into some form that would uplift others.[6] Obviously inspired by his own sea voyage, he declared, "When the Sea was stormy the disciples awoke Christ. Let us do so.—" (*JMN* 3:82). As he returned home Emerson was readying himself to awaken not only the Christ whose sublimity he found so fascinating, but also the heroic springs of his own personality.

Part of Emerson's new assertiveness derived, ironically, from a resolve *not* to commit himself to a new course of action for the present and from a firm retrenching into Boston provincialism.[7] On 7 April 1827 he rejected once and for all William's suggestion that he seek a position in New York: "I am a bigoted Yankee," he wrote with blunt pride (*L* 1:195). Again on 3 May, while he admits that being "so bigoted a Yankee" may have blinded him to the beauty of Charleston, he expresses a liking for Baltimore—because it looks like Boston (*L* 1:196). In mid-May, he is writing his brother Charles in an encouraging tone that stands in sharp contrast to the self-critical letter to William in late January. He advises Charles: "Give yourself to study with boundless ambition. Despising as much as you please the primary & vulgar landmarks of success in the consciousness y^t you aim to raise your rank not among your compeers alone but in that great scale of moral beings which embraces the invisible & the visible" (*L* 1:200). Emerson, working his way back north, was clearly expressing here his own newfound confidence based on his conviction that there are different measures of success, that one finds greatness in being and in performing according to one's nature; worldly success will follow, if it is to follow, in due order.

Pivotal in Emerson's evolution from the self-flagellation of the letter to William to the hope of the letter to Charles is a letter to Aunt Mary from Saint Augustine in late March 1827. Here Emerson comes to grips with the self-pity that attended his vocational/personal crisis, identifying with the stance of Jesus in the Lord's Prayer in terms that were to reverberate in Sermon No. V:

> It is certainly very easy to conceive of cases wh require more
> than the exaltation of the martyr's virtue who triumphs at the

stake. I mean . . . and who nourishes in silence far from fame the secret virtue the gift of which was accompanied with a consciousness of its worth [*sic*]—than it is for such a youth meekly to surrender his hopes in the outset of his career to forego all these fairy visions & say with uncompromising self devotion Thy will be done. Many a man has died with firmness who yet had never broke his spirit or rather sublimed his spirit to such resignation. Resolution was on his face but regret sat on his heart. Yet we can conceive of one so united to God in his affections that he surveys from the vantage ground of his own virtues the two worlds with equal eye & knowing the true value of the love & praise of men challenges rather the suffrages of immortal souls. And what we can conceive of virtue, it may be we can exhibit. (*L* 1:195)

As this passage makes clear, Emerson is not denying his anxiety that the world will never know his gift; indeed, the contrast he draws between outward "Resolution" and inward "regret" suggests what had until now been his own situation. Yet he envisions a creative solution: What Emerson is here recommending is neither the glory of martyrdom nor the simple verbal acquiescence of "resignation," but the discovery of that inner resource, that security and maturity of personality, whereby earthly fame and eternal principle are seen in perspective. This, implicitly, is to experience personally the "vantage ground" of Jesus himself. Emerson's stance here reaches back to the Pauline notion that one can *know* only what one *is*; it derives from Emerson's Puritan heritage that insisted that true sanctification proceeds from justification; and it was nourished by the liberal-Christian ethic of his own time that insisted that deeds and appearances must be judged by the motives that prompted them. On a personal level it signified for Emerson a glimpse of self-acceptance, a faith in himself that would "exhibit" its fruit to the world. Instead of worrying about becoming a "great man," he would *be* one by comprehending the very struggles that had before seemed to stand in the way of success. In overcoming anxiety and self-consciousness, in conceiving of vision and the manifesting of virtue as one, Emerson sensed a new security of personality.

While much has been written about the importance of Emerson's European trip following his resignation of the Second Church pulpit, the southern journey of 1826–27 was crucial as a moratorium allowing the prospective minister to assess his theological and personal doubts and to commit himself to a profession that would profoundly affect the stamp of his future thought. Sermon No. V incorporates the major motifs we have found in the early journals and letters and reveals the constructive impact of Emerson's ministerial training, which enabled him to identify with the heroic "character" of Jesus and, in preaching his virtues, to assume the mantle of eloquence crucial to his own sense of greatness.

III

Sermon No. V, which covers the better part of sixteen manuscript pages, takes as its text part of 1 Corinthians 1:23: "We preach Christ crucified." Conventionally, the sermon promises to "open" the Scriptures to show how we may rightly appropriate Christ. Emerson's opening, which derives from a journal entry written at Concord on 19 June 1827, just five days before the sermon was first delivered, is stern: "It is better, said Solomon, to go to the house of mourning than to the house of feasting. There is something more safe & salutary to our virtue in the influences of sorrow, than in the enticing splendor of scenes of joy. Man does not stand firm in a high & giddy prosperity. The tender eye of the mind is dazzled by excessive sunshine. 'We are purified by pity & terror.' " Ralph L. Rusk, in his biography of Emerson, suggests that the sermon "was full of the sense of the tragic; yet it too implied compensation" in its Aristotelian posture (*Life* 123). Indeed, Emerson elaborated on the journal material, following the reference to Aristotle in the sermon with five new sentences, explaining just how "[b]y these passions our attention is arrested, our faculties are startled from their sleep into strenuous exertion."[8] Perhaps rationalizing his own earlier enervating introspection by projecting it onto his congregation, he argues that one need not fear the results of contemplating "affliction," "[f]or the animal spirits are not to be long repressed."

The young preacher then takes a direct shot at liberal religion, declaring on the second page that "[t]he religious service of this day seldom has too morose an influence on the rest of the week. That danger departed with a former age." He finds fault with the "great abundance of smooth & pleasant speculation on the agreeable topics" of the day and goes on to question, without really establishing his grounds, "the congratulations that are cheerfully exchanged from every quarter on the distinguished advancement of the age." The gladness of the modern philanthropist and Christian is "just & blameless" (a toughened revision of "just & beautiful" in *JMN* 3:92);

but Emerson discovers sufficient chink in the armor of the popular mind to suggest that, as the wealthy "heir" ought to recall his "benefactor," so "it is a natural & reasonable gratitude on our part which sometimes carries us back in devout recollection to the founder of our spiritual privileges."[9] (Here concludes the material borrowed from *JMN* 3:91–92.) However gratuitous the pretext for this sermon, it enables Emerson to establish a stance of moral superiority and in purple dramatic tones to invite his congregation away from familiar "pleasant places," "to the field of blood, to a ghastly & atrocious spectacle, to the hill of Calvary & the passion of Christ."

Now, in the middle of the third manuscript page, Emerson announces the moral value of this dramatic reconstruction: "It is good to refresh our virtues by the example of perfect innocence." He focuses attention on Jesus, borrowing, with minor revisions and much amplification, that journal entry from November 1826 (*JMN* 3:55) in which he desired to "write something worthily on the most affecting of topics": in the sermon he turns

> to that most affecting page of human history which pourtrayed in living lines the personal character & the death of Jesus Christ. a being whose character has taken such strong hold of the mind as to divide the opinions of men as to his nature & office more than did ever any question. one so great as to leave foundation for the opinion that he was a portion of the Deity & in the opinions least reverent that he was first of men—a being who would be called renowned did not fame & what men call glory sink before the majesty of his character into things offensive & ridiculous; one whose effect on the fortunes of human society, taking out of account what may be called supernatural influence, has been far the most powerful impulse that ↑ of those y^t ever wore the human form ↓ ever acted thereon & yet whose influence on the world is now I had almost said but *beginning* to be felt.

The passage is worth quoting at length because it reveals the theological significance of Emerson's Jesus, the literary nature of the sermon, and the kinds of values he found in Jesus worth appropriating to his own life. Twice he skirts, without explicitly denying, the divinity of Jesus. The focus is on the "character" of Jesus, a character whose "majesty" captured the attention of mankind without the kind of overt achievements and conquests we normally associate with heroism; most important for Emerson, we shall see, is that while Jesus appeared a failure by the world's standards, he was "*beginning*" to have "influence on the world."

Emerson's purpose clearly is to refresh his congregation's sense of one who, while perhaps not a savior in the conventional sense, is the great model of moral growth. Emerson's attempt to reach this end is couched in strikingly literary terms. Where in the journal he longed to "write" on the "most affecting of topics," he now turns "to that most affecting page of human history which pourtrayed in living lines the personal character & the death of Jesus Christ." The layering of imagery of storytelling enables Emerson to play up the "sublimity" of Jesus' life and to work on his hearers' emotions without committing himself to technicalities of theology; indeed, he sets aside the "supernatural influence" of Jesus, emphasizing instead his "human form." The dramatic unfolding of Jesus' life and crucifixion marks this sermon as an early example of what Lawrence Buell sees as a "genre" developed in Unitarian preaching: "biblical fiction."[10]

Not only can Sermon No. V be placed in this genre; the "story" it seeks to tell is not all that original. William Ellery Channing, for example, had anticipated both theme and approach some six years earlier in "The Evidences of Revealed Religion" (1821). Channing had provided the obligatory biographical sketch of Jesus' "humble birth and education" as background to describing his grand "character."[11] More concerned than Emerson to establish rational proofs of Christianity, Channing did not depict the melodrama of the Crucifixion as Emerson does; but he set an example of validating Christianity by appealing not to miracles but to the benefits of moral development and "character."

While Sermon No. V partakes of a "genre" and expresses ideas that were current in Unitarian circles, it remains an important statement in Emerson's growth. However common Emerson's techniques and sentiments, his depiction of Jesus represents a turning point in the identity crisis of his mid-twenties.

We have seen that Emerson was impressed by the "influence" exerted by Jesus. On the fifth page he goes on to say that most of us pay heed to "signs of outward splendor" and are influenced "by the pomp of wealth & power." "But we judge in this matter according to the flesh," he declares; indeed, Christianity "seems to have been designed to correct this ancient error." While hardly a novel religious idea, the notion that this truth is taught not by success but by "affliction" (p. 6) enables Emerson to assert a professionally and socially approved code that would legitimize his constitutional introspection, his fear of failure, and his lack of real power. In this sense, his declaration that "[t]he emblem of our faith is not a crown but a cross" both certifies his acceptance of general Unitarian doctrine and announces that henceforward he will not be judged by the world's standards.

To a considerable extent, Emerson's ministry, far from being a stifling sidetrack from his real literary ambitions, sheltered him from overwhelming personal crises. Ostensibly, Emerson was *committing* himself to an acceptable adult role in assuming the ministry.[12] But the dialectics of Unitarianism also enabled him to redefine the nature of action and heroism in ways that suited his temperament and convictions. He asks rhetorically, for example, if Jesus was "born in the lap of grandeur, the child of the Caesars," or pampered "to an effeminate manhood"; and in terms reminiscent of his early journal criticism of military heroes, he asks in swelling phrases if Jesus was "like the renowned conquerors" who achieve fame through the misery of others. The obvious implication is that the world's is not the only measure of greatness.

The familiar details of Jesus' "humble" origins are rehearsed on the seventh page. This assessment of the power of Jesus' character, while it is a conventional Unitarian character sketch, is an epitome of Emerson's evolving personal and professional self-image: "All that was simple & unpretending in his circumstances was made to show in stronger relief the majesty of his life: all that was distressing & terrible in his lot to disclose more manifestly the purity & sublimity of his virtue. It was designed to set the greatness of the world at nought. It was designed to give us a perfect pattern of obedience to God at the same time that a confirmation was added by a holy life as well as wonderful works to the authenticity of his mission, & the truth of his tidings."

Though he stops short of attributing divine qualities to Jesus, Emerson finds him a staunch model of that sentimentalized revision of Protestant justification, "sublimity." Jesus achieves the lofty stance Emerson had suggested to Aunt Mary in the letter from Saint Augustine (*L* 1:195). Jesus wins greatness without becoming contaminated by the world (an admirable trait to a young man with a highly refined sense of moral discrimination). And the holy "confirmation" of Jesus' "mission, & the truth of his tidings" had special appeal to one who ministered the faith of Jesus yet longed for validation of his own high calling and the eloquence of his own "tidings," which he had morbidly feared would never find vent or audience.

In the short paragraph at the bottom of the eighth page, Emerson invites us again to the scene of the Crucifixion, the detailed description of which extends from page nine through the middle of page fifteen. This description, while interesting as a melodramatic *tour de force* unusual in Emerson, is as we have seen conventional "biblical fiction." What is more significant is the further elaboration of Jesus' character, so revealing of Emerson's self-image, and its application to the congregation. Jesus exhibits the kind of transcendence of the shabby material world that Emerson was later to attribute to the poet, naturalist, or scholar. By contrast, Herod and the crowd present at the Crucifixion display a stupidity and viciousness in keeping with Emerson's habitual depiction of martial "heroes" and the "mass" of mankind: "They were unable to comprehend in their pitiful ferocity that there is a greatness of soul to which evil fortune & good are accidents . . . a magnanimity so high & serene that mockery & scorn cannot touch its composure. . . . It sleeps to the things of this world in a vision of divine contemplations, an elevation of the soul too sublime to waste itself in idle vaunts & bravado. It is clothed in humility. It walks with God" (p. 9).

We have seen in earlier journal entries Emerson's tentative positing of a stoical equilibrium that provides an impregnable defense against the world's adversities. While it can be argued that Christian revelation transcends the stoic stance, Jesus clearly exhibits the stoical fortitude we find Emerson admiring in the journals. Reverting to the imagery of drawing and storytelling (whether to back off from theology or to emphasize the affecting power of Jesus' life), Emerson continues: "They were skilful hands that sketched in our Scriptures the tragic events of that memorable day. They have told with sad fidelity the story of his sufferings[,] the insane vindictiveness with which his countrymen thirsted for his blood." But while Emerson's vision of transcendence presupposes a hostile mass of men grotesquely waiting for the destruction of the oppressed hero, Emerson is meliorist enough to acknowledge the "consolation" that at the time of man's "deep depravity" (p. 10) Christ "was not wholly abandoned by the sympathies & admiration of men." The mass of mankind may be depraved, but Emerson knew that the congregation at hand must have some hope to hold to, else Christ's life and Emerson's eloquence were for naught.

Accompanying Jesus' noble compassion (he tells his sympathizers to "weep for yourselves & your children") is an ability to perceive the future. Indeed, that Emerson is identifying closely with Jesus here will be obvious to students of Emerson familiar with the importance of eye imagery in the great essays. Jesus' "eye went forward to

the future" and "his merciful spirit contemplated" Roman domina-
tion, civil turmoil, hunger.[13]

As a seer, Jesus comprehends and transcends the human predicament even as he is victimized by it. In sharp contrast, the "cruel
enemies" of Jesus are "ignorant of the future & blinded by passion
even to the present" (p. 11). Immediately following this juxtaposition
of the man of vision and the uncouth mob comes the journal entry
written in Charleston on 6 January 1827 (*JMN* 3:62–64) and compris-
ing pages eleven through thirteen. The sermon manuscript reveals
that Emerson carefully polished the expression of the journal entry
and inserted two substantial passages to emphasize the mission of
Jesus and the lesson to be drawn from his life and death. The result
is an extended passage of antitheses which points up the contrasts
between man and Christ, materialism and vision, body and soul,
mob and man of vision. "I am anxious," Emerson had begun the
journal entry, "to sketch out the form of a sermon I have long had
in my head upon the <affecting character> events of the Crucifixion" (*JMN* 3:63).[14] Despite the cancellation, the sermon makes clear
that the "events of the Crucifixion" are graphically presented to
throw the "affecting character" of Jesus into sharper relief. Emerson
presents the "majesty" of Jesus' agony and describes the sufferer's
thoughts of "the painful picture of all the past." In four sentences
added to the journal entry he emphasizes that "[m]an had not found
out his immortality, had not found out the God who made him."
The mission of Jesus was to restore man to God and to "the purposes
to which we exist." Now, "[t]o add to his works of wonder the last
testimony he brings his life to bear witness that his doctrine is true."
The next sentence, from the original journal entry, states that "now
he offers himself a silent victim & feels that he is accomplishing a
mighty destiny"; the foregoing new sentences make it clear that to
bear witness, to be "a silent victim," is not to be inactive. In a new
sentence, Emerson continues that as Jesus "walks amid that raging
multitude" his eye looks beyond the "spectacle around him," seeing
(in a series of sentences from the journal) "into the future" to perversions of his doctrine "to an unhallowed use of power & pride" (p.
12), until "his calm eye . . . rests on the faithful who in this latter
day shall consecrate themselves with pious self devotion" to his
cause. Though Jesus is depicted as a passive perceiver, he is a precursor of Emerson's more "active" heroes of the 1830s in that his vision
cuts across history. In a long added passage Emerson stresses the
ongoing legacy of Jesus' Crucifixion ("the death which he is finish-

ing") and emphasizes the imploring invitation of Jesus to "overcome the body in seeking the welfare of the soul." But the implication is that, despite the Christian revelation, history will continue to show the human condition "borne down to the earth" by a "tremendous load of moral depravity." The peace of Christ, always at hand, must forever be won by the select person who responds to Jesus' offer "in imitation of him, to lift that weary head towards God & Heaven" (p. 13).

The moment of moral commitment transcends history, uniting man with Christ, though that commitment must occur within time. Emerson sustains his pattern of antithesis, sharply breaking up even this reverie: "But it was not the hour for meditation; it was the hour of blood. The cry of Crucify him! Crucify him! burst from the savage lips of that enormous multitude & the hills of Judaea rang with the ominous echoes. Then the cross was planted in the earth; & He,— the man who came from God, was hung thereon." The effect of "biblical fiction" in the sermon is to dramatize Christ as an *active* hero despite his outward passivity. The outward action points to death, defeat; the internal spiritual action takes on an heroic sweep that encompasses both history and heaven. Emerson's audience is moved to take sides by emotionally identifying with the victim who is also conqueror, and by making the moral commitment to *imitate* the hero. The pages derived from the Charleston journal entry conclude with a final contrast between the "scoffing" and the "dismal shouting" of the mob, and Jesus' appeal to God to forgive his persecutors.

The "story" of the Crucifixion continues in terms interesting less for originality than for the delight and gusto Emerson takes in completing the sermon. Jesus "is at peace his sufferings are ended, his warfare is accomplished" (p. 14). Emerson declares in apparent imitation of Jesus that our tears should be for Pilate and the priests who now fear Jesus' body may be stolen by disciples to prove his promise of resurrection, but his tone is unmistakably one of aggressive exaltation: "Alas poor pigmy actors in this scene of madness & crime." The narrative proper ends not surprisingly with the Ascension in the middle of page fifteen. What is surprising, in view of Emerson's earlier tacit denial of Jesus' "supernatural influence," is that his ecstatic vision of transcendence (or conquest) of the cruel world betrays him into a literal assessment of the Resurrection. Of Jesus' persecutors, Emerson declares, God "will baffle you in your folly, & raise him from the dead. He has burst the bonds of death. He has put on the garments of glory for a putrid shroud. Ministering angels rolled away the stone from the door of the sepulchre: the soldiers that watched became as dead men. He has appeared unto men. He has ascended to his Father in Heaven."

In the remaining page and a half Emerson winds down the intensity of the sermon by explaining the uses of the story. Still taken by the glory of the Resurrection, he suggests rather morbidly that our deceased friends continue to observe our behavior and thus act even in death as moral guides. This view derives, he claims, from the scriptural promise of Jesus: " 'Lo! I am with you alway, even unto the end of the world' " (p. 16). We begin to wonder to what extent Emerson is preaching a religion of miracles. His final emphasis, however, is on Jesus' moral legacy. "You can enter into a sublime sympathy with him," he proclaims (in a line that originally concluded the Crucifixion passage of the Charleston journal entry [*JMN* 3:64]), for Jesus provided us with "an example that we should follow in his steps." Emerson concludes the sermon by declaring how we achieve "sublime sympathy" with Jesus: "Whensoever you breathe a pure affection to heaven when you forget yourself to spend your strength in promoting the happiness of others in every blessed moment that you resist & overcome the temptations of the world in the pure hope of becoming more like to our Master, more acceptable in the eye of God,—in that moment be assured, his heart goes with you, his gentle spirit commends you, he sees that you acknowledge him on earth & he shall acknowledge you before his Father in Heaven." The impression is an odd mixture of genteel sentimentality and evangelical fervor. Emerson is clearly uneasy espousing traditional Christian doctrine. But the intensity of his feeling reveals a powerful identification with Jesus that surpasses the bounds of doctrine. It may be true of Emerson as of his Unitarian contemporaries that, as Buell charges, melodrama was a way of evading the details of doctrine. What is obvious in reading Sermon No. V is Emerson's enthusiasm in embracing the heroic Jesus who overcame the adversities of sin, mutability, and the spite of men, achieving an inner peace and vision, and setting an example, which Emerson craved both personally and philosophically. Moreover, proclaiming Jesus' message—or, in this case telling his story—constituted a socially acceptable career that provided an outlet for the eloquence and power Emerson had earlier despaired of achieving. Emerson had assumed a variety of personae—stern Jeremiah, melodramatic storyteller, hopeful evangelist.[15] In so doing, he assumed masks of moral superiority and vision that permitted him, in preaching to men and women who could not but endorse his views, to exorcise the demons of coarse, bloodthirsty mobs who had seemed to threaten his own ideals and aspirations, and to establish a sense of purposeful identity that would endure, with modifications, long after his formal ministry had ended.

IV

Why Jesus could not long serve Emerson as a "hero" is perhaps best exemplified by Emerson himself in "Uses of Great Men" (1850). "Great men," he argued in his middle years, are "a collyrium to clear our eyes from egotism, and enable us to see other people and their works" (CW 4:15). As such, great men rescue us from the stifling confines of our own claustrophobic personalities; they spur us into new action and discovery by making us aware of the otherness of man and nature. The "danger," according to Emerson, is that influence may become subjugation. For the healthy person, "[e]very hero becomes a bore at last. Perhaps Voltaire was not badhearted, yet he said of the good Jesus, even, 'I pray you, let me never hear that man's name again.' " This reaction Emerson sees as "human nature's indispensable defence" (CW 4:16), each man having the *potential*, typified by the hero, of "ascending out of his limits into a catholic existence": "We have never come at the true and best benefit of any genius, so long as we believe him an original force. In the moment when he ceases to help us as a cause, he begins to help us more as an effect. Then he appears as an exponent of a vaster mind and will. The opake self becomes transparent with the light of the First Cause" (CW 4:20).

After a year of preaching the crucified Jesus in Sermon No. V, Emerson came to feel that *this* "great man" was thickening into an opaque statue produced by dogmatism. Not that Jesus ceased to interest Emerson in later sermons. But these were different versions of Jesus, designed to meet new emotional and intellectual needs, with fewer references to the specific suffering of the Crucifixion.[16]

The tentativeness of Emerson's satisfaction with the Jesus of Sermon No. V is already suggested in a letter to his brother William on the very day he first delivered the sermon. Emerson writes that he has supplied the pulpit at First Church, Chauncy Place, but that already vocational doubts are reasserting themselves: "Meditate now & then total abdication of the profession on the score of ill health . . . . Very sorry—for how to get my bread? Shall I commence author? of prose or of verse. Alack of both the unwilling muse!" (L 1:201).

Aesthetic honesty for Emerson is inseparable from his craving for

personal and vocational "power." The timing is perhaps coinciden-
tal, but on 15 July 1828, twelve days before Emerson used Sermon
No. V for the *last* time, the theme of aesthetic power reappears, this
time in a letter to his brother Charles, whose "valedictory oration"
Waldo criticizes on the grounds that for all his gifts, Charles is "a
fine show at which we look, instead of an agent that moves us." In
what again is clearly as much self-criticism as criticism of Charles,
he anticipates his careful definition of the uses and limitations of
great men: "Let him [Charles] remember that the true orator must
not wrap himself in himself, but must wholly abandon himself to
the sentiment he utters, & to the multitude he addresses;—must
become their property, to the end that *they may become his*. . . . Let
him for a moment forget himself, & then, assuredly, he will not
be forgotten.—" (*L* 1:238–40). For Emerson, vision, sincerity, and
eloquence had become one. Judged by his own standards, Sermon
No. V, however it may have expressed earlier needs, represented now
a theological hardening which in turn was restricting him from freely
giving of himself as preacher, a situation that in four years would
cause him to resign his pastorate altogether to seek new relationships
to nature and new modes of expressing those relationships.

In 1826 a painfully introspective young Emerson was dedicating
himself to follow his hero, Jesus; increasingly he came to discover
traits in Jesus that he wished to emulate. By 1836 in *Nature*, as Joel
Porte has brilliantly shown, he was actually *identifying* with the
visionary *voice* of Christ. (Porte's observation that the first paragraph
of *Nature*, with its echo of Christ's warning to the lawyers [Luke 11],
"is laced with more anger than we are normally willing to hear"
reveals how important Jesus was to the evolution of Emerson's sense
of identity: The defensiveness/aggressiveness suggested by his depiction of militant religious heroism in the early journals had become
by 1836 forthright and confident, if angry, prophecy.)[17] In this sense
Nature represents the ultimate stage of Channing's call for man to
achieve "likeness to God." Emerson was usually careful to define,
as had Channing, Jesus' "inferiority" to God. But the transition from
Unitarianism to Transcendentalism is perhaps nowhere better illus-
trated than in Emerson's movement from speaking *about* Jesus to
speaking *as* Jesus. *Nature* thus marks an exercising of aesthetic
power he began to feel was stifled by writing sermons. This evolution, however, was more gradual than is usually supposed. It would
be melodramatic to claim that Emerson, in discovering the liberation
of Romantic expression, was rejecting the essential discoveries he
had made while a divinity student. If Emerson's new profession and

concept of the hero in 1827–28 could not provide final solutions to his anxieties, they provided at least a momentary stay enabling him to build self-confidence and a sense of power even as he denied the "supernatural" properties of Jesus and found the ministry increasingly tedious.

Emerson's satisfaction with the sentiments expressed in Sermon No. V is implied, nevertheless, in his journal five days after first preaching the sermon. He expresses the consolation, the compensation, that one grows from adversity: "The man who bates no jot of courage when oppressed by fate[,] who missing of his design lays hold with ready hand on the unexpected event & turns it to his own account & in the cruelest suffering has that generosity of perception that he is sensible of a secret joy in the addition this event makes to his knowledge—that man is truly independent . . . of time & chance" (*JMN* 3:92–93). He continued to maintain, with stoic fortitude, that "these doubts of ours" are "hints God has interwoven in our condition to remind us of the temper that becomes us; that diffidence & candor suit us better than arrogance & dogmatism" (*JMN* 3:103).

Philosophical integrity continued to clash, to a painful degree, with Emerson's expectation that a minister exists to "combat prejudices" (*JMN* 3:108). The old defensiveness concerning what constitutes power resurfaces in the journal on 10 March 1828. Ministers, he explains, are expected by the common folk to appeal for "*Contemplation*"; "But it is not so," Emerson declares. "*We* call them to a life of action" (*JMN* 3:110). That Emerson was still not equating such a life with a formal occupation is suggested in his letter to William on 3 April 1828, in which he expresses satisfaction at "escaping all engagements at the New Church in Boston." He goes on: "I am embarrassed at present whenever any application is made to me that may lead to permanent engagements. For I fancy myself dependent for my degree of health upon my lounging capricious unfettered mode of life & I keep myself & I slowly multiply my sermons for a day I hope of firmer health & solid power" (*L* 1:229–30). We find traits of the quiet, inward-looking Jesus of Sermon No. V and glimpses of that peculiar Transcendental inversion of the value of action in Emerson's assertion that "[t]here are two men in the world: the man of passion, & the man of principle" (*JMN* 3:129). Indeed, "the silence of a good man" often bespeaks "character" (*JMN* 3:132). Emerson's new sense that he could learn from adversity and need not force final conclusions on complex reality did not preclude his recourse to terse antithesis and aphorism to justify his passivity.

The "formation of Character," and not outward action, constituted moral development for Emerson. What would seem antisocial under other circumstances he converted into an unimpeachable code. In moments of enthusiasm, he found this vision embodied in his "Idea of the Christian Minister: a man who is separated from men in all the rough courses where defilement can hardly be escaped; & who mixes with men only for purposes that make himself & them better; aloof from the storm of passion, from political hatred, from the jealousy & intrigue of gain, from the contracting influences of low company & little arts" (*JMN* 3:152). This disembodied figure could be accused of a cloistered virtue only if we forget his antecedents in Emerson's descriptions of Christian heroism in the journals and in Sermon No. V. The virtues of this "Christian Minister" can be found in substantially the same form in the "poet" and "scholar" of the 1830s and beyond. That the "Christian Minister" is not bound by denominational orthodoxy is already suggested in a journal entry in late November 1828: "I take a pleasure greater than I can express in finding among men out of the influence or [*sic*] Xty the light of Xn sentiment" (*JMN* 3:144).

Yet the sterner vision expressed in "Christ Crucified" is not the antithesis of Emerson's new hero of the 1830s and 1840s. The concept in Sermon No. V of the hero and his relationship to society and history continues to inform the great essays. In "Self-Reliance," for example, "we are . . . guides, redeemers, and benefactors, obeying the Almighty effort, and advancing on Chaos and the Dark" (*CW* 2:28). But the hero still stands against the opposition of a vampiric society: "Society everywhere is in conspiracy against the manhood of every one of its members" (*CW* 2:29). "Whoso would be a man, must be a nonconformist" for which "the world whips you with its displeasure" (*CW* 2:32). Images of mobs like those in Sermon No. V depict "society": "the sour faces of the multitude," "the discontent of the multitude," "the unintelligent brute force that lies at the bottom of society" (*CW* 2:33). To be "misunderstood" becomes not just a right but an obligation if one is to be like Jesus "and every pure and wise spirit that ever took flesh" (*CW* 2:34). While in the moment of vision the soul "shoves Jesus and Judas equally aside" (*CW* 2:40), Emerson seems to assume the voice of Jesus sending out the twelve apostles (Mt 10:35–37) when he urges: "Live no longer to the expectation of these deceived and deceiving people with whom we converse. Say to them, 'O father, O mother, O wife, O brother, O friend, I have lived with you after appearances hitherto. Henceforward I am the truth's' " (*CW* 2:41–42).

Emerson's growing self-confidence and evolving concept of heroism would make him define Jesus in new ways until he would seem but one more "representative man" for the whole person to use selectively.[18] But even by 1838 there are still echoes of the Jesus of Sermon No. V in the Divinity School Address; now Jesus is praised as "a true man" (*CW* 1:81). Moreover, the "formalist" minister, less "real" than the snowstorm because he gives nothing of himself (*CW* 1:85) is but a version of the orator Emerson had criticized in Charles—and in himself—in 1828. The obstacle here to fulfillment of the minister's office is, as Emerson had believed for over a decade, reliance on historical Christianity. It is the task of preaching, he goes on, to rediscover "the resources of astonishment and power"; otherwise, "[t]he pulpit . . . loses all its inspiration, and gropes after it knows not what. And for want of this culture, the soul of the community is sick and faithless. It wants nothing so much as *a stern, high, stoical, Christian discipline,* to make it know itself and the divinity that speaks through it" (*CW* 1:87–88; emphasis mine). Though Emerson here completes his early tendency to distill the essence of Christianity from Christ, the Stoic/Christian stance continues to mean self-knowledge, transcendence, impregnable security. Despite the revolutionary reputation of the address, there is also a touch of pathos in Emerson's decree: "Discharge to men the priestly office, and, present or absent, you shall be followed with their love as by an angel" (*CW* 1:90). As a minister Emerson had craved mission, eloquence, acceptance. The role of minister had provided him with a mask that helped him achieve a "vantage ground" by which to uplift others even as he overcame his own fear of them. His new quest for a broader "congregation" makes poignant his disembodied version of the "priestly office" as a means to win "love," especially in view of his ongoing distrust of "society."[19]

Though he had left his own pulpit, Emerson continued to find hope in the heroic image of Jesus he had conceived in 1826–28, an image of courage and steadfastness, of militant alertness and lofty commitment to truth despite the vagaries of nature and the derision of mankind. Believing vision to be moral action, he found the essence of Christianity a significant touchstone. Though he had rejected the value of the historical Jesus, Emerson continued to find great importance in the "uses" of his first hero—and still representative "great man."

In devoting himself to Jesus, Emerson in a curiously personal way had reenacted the classic Christian experience of finding oneself by losing oneself (Mt 10:39). Ostensibly, Emerson's intense devotion is a form of subordination of self to a more powerful and perfect hero.

The vehemence with which Emerson preaches "Christ crucified" is also a form of defense, if not aggression. But the final meaning of Jesus in Sermon No. V is not simply the "Christ crucified" suggested by the short title and by the lurid descriptions and harsh judgments of the sermon. The persecuted Jesus, to be sure, found sympathy from a young minister who needed to project his fears of failure onto a hostile world that could not understand his true gifts. However, Jesus is, in the end, an affirmative image not of passive suffering but of successful heroism. The whole Christian vision, which implies that resurrection follows crucifixion, is expressed in the full context of 1 Corinthians 1:23, which provides the text of Sermon No. V: "But we preach Christ crucified, unto the Jews a stumblingblock, and unto the Greeks foolishness." Paul had continued, "the foolishness of God is wiser than men; and the weakness of God is stronger than men. . . . and God hath chosen the weak things of the world to confound the things which are mighty. . . . But of him are ye in Christ Jesus, who of God is made unto us wisdom, and righteousness, and sanctification, and redemption." Emerson's Jesus may have been stripped of "supernatural" power. But transformed as he was into the stuff of Unitarian and, later, Transcendental myth, Jesus remained in a most important personal way for Emerson the essence of wisdom, righteousness, sanctification, and redemption.

2

Power in the Pulpit:
The Unitarian
Problem of Vocation

"What is the office of a Christian minister?" Emerson asked in his journal sometime in mid-1829 (*JMN* 3:152). His well-known "problem of vocation" in the mid-1830s would be, of course, a Transcendentalist search for a calling outside the pulpit. But this "professional" dilemma was not so much a departure as an extension of his continual reflection on the clerical office and of his sermons on the subject that stand as virtual bookends to his formal career as minister.

Moreover, what we have been accustomed to seeing as the unfrocked Emerson's personal ordeal to reconceive his mission and to empower his voice grows directly out of a collective "identity crisis" in which liberal Christianity had been simmering for three decades. Economic and political, as well as theological, issues had been forcing the ministry—liberal and orthodox alike—to redefine its role in a rapidly changing world. The resulting ongoing debate attracted both professional and public attention, a fact that only heightened the clergy's anxiety to establish its purpose and exercise its power.

Unitarians struggled to articulate their differences from orthodox Congregationalists while defensively insisting that they were still a Christian denomination. But Unitarians, in challenging the very doctrines that had largely invested the New England ministry with an aura of power, had left themselves open to a gnawing question: What was the source of the liberal minister's authority? Emerson's concept of the ministry and his vision of the ideal minister, the products of intensely personal soul-searching, were also characteristic of the age.

When in the spring of 1824 Emerson had played in his journal with the career options available to him, he had, we have seen, ruled out law and medicine; he had already dismissed teaching, which he found stultifying. Divinity meant more to young Emerson than an arena for verbal self-expression and a feeling of control over others; it also meant devotion to a high "calling" that, we shall see, was crucial to his sense of identity. In November 1824, he was dedicating himself to a rigorous moral standard that he already associated with the ministry: "Let me not be esteemed the prophet of lukewarm doctrines betraying my sacred cause to the desire of conciliating ease & worldliness" (*JMN* 2:292).

Not coincidentally, a similar high earnestness appeared a few months later (four years before Waldo's ordination) in the *Christian Examiner*, Winthrop Bailey stressing the clergy's "peculiar necessity for excellence of character" resulting from "the grand moral purpose, which they are designed to accomplish."[1] The minister was obliged to "exemplify the common virtues, which Christianity inculcates" (163) as well as to carry out faithfully "the appropriate duties of his office" (165). This bland-sounding call for clerical exemplariness is actually neither conventional stereotype nor inflated idealization, for it expresses denominational pride that masks a real anxiety. Moral excellence was especially needed, Bailey argued, because liberal Christians did not regard their clergy with fear or awe: "Among us there is nothing but these moral ties, to bind a Christian society to their minister" (166).

The concern about clerical influence, of course, was not new in New England. Throughout the eighteenth century, ministers increasingly had been creatures of both their profession and the secular world. Still, the minister's personal, daily pastoral work had been a stabilizing force within the Congregational clergy and the larger community even during the Great Awakening. For generations, moreover, the minister's power had been based less on the inherent authority of office than on "a principle of consent."[2]

The post-Revolutionary years, however, saw a marked decline in the sense of "permanency" in the ministry as a profession. Economic inflation and a popular "libertarian" mood, Daniel Calhoun has said, joined with "external factors such as the frontier and revivalism and denominational competition" to shake the time-honored image of the minister "settled" for life over a specific congregation.[3] Traditional

Puritan concepts of the political power of the pulpit were also giving way as the clergy faced, in Donald Scott's phrase, a "growing sense of fissure between sacred office and civil office."[4] So far had conventional relationships deteriorated that in the early years of the nineteenth century, Calvinist Timothy Dwight peevishly dismissed the stereotype— held by non-New Englanders—of the supposed power of the New England pulpit: *"The real weight of clergymen in New England,* particularly in Massachusetts and Connecticut, *consists wholly in their influence:* an influence derived from their office and their conduct."[5] Indeed, the emerging Unitarian faction quickly recognized that, with their softening of Reformed dogma, they had forfeited much of the aura of awe and power that lingered in the Calvinist pulpit as a source of authority. The more urbane and educated liberal congregations were turning to *conduct*—encompassing deportment, learning, and literary and social attainment as well as moral reputation—as the basis for weighing clerical "influence."

Increasingly, this influence, these "moral ties" between Unitarian minister and congregation, were cemented by the acknowledged literary superiority of the liberal clergy, as Lawrence Buell has definitively shown.[6] From the perspective of literary history, the Unitarian cultivation of *belles lettres*—ultimately a seedbed of Transcendentalist theory and practice—had a broadening cultural impact and would seem to have won the day over the typically rural Calvinist rearguard action. In its contemporary context, however, emerging Unitarian cultural supremacy was a mixed blessing. The literary calling on the one hand opened new horizons, but on the other it signaled a narrowing base of clerical influence.

Ironically, though the Calvinist pulpit retained more of the traditional power of "office," Calvinists were disdainful (and openly jealous) of the literary prominence of their liberal rivals. Timothy Dwight was particularly sensitive to unflattering comparisons of the intellectual sophistication of New England and British clergy. He tried to strike a pose of moral superiority, but his tone betrays envy: "[A]ny considerable opportunity for pursuits merely speculative," he explained, is virtually ruled out on this side of the Atlantic by the heavy preaching and social duties of our ministers; "[t]he business of a clergyman, it is here believed, is to effectuate the salvation of his flock, rather than to replenish his own mind with that superior information which, however ornamental or useful in other respects, is certainly connected with this end in a very imperfect degree."[7] Liberal ministers, meanwhile, felt no guilt about being men of culture; their constituencies were demanding as much.

But Unitarian ministers in the 1820s had reason for more urgent concern with the reputation of the clergy. Their writings reveal their own defensiveness as a sect, a raw sensitivity to orthodox charges that their humanizing of Christ and exalting of human nature were, in Bailey's words, "hostile to the interests of true religion, and fatal to all genuine piety." Liberals held their own in the bitter pamphlet warfare with Calvinists that lingered into the 1830s. (The acrimony of the debate is epitomized in a pair of pamphlet titles: Calvinist Jedidiah Morse pointedly asked, "Are You of the Christian or the Boston Religion?" only to have liberal John Lowell retaliate with "Are You a Christian or a Calvinist?") But liberals were particularly stung by the snubbing from orthodox ministers who steadfastly refused to exchange pulpits with Unitarians on the grounds that they were not true ministers of Christ. "[H]ow can we hope to maintain our ground," Bailey asked, "unless we are well protected by the armour of righteousness, on the right hand and on the left?" (168). The liberal minister was expected not only to be the traditional pastor and teacher to his flock; he had also, with exceptional character, to deflect from himself and his entire sect suspicions of evangelical coolness and doctrinal and moral looseness.

The conventional thumbnail history of American Unitarianism conveys a misleading image of swift, confident, progressive growth: The denomination's power and respectability in eastern Massachusetts were certified with the naming of Henry Ware, Sr., to the Hollis Chair of Divinity at Harvard in 1805; liberal Christians by 1815 were unashamedly calling themselves Unitarians; the vicious pamphlet exchanges with dour, repressive orthodox Congregationalists subsided by the early 1830s, after which Unitarianism continued its upward spiral, facing a significant threat only in the internal agitation of Transcendentalism. (And, as we shall see, by the time of Emerson's death, Transcendentalism too had been comfortably absorbed into Unitarian historiography.) These are useful touchstones, and certainly the Unitarians themselves conceived of both human moral cultivation and denominational fortunes in images of continual progress and ascent. But such images fail to capture the real anxiety of the liberal clergy into the 1830s.

The plight of the liberal ministry in the early years of the new century was put most starkly in 1811 by Joseph Stevens Buckminster in, significantly, his funeral sermon for Waldo's father, William. After praising Emerson's virtue and dedication, Buckminster confronted the ministers in the audience: "[O]ur ranks are fearfully thinned. Great is the interval between the elder and the younger clergy in this town; an interval now left almost empty." Worry about the very survival of the liberal clergy in Boston was intensified by Buckminster's keen awareness of the precariousness of human affairs in general and by his reminder that absolute consolation belongs only to "him who has the eye of faith." (The death of the young, gifted, charismatic Buckminster himself the following year would thin the ranks even more fearfully.)[8]

Eight-year-old Waldo may not have grasped the significance of Buckminster's complaint, and of course he never outwardly had sympathy for his father's generation. But he would cast his professional lot with a clergy for whom the issue of influence was never fully resolved and for whom, indeed, the spectre of extinguishment would not be dispelled for over a decade. Seemingly mundane but genuine expressions of vocational self-doubt persist in the Unitarian literature throughout the period of Waldo Emerson's ministry. Unitarian morale suffered continually as a result of the greater success of evangelical sects in attracting new members and spreading their missions.[9] Disestablishment of the Congregational and Unitarian churches in Massachusetts in 1833 would provoke new fears that church membership and attendance would slide, forcing ministers to compromise their calling by currying favor with financial backers.[10]

Unitarian pronouncements about the nature and office of "The Christian Minister" might sound to the modern ear like rarefied, flattering self-portraits. But they must be judged in the context of high early-national demands of the ministry coupled with sectarian, economic, and political challenges to traditional assumptions about the structure and role of the clergy. Pronouncements about the *difference* between the liberal minister's mission and that of his Calvinist counterpart can be found in any number of ordination sermons in the early years of the nineteenth century. Delivering the "charge" to the Reverend Nathaniel Langdon Frothingham (whom the young Emerson admired—see *JMN* 3:141), the Reverend John Lathrop related "the office, and character" of the ministry to Paul's time-honored charge to Timothy and Titus. The terms of Lathrop's charge, in fact, remind us of an essential element we are accustomed to overlook in stressing the Arminian and secular implications of Unitarianism: that in exalting the moral law above the person of Christ the mediator, liberal theologians viewed themselves, with their own brand of evangelical intensity, as rediscovering the pure spiritual strain of the Gospel:

> You have a commission to preach the gospel to every creature. The gospel is the most generous proclamation that ever was made. It is limited to no particular nation. The blessings of it are confined to no particular *sects*, or denominations. Although the advocates for particular systems, and the framers of particular creeds, may exclude from their communion all who cannot embrace their *dogmas*, or subscribe their *formulas*, they cannot bar the gate of heaven against the humble christian, who repents of his faults, who loves the Saviour, and endeavours to obey him.

The liberal Christian Minister claimed neither supernatural power nor special privileges of office. As Lathrop encouraged Frothingham, "you will inculcate obedience, by all the motives which can be drawn from the purity and rectitude of the divine law; from the mercy of God in appointing a Saviour; from the obedience, the sufferings and the death of the Messiah; from the hope of happiness, and the dread of misery in a future world." The minister is "an ambassador of Jesus Christ," "a steward of the mysteries of God," "a scribe," "a watchman," "a soldier of Jesus Christ." He is a man not of aloofness but of engagement; but his "conscience" in any given question obligates him to be free of all human opinion—including that of the most revered Church Fathers—and to ask only, " 'What saith the Lord? what say the scriptures?' "[11]

Waldo Emerson would depart, of course, from Lathrop's almost Calvinist high regard for Christ as Saviour, subordinating Jesus' suffering and atonement to his moral purity; and, with the more "progressive" Unitarians, he would come to regard the "future world" not as a place of reward or punishment but as an arena for *continuing* human moral growth. But he inherited the vision, widely held in Lathrop's day, of the unity of moral truth and the preeminence of "conscience" as religious barometer. Emerson would zealously embrace this cornerstone of liberal faith in his ministry, and it would permanently be central to his thought.

The Unitarian concept of the minister as moral and cultural exemplar to a congregation *innately* capable of moral and cultural refinement led to some uncomfortable ironies that in the 1820s began to be apparent outside clerical circles. Ministers might worry about the direction of their profession and the source of their authority. But in Boston, at least, the ranks of the clergy had thickened in the decade since Buckminster's death; the ministry, moreover, retained considerable prestige—in its own mind as well as in that of the public.

Emerson's Harvard classmate Josiah Quincy, who had bested him in the Boylston Prize competition, recalled in old age that "[o]n the topmost round of the social ladder stood the clergy; for although the lines of theological separation among themselves were deeply cut, the void between them and the laity was even more impassable." Indeed, he went on, "I find, in my journal for January 8, 1826, an abstract of a sermon preached that day upon 'Sanctity of Persons,' wherein Dr. Channing thought it necessary to maintain the thesis that ministers, merely in virtue of their office, were no holier than the rest of mankind, and that the reverence accorded them should not differ from that due to Christian laymen whose influence tended to the elevation of our characters."[12]

The gospel of self-culture, it would seem, was a heavy burden, and traditions of neither Puritan piety nor political democracy in New England had dispelled the human propensity to hero worship. Quincy's retrospect hints that the political power of the clergy was ebbing even as the social status of ministers was at its highest point. At the very time when Emerson was preparing to enter the ministry, the profession was straddling the line separating lean years when the struggle for identity and empowerment had built character, from a new age when survival might be expected but at the expense of its vital piety being sucked by the veneration of the genteel. Though he adds an even broader paradox, Moncure Conway recalled that Emerson knew as much: "Emerson's remark, that there was more progressiveness and more enthusiasm in Unitarian ministers of orthodox antecedents than in those of Unitarian birth, is true. They whose freedom has involved struggle carry heat into their ministry. But this is at some cost."[13]

The cost of social prestige without power, however, was what continued to bother the most discerning of the new generation of liberal ministers. The problem was best put by the Reverend Orville Dewey, two of whose most explicit articles on the subject appeared in the *Christian Examiner* near the beginning and end, suggestively, of Emerson's brief career at Second Church. Dewey, who was married to a cousin of Emerson, attacked the false deference given ministers which, in fact, deprived the clergy of *real* influence in the affairs of society. He warned that "there is *a factitious importance ascribed to the official duties and to the whole conduct of a clergyman.*" The ministry, he agreed, is a lofty office, but he objected to bestowing "an unnatural importance, an artificial value" on the minister's specific functions.[14] The minister's benediction is not magic, his social "deportment" that of a normally good man (106–7). In particular Dewey criticized "the ado and formality that often attends" visitation of the sick and dying (110). The key to Dewey's complaint lies in his sense of the hypocrisy of a smug congregation that took advantage of the Unitarian relationship between pastor and flock. Ministers no longer claimed any special divine power, but congregations, abusing the looser requirements of the liberal church, were becoming downright heathenish in shirking *their* responsibility: "It is the duty of the clergyman to *preach;* but not a whit more than it is the duty of others to hear; not a whit more than it is the duty of others to profit by his preaching" (104–5).

Dewey's distemper with liberal congregations is, in a sense, simply in the tradition of New England Puritanism, which always placed heavy responsibility upon the hearer of the Word.[15] But there is a distinctly liberal background to the lament. Buckminster also had laid the principal blame for Christianity's loss of moral influence not on the clergy but on liberal Christians who had stopped reading the Bible and expected to imbibe passively from sermons all they needed for salvation. Nearly a cult figure himself, Buckminster lambasted lazy congregations: "We go to be entertained at our ease. If the speaker fails to effect this grand object," he charged, "we consider ourselves disappointed, and return vacant and uninterested to the occupations of life." The hearer, Buckminster had continued, must give the minister "cooperation" by "personal application" of the sermon's truth to his or her own life, for "[t]here is no miraculous efficacy accompanying the words of any preacher, which will convert an auditor against his choice."[16] The liberal clergy had not anticipated that their congregations would have to be prodded and dragged into the brave new world of human worth and dignity.

Waldo Emerson's regard for oratory and his high sense of the ministry combined with his disdain for the "crowd" to make him receptive to the common Unitarian critique of modern congregations. In early 1826, several months before he was approbated to preach, he wrote in his journal: "The language of the pulpit must seem to many men laborious & extravagant; too strong for the ideas it is designed to convey & appealing to emotions with which they have no sympathy." The average person, he felt, lacked the intellect and the spiritual discernment—indeed the taste—to appreciate the fine discourses created by the liberal clergy. Young Emerson's critique resembles Buckminster's and Dewey's, but his elite sense of spiritual perception merges with a condescending, almost languid aestheticism: Sermon listeners cannot properly value "the expostulations of preachers or the descriptions in which they attempt to clothe ideas beneath which language sinks and is unequal & vain"; indeed, "[t]he minister & the hearer are in two different moods of thought," the one lofty, the other sensual (*JMN* 3:9). No longer mere defenders and "openers" of doctrine, liberal ministers were keepers of precious moral insights that, theoretically accessible to all people, sometimes beggared adequate expression; the minister's self-endowed esoteric discipline could end in exasperation at the obtuseness of his flock and a feeling of isolation.

The experience of preaching, however, tempered Emerson's scorn for those who had not attained his level of spiritual discernment. Just as Dewey had been calling for more realistic conceptions of the clerical office and a corresponding naturalness of pulpit speech, Emerson too began to value direct speech, discovering first hand the moral and civic implications of preaching in a democracy. The tone of his journal entries on the ministry became less haughty; his sense of both the urgency and the problems of communication became less effete, more compassionate. On 10 March 1828 (a year and a day before he was ordained at Second Church), he admitted that preachers "ought perhaps to state explicitly the magnitude & present danger of this enemy [popular prejudice]. But to combat prejudices is all that preaching is for" (*JMN* 3:108). By "prejudice" he meant simply habitual immersion in the things of the world that blunt one's perception of moral right. "Now men entertain very gross prejudices touching the very nature of Religion"—not atheists or the depraved but "good plausible people that go to church for decency's sake but do not obey the Commandments nor observe the Ordinances. . . . They are on a wrong scent, they are undoing themselves, they are living like *animals*. We would have them live like *men*" (*JMN* 3:109–10). Emerson saw the "enemy" facing human reform as no less menacing than he had a couple of years before. But now the pose of disgust at the unregenerate and personal remove from human frailty ceased to satisfy him. His voice becomes more confident, his analysis of the human condition more incisive.

At the same time a more serene sense of vocational purpose begins to emerge in Emerson's journal. In terms that foreshadow his early Transcendentalist interest in correspondence, he proposes "as a question whether the business of the preacher is not simply to hunt out & to exhibit the analogies between moral & material nature in such manner as to have a bearing upon practice" (*JMN* 3:130). And with his new maturity of voice and confidence in his vocation, there emerges in the journals a more generous view of audience. "I am always made uneasy," he wrote on 10 July 1828, "when the conversation turns in my presence upon popular ignorance & the duty of adapting our public harangues & writings to the minds of the people. 'Tis all pedantry & ignorance. The people know as much & reason as well as we do. None so quick as they to discern brilliant genius or solid parts. And I observe that all those who use this cant most, are such as do not rise above mediocrity of understanding" (*JMN* 3:136).

In early journal entries Emerson had entertained a scornful image of audience as wholly *other* than preacher in intellectual grasp, delicacy of perception, and fluency of expression. And some of his early sermons indulged in hothouse rhetoric worthy of Edward Everett that betrayed not simply callowness but real disdain of others. But he came to see, as had Buckminster and Dewey, the risks of an effetely literary ministry, challenging his hearers as well as himself in Sermon No. LV (first delivered 15 November 1829):

> The taste of the times is grown fastidious, & if the preacher does not gratify the imagination or enlarge our conceptions of God, we go away unedified, unsatisfied, & possibly chagrined. My brethren, if the preacher was in fault so is the hearer.

Emerson too had come to see the twin dangers of assuring congregations of the inherent worth of human nature while treating them to merely "literary" sermons. This combination threatened to turn Unitarians from Christians concerned with spiritual growth into casual critics of a kind of dramatic monologue. As had Buckminster, Emerson went on, in Sermon No. LV, to place the burden where it belonged:

> The mind that is in a religious frame, in a highly excited state—welcomes with delight every new truth which the reason or learning of the pulpit can bring to the cause of religion but it does not depend on them for its devotion.

Emerson's change of heart, based on his early experience in the pulpit, also belongs to an ancient tradition of rhetorical theory that distinguishes true eloquence from mere *tour de force*. As Emerson's senior colleague at Second Church, Henry Ware, Jr., put it, pulpit eloquence is not a "high and singular gift," nor "that which conforms minutely to certain rules; nor that which in vulgar estimation is accounted eloquent,—the loud, sonorous, and showy. It is that which best brings out the meaning of the discourse, and leads the hearer so directly to the sentiment, that the manner of its utterance fails to attract remark."[17] Ware's aim was not inoffensiveness or self-repression, for he goes on in tones almost Romantic: "Let him give way to the impulse of his situation, and nature, truth, and feeling, will make him eloquent—that is, will make him effective. The fetters of his unnatural schoolboy habits will relax and drop off. He is once more a man, independent and self-moved." Ware could be offering an antidote to the dull formalism Emerson decried in the Divinity School Address when he declares that when true eloquence appears, "[t]he drowsy, dronelike monotony of indifference, and the artifices of affectation, and the graces which seek applause,—all fly before the business-like sobriety of actual zeal" (187–88). This tradition can be traced back through the *Dialogues on Eloquence* of the French cleric Fenelon, whom Channing, Ware, and Emerson admired, to St. Augustine, Cicero, and Plato, all of whom defined eloquence not as show but as an expression of, and means of shaping, character.

Emerson's concern with sermonic language and the moral dialectics of preacher and hearer remind us that from the very start of his ministry, he regarded eloquent preaching as a higher calling than pastoral tasks. Notwithstanding the Unitarian tradition of upbraiding passive congregations and the public's corresponding growing appetite for literary sermons, liberal Bostonians still craved individual pastoral attention from their ministers. As practical matters, not all Unitarian preachers *were* articulate, and some—articulate and otherwise—were slighting pastoral duties to pour all their energies into belletristic and other cultural endeavors. This especially distressed Henry Ware, Jr., who wrote at length and with feeling that preaching and pastoral duties are mutually enriching, that the effectiveness of the one could not finally be judged in isolation from the other.[18]

Lynde M. Walter's Boston *Evening Transcript* made one of the bluntest assaults on the emerging literary ministry, finding especially obnoxious those *"Puffing Preachers"* who shamelessly hawked public lectures pandering to "Passing and popular subjects": "The whole thing is rank, it smells to heaven."[19] Only slightly less rank to the *Transcript* were the many ministers who, investing all their talents and enthusiasm wholly in the sermon and the worship service, missed the real value of religion. Seething with sarcasm, the *Transcript* recommended that these clergymen read from the pulpit "printed discourses" by *other* authors instead of wasting time writing elegant sermons of their own: "There is no point in which Clergymen so often err, as in negligence of the parochial obligations that require

of them to *visit* their parishioners . . . [to] arouse a feeling of veneration and love." Too many exhibited "cold, repulsive manners"; "the
time has come when Clergymen must occasionally consent to be,
themselves, the auditors, and listen to the Lectures of Laymen."[20]

Too much has been made of Emerson's distaste for pastoral duties.
What needs to be stressed, however, is that his preference for preaching was not unusual within Unitarian circles; moreover, few "literary" ministers were so self-indulgent as to be unconscious of the
special obligations and pastoral dangers inherent in this trend. While
many were criticizing the excesses of literary sermons, Orville
Dewey, in the second of his two articles on the ministry cited earlier,
was warning that sermons *as* literature are "oftener disparaged than
otherwise." Anticipating Emerson's critique of dryasdust preaching
in the Divinity School Address, he called on preachers "to give
themselves up, more than they do, to the bent of their own minds."
Mere "correctness" was deadly. "The best discourses," Dewey believed, "are those which take the form of a personal argument with
the people."[21]

Dewey's terms require careful definition, for Emerson's well-
known aversion to "argument" was already apparent during his ministry. He would have concurred fully with Dewey's concept of "personal argument"—a natural expression of felt truth—as a measure
of integrity. For Dewey the very authority of the ministry was at
stake. Indeed, in "Clerical Office," published only three months
before Emerson's resignation was formally accepted by Second
Church, Dewey returned to his old complaint about the artificial
deference, the popular distinction between *"secular"* and *"sacred"*
careers that had dessicated the influence of the liberal ministry (353).
Dewey sensed a genuine crisis of professionalism, one that Emerson,
with his aspiring after oratorical power, instinctively felt. The contemporary pulpit, Dewey declared, "does not seem a sufficiently
lofty sphere" to men of the world (352). Instead of being placed on
pedestals or under glass as ornaments of society, "[l]et clergymen
stand where other men do" (355). For Dewey, this meant an end
to "our political disenfranchisement"; it meant freedom to hold
property and choose a residence, a reasonable, competitive salary . . .
and an audience worthy of a good minister's talents (357–61). Dewey
demanded virtue of all ministers, but he scorned the genteel attitude
that expected ministers to renounce real power, to be only "examples
of moderation, and simplicity, and indifference to worldly possessions" (364).

While lamenting the clergy's impotence and noting that the ministry too often was a quicker route than law and medicine to obscurity, Dewey came full circle in identifying the ministry's supreme consolation for one seeking immutable fame: "[I]t is mind only what enjoys a distinction that lives; and that mind spread out in immortal productions. . . . Success in authorship, and not success in politics, furnishes the best title to being remembered." And what profession better than the ministry for providing the opportunity for the "intellectual improvement" and "studious leisure" necessary to such achievement. The context for Emerson's career deliberations is evident. Despite his resentment at the vocational emasculation of the clergy through false deference, Dewey viewed the ministry as different in kind from other professions, as higher in calling: "Not only are its opportunities for study great, but the grand object of its cares and labors is one of the noblest of all objects,—to understand and improve the human soul; its themes, too, are all lofty, and the motives urged upon it are of the purest kind" (367–68).

More than Dewey, Emerson was repelled by the sensualism of the laity even as he required them, conceptually and literally, as the object of his uplifting eloquence. And he found the most stirring, heroic model of the clergy in William Ellery Channing. Preaching on "The Christian Ministry" at the dedication of Divinity Hall in 1826, Channing announced that "this edifice is dedicated to the training of ministers, whose word, like their Master's, shall be '*with power,*' " by which he meant "that strong action of the understanding, conscience, and heart, on moral and religious truth, through which the preacher is quickened and qualified to awaken the same strong action in others."[22]

Professional anxiety and evangelical urgency mingle in Channing's declaration: "We want more than knowledge. We want force of thought, feeling, and purpose. . . . Power is the attribute, which crowns all a minister's accomplishments. . . . We want powerful ministers, not graceful declaimers, not elegant essayists, but men fitted to act on men, to make themselves *felt* in society" (3:259). Trying to reclaim the lost authority of the Puritan pulpit while spurning the old theology, he insists that he does not seek *political* power for the clergy "suited to barbarous times," nor does a minister exist to arouse "terror" (3:260). The liberal minister relies instead on "power to act on intelligent and free beings, by means proportioned to their nature" (3:262). Though we are used to reading democratic and Arminian tendencies into such remarks, Emerson would offer staunch reminders that the "liberal" ministry could be spiritually Pauline, politically conservative, in its assessment of human nature.

And for Channing, the minister's essential themes continue to be Christ, transcendence, "the coming of the Son of Man, the resurrection, the judgment, the retributions of the last day. Here are subjects of intense interest. They claim and should call forth the mind's whole power, and are infinitely wronged when uttered with cold lips and from an unmoved heart," he proclaimed in yet another precursor of Emerson's critique of the "formalist" minister more than a decade later (3:263–64).

Avoiding the "morbid" element latent in "fervent" religion (3:268), the liberal minister carries on conventional duties: "to rouse men to self-conflict, to warfare with the evil in their own hearts" (3:269), and "to call forth in the soul a conviction of its immortality" (3:270). After listing the attributes of the clerical personality, Channing stresses that conversion is still the aim of preaching and that "[t]o preach with power, a man must feel Christianity to be worthy of the blood which it has cost." As genuinely as for a revivalist, "[t]his spirit of self-exposure and self-surrender, throws into preachers an energy which no other principle can give. . . . New faculties seem to be created, and more than human might sometimes imparted, by a pure fervent love" (3:284). Channing reminds us that Unitarianism's progressive views of human nature and divine attributes did not require a coldly rational concept of preaching or the ministry but could indeed tap new springs of evangelical intensity.

On 15 March 1829, four days after his ordination at Second Church, Emerson publicly announced his own concept of the Christian Minister, in Sermons No. XXVIII and XXIX. These sermons are, we have known since their publication in *YES*, deeply personal statements of self-image and mission; we are now in a position also to see their fundamental debt to a tradition of perennial Unitarian vocational self-analysis and justification. More than in any other sermon except perhaps No. V, Emerson in Sermon No. XXVIII celebrates heroic Christian martyrdom—in this case St. Paul's—to emphasize the solemn grandeur of the ministry. Paul's "declaration of a valiant heart" ("I am not ashamed of the Gospel of Christ . . ." Rom 1:16) was "no superfluous tender of adhesion to a cause already strong enough nor arrogance of courage where no danger was. It was a challenge that a martyr gives to all manner of pain." In a portrait resembling that of the persecuted Jesus of Sermon No. V, Paul is depicted as standing in the face of cruel abuse: "The Jew & the pagan cried Blood! . . . & where he went, he heard the hisses of the world." Though he sustained this melodrama in the earlier sermon, Emerson abandons this tack early in Sermon No. XXVIII, saying he intends not to revive "a departed indignation" at Nero's having killed Paul, but, more importantly, to inquire into the grounds of Paul's faith.

Emerson wants us to know, however, that he is heir to a conviction no less dangerous in its own way in 1829 than it was in Paul's day,[23] and—following years of educational preparation and apprenticeship—he reaffirms his own "faith" in the high office whose "principal public performances . . . are prayer & preaching." He is already defining prayer not as a formal ritual but as "a fruit of a frame of mind," not of the "intellect" but of the "affections." Preaching, on the other hand, is "a high & difficult office" by which the minister "undertakes to instruct the congregation, himself an erring man . . . to encourage . . . to persuade . . . to melt the obdurate, and to shake the sinner."

Anticipating his criticism of Barzillai Frost in the Divinity School Address, Emerson chastizes ministers who fail to make the most of "eloquence," "[t]he mightiest engine which God has put into the hands of man." As with his concept of prayer, he suggests a key article of Transcendentalist faith that has both democratic and Pauline implications—that despite differences in talent, *all* share in some degree the power of eloquence; and that eloquence, moreover, is not merely verbal but moral: "[E]very man who gives himself wholly up to a just sentiment which he lives to inculcate, will be eloquent." In hindsight he seems to portend his rejection of formal religion, declaring in terms echoed in the Address, that "preaching must be manly & flexible & free beyond all the example of the times before us." Emerson insisted that such a brave freedom was as essential to preaching as it had been to Paul. That Christianity had made so little positive impact in 1,800 years was "not a defect in Christianity itself but a defect in its teaching. Christianity is true." The basis for Emerson's preaching, this conviction was central to his sense of revelation both as a preacher and as a Transcendentalist "sage." Complaining that "our usage of preaching is too straitened," that it "harps on a few & ancient strings," he appeals for the minister to eschew doctrinal and textual logic-chopping and explore the "infinite & universal law" that is true Christianity. Expansively, he announces that he will use "new forms of address, new modes of illustration, & varied allusions"; "I shall not certainly reject them simply because they are new. I must not be crippled in the exercise of my profession."

Emerson was not merely evading vocational constraints and habits, nor was he conceiving his Christian Minister around narrowly personal, literary interests. The minister, he believed, must embrace not only Scripture but also experience, "intellect," and most important, the "affections." Sounding Hawthornean to a modern ear, he declares, "Any defects can be excused but the defect of a pure heart & a good life." It was a cause of deep regret, he believed with Buckminster, when the congregation praise only the minister's style, "his manner, his language, & his voice . . . & then go away & remember the service no more." The real measures of clerical success are the virtue, "solace," and "hope" instilled in the audience.

In Sermon No. XXIX, delivered the same afternoon, Emerson balances his description of the Christian Minister by stressing the pastoral duties. With his well-known concluding appeal for the congregation not to expect too much of him—capped off with formulaic self-deprecation—it is easy to read too much into Emerson's antipathy toward pastoral work. The sermon indeed complements its companion piece by picking up the theme of the minister as "a man of feeling" who engenders feeling in others. Acting in this spirit, the minister, in conducting marriage and baptism, links the secular to the divine; he presents the Lord's Supper not as "a melancholy memorial" but as a ceremony that "commemorates [Jesus'] love." Emerson finds himself called "to affectionate & *domestic* relations as your pastor." He hopes to be regarded not as "an austere zealot" but as "the mild & blameless friend who would win you to a life of purity by the shining example of his own." Though Emerson would not carry out all pastoral duties with gusto, he stressed in his sermons, at least, the "domestic" nature of true virtue and the supremacy of moral "example" over abstract appeal to doctrine. His sense of "society," to be sure, already seems more spiritual than corporeal, but in large part this is owing to his own brand of evangelical zeal that made him acutely sensitive to mutability, to "the symptoms" of death that lent urgency to his profession, to his conviction that in the end only Christ's "sweeter society" could avail much.

Emerson's preference for preaching over pastoral duties is reflected, certainly, in his tone: he sounds more dutiful than enthusiastic when he pledges to tend and uplift the dying ("it is the reason why pastors are made"). But the legacy of Federalist hope in the power of the pulpit as an agent of social control made young Emerson assent, in principle, with Henry Ware, Jr. A preacher must also be a pastor, Emerson believed in 1829, because human contact provides themes for sermons which, in turn, will find a receptive audience of friends.

Emerson sought to carve out a vocation within a profession that for decades had been groping for an identity, alternately confused and sublime in its self-image. Privately, as we have seen in the context of his emerging sense of identity, he was answering the question "What is the office of a Christian minister?" in more Olympian terms than in his sermons (the entry in *JMN* 3:152–53 appears to have been written four months after he preached Sermons No. XXVIII and XXIX). In imagery of aloofness, insulation, Emerson envisions transcendence of the petty emotions and desires that corrupt social life. But these "retired thoughts" follow in the context of a public mission that incorporates reflection and utterance, the minister as seer:

> 'Tis his to show the beauty of the moral laws of the Universe; to explain the theory of a perfect life; to watch the Divinity in his world; to detect his footstep; to discern him in the history of the race of his children by catching the tune from a patient listening to miscellaneous sounds; by threading out the unapparent plan in events crowding on events.

As an inspired watchman, Emerson's minister resembles Lathrop's of a generation earlier. Moreover, Emerson retains a commitment to Scripture as revelation of God: "The world to the skeptical eye is without form & void. The gospel gives a firm clue to the plan of it. It shows God. Find God, & order & glory & hope & happiness begin. It is the office of the priest. It is his to see the creation with a new eye" (*JMN* 3:152).

Emerson's significant point of departure from earlier liberals like Lathrop, however, is his exalting the minister's perception. Already Emerson attributes to the minister much of the orthodox role of Christ. In a passage that epitomizes his goals as a preacher, he sees the minister as "set apart to the office of walking between God & man; of concentrating his mind upon Divine counsels; to come bearing in his hand the immortal Word itself which when this visible world & the heaven itself shall pass away from which others drew their evidences that wax not old shall in no jot or tittle pass away— to hear the Reason of God speaking to the reason of Man, to be familiar with what is holy" (*JMN* 3:152–53).

Such a stance had become familiar in Unitarian circles long before Emerson's heretical pronouncements in the late 1830s. Rejection of the Trinity tended obviously to diminish the role of Christ as an object of worship while, correspondingly, the role of the minister as sensitive recorder of universal truth was enhanced. In Emerson's private musing, only after he has warmed to the image of the minister quivering with divine insight does he introduce the pastoral duties: visiting the "dying" and "bereaved," conducting marriages, and administering baptism and the Lord's Supper. Emerson did not loathe these responsibilities so much as he had conjured up for himself a vision of his flock falling into order eagerly and appreciatively catching his fine pearls of wisdom. With such views of the ministry encouraged by the age's high expectations of pulpit eloquence, the reality of pastoral duties could not but seem secondary to one of Emerson's temperament.

Most significant for the rise of Transcendentalism, Emerson's definition of the Christian Minister presses beyond both denominational and vocational boundaries. Eight years after asking himself "What is the office of a Christian minister?", and while still acting as a supply minister, Emerson would define "The American Scholar" in terms not of occupational "functions" but of integrative activity— as *Man Thinking.* In "the *divided* or social state" one is "seldom cheered by any idea of the true dignity of his ministry" (*CW* 1:53). The scholar—like the Christian, who never achieves perfection, and the minister, who cannot sustain constant eloquence—has not been wholly realized. But the scholar's "duties" *are* a sacred "ministry" because they restore others to themselves: "The office of the scholar is to cheer, to raise, and to guide men by showing them facts amidst appearances." Though fulfilling a crucial role, the scholar enjoys no artificial distinctions but "raises himself from private considerations, and breathes and lives on public and illustrious thoughts" (*CW* 1:62).

In working out his "problem of vocation," Emerson has reversed the terms of his private reflections on the ministry. Instead of retreating from the squalid world to protect his pure sensibility, as the Christian Minister had done, the scholar, in his very freedom from a specific career, is somehow carrying out a *public* mission. The scholar yokes the spiritual insight of a Swedenborg, who "endeavored to engraft a purely philosophical Ethics on the popular Christianity of his time," with the corresponding political acknowledgement of the dignity of "the single person" (*CW* 1:68). "The American Scholar" is, to be sure, a creative if somewhat tentative solution to a unique case of vocational anxiety. But while the address would transcend its immediate occasion to be celebrated as America's cultural "declaration of independence," the vision it offers is one of integrated personality, the mission it outlines, nothing less than a reformulation of the office, character, and duties of the previous decade's "Christian Minister."

3

The Evidences of Christianity
and the Nature of Belief

On 30 December 1826, two and a half months after he began preaching, Emerson wrote humbly to his brother Charles, "The search after truth is always by approximation" (L 1:181). Soon, however, his sermons would proclaim the unshakable trust in the indwelling God that forms the basis of his notorious optimism. Before it was a literary or social "movement," Transcendentalism was an outgrowth of Unitarian epistemology. Emerson's version of Transcendentalism may be said to have sprung from his deep commitment to live out the implications of what was arguably his favorite Scripture verse, "the kingdom of God is within you" (Lk 17:21).

Perhaps the characteristic theme of nineteenth-century Anglo-American literature is the problem of belief, the loss of faith in an age of rationalism, science, utilitarianism, revolution. Emerson's apparent serene indifference to this plight, reflected in his secular gospel of the Over-Soul and his celebration of the age of the first-person singular, has alternately uplifted or exasperated his readers. We are now, of course, more keenly aware of Emerson's private agonies, and of the tensions that underlay his creative work and public life. But in an important sense—and this can be said without disparaging his intellectual complexity or integrity—Emerson never underwent a major crisis of belief.

Understanding the sources of Emerson's Indwelling God demands reconsideration of the major theological—and critical—charge against Emersonian Transcendentalism: that its emphasis on insight was narcissistic. Critics have repeatedly accused Emerson of concocting a system of Idealism as, in Joel Porte's phrase, "primarily a personal stratagem and only secondarily a metaphysical position." Santayana believed that Transcendentalism considered nature a flattering "mirror" in which one would see one's own virtue reflected. And F. O. Matthiessen worried that, because Emerson's "inwardness" lacked external restraint, it was in danger of becoming simply his own "impulse and will."[1] But however personal his quest for religious assurance, Emerson drew on a Unitarian category of thought a generation old and grounded his solution on years of meditation on key Gospel verses.

His appropriation of the character and role of Christ was the product, we have seen, of insecurity. But having settled his sense of identity, he was remarkably consistent for the rest of his life in the view that "[i]nternal evidence outweighs all other to the inner man" (*JMN* 3:214). And having settled the basic question of the ground of religion, he could declare—with no sense of arguing in a circle— "Christianity has this peculiarity that its doctrine is incompatible with imposture & therefore its miracles are real" (*JMN* 3:215). Nowhere in Emerson's early thought is the origin of his Romanticism more evident than in his discovery that the solution to the problem of belief is innate, a vision deeply rooted in New England theology and distinctively refocused in contemporary Unitarian discourse.

I

The hunger for Christian evidence, as old as the religion itself, normally asks two distinct but related questions: *Is* there a God, and Am *I* to be saved by him? These questions were fundamental for the first American Puritans, whom the anxious nineteenth century, while scorning their intolerance, envied because of their perceived lack of doubt. Though Puritans tended to value evidential questions as a preparatory exercise in "humiliation," looking *within* for assurance had always been characteristic of New England religion. When orthodox and liberal Congregationalists quarreled over the nature of revelation in the early nineteenth century, they were simply reviving the terms of an age-old debate.[2]

According to Conrad Wright, it was Locke who "shifted the whole issue of Christian faith, from inner conviction to external testimony." And though the early Unitarians were, as Wright says, "almost wholly derivative" in their formulations of the Christian evidences, they deemed this line of thinking crucial in distancing liberal religion from Deism.[3]

Bishop Butler, whose *Analogy of Religion* young Waldo admired, had attempted to shore up Christian revelation by appeal not to human reason but to miracle and prophecy, proofs supposedly transcending human frailty. Indeed, J. K. S. Reid has argued, before 1800 miracles were invoked not to support belief in God per se, but to establish the divine origin of revelation. The Deist attack was aimed primarily not at the question of God's existence but at revelation as a source of authority. Hume, for example, did not deny miracles but that miracles can "be used to provide evidential proof," since human perception itself is so fragmentary.[4]

Responding to Hume, English apologists like Soame Jenyns and William Paley began to treat prophecy and miracle not, in Reid's phrase, "as external proofs, like flying buttresses," but as fundamental to "the substance" of Christianity. Paley's famous "watchmaker" God, presented in *View of the Evidences of Christianity* (1794), was not an original concept, but it marked a new emphasis on evidences not simply as support for the divine origin of revelation, but as justification for belief in God's very existence. Paley is often viewed as a rationalistic logic-chopper at the dawn of Romantic sensibility. But the real irony of his argument from design was that his analogies on the one hand led *away* from rationalist objectivity into, quoting Reid again, a "subjective fog of anthropomorphism,"[5] and on the other hand tended to vitiate the emotional and spiritual grounds of belief.

Undaunted by these ironies, American Unitarians waged the battle against Calvinism in large part on the basis of scriptural "evidence." Calvinists like Buckminster's imposing father had tried to preempt Scripture altogether as a ground on which to engage the liberals, professing astonishment at their casual preaching of soft views of human nature and of our relation to Christ: "I don't know but many may do this from an honest, but, in my view, very erroneous apprehension, that it will serve to remove the objections of some amiable moral characters, and conciliate them to the Gospel. But what advantage is it to conciliate them to a Gospel that is not the Gospel of Christ, and fails of the energies necessary to make them holy and happy?"[6]

Though literary historians are interested in Unitarianism chiefly as a forerunner of the American Renaissance, it is a mistake as great as the elder Buckminster's to ignore at face value what the liberals vehemently insisted was the ground of their religion: a truer reading of Scripture. The notion of depravity, Henry Ware argued, was inconsistent with Scripture, with experience, and "with the moral perfection of God."[7]

Liberals were adept at arguing verse and line with Calvinists, being especially eager to point out that the Bible alludes only once to the notion of the Trinity (Mt 28:19), and even there is "wholly silent as to the requisite distinction of their perfect equality and perfect unity."[8] And they were confident that an enlightened reading of the Bible, far from being lax and self-serving, was actually saving Christianity from the repellent encrustations of Calvinist theology, which was wholly out of keeping with the modern temper. Scripture, James Diman Green wrote during Emerson's ministry, holds up to critical scrutiny. We should neither fear the rumblings of the orthodox nor demand uniformity in the Gospels. Just as Emerson would later decry a "foolish consistency," Green claimed that diversity is a human virtue, and that the credibility of the Gospels is best established by regarding each writer as a real man. Otherwise, we call into question "the character and competency of the sacred historians." Indeed, he argued, the notion of "continued miraculous superintendence and suggestion" actually "destroys all internal evidence of genuineness and authenticity," leaving Scripture's defenders helpless against skeptical charges of "discrepancies in the accounts of the Evangelists." The Gospel writers were "divinely illuminated upon the great truths of the religion, but . . . in giving an account of our Saviour's life, they were left to the exercise of their natural powers."[9] Thus did many Unitarians seek to uphold the religious truths of the Gospels by celebrating the very diversity of their witnesses—not by demanding an externally imposed consistency in the synoptic texts but by stressing the "internal" coherence of each as an inspired but human product.

The authority of the Bible, recent studies of Unitarianism have demonstrated, underwent drastic redefinition at the hands of liberal Christians. From the beginning of the nineteenth century, liberals with mounting eagerness yoked European "Higher Criticism" to their more generous view of human nature, enthroning morality—established by reason and sentiment—as the essence of religion.[10] But biblical scholarship, which the liberals tended to value as rescuing Scripture from the absurd anachronism of Calvinist literalism, served ironically to undermine its authority altogether. Ultimately, the expectation that a Christian should be not simply devout but also critically astute contributed to the reputation of Unitarianism—

not dispelled in our own day—as an elite enclave of intellectual snobs.

From the outset many Unitarians saw historical criticism as emotionally unsatisfying, as threatening the moral basis of religion. One solution was to superimpose over the rationalist view of Scripture a doctrine of special providences, or miracles, a stance obviously open to suspicions of arbitrariness and special pleading. Emerson's well-known denunciation of this position in the Divinity School Address ("the very word Miracle, as pronounced by Christian churches, gives a false impression; it is Monster. It is not one with the blowing clover and the falling rain." *CW* 1:81) is only the most famous critique of using miracles lodged in the musty past as the basis of faith. The "miracles controversy" intensified in the wake of Emerson's Address, but it had been brewing for at least fifteen years.[11]

Approaching the Bible poetically as well as rationally, many liberals found a satisfying ground of religious authority in positing the true Christian as one possessing innate moral sensibilities that would blossom under the influence of uplifting preaching. The "basis of belief" for most Unitarians was "a vague but ardent core of poetic feeling," says Lawrence Buell, who points to the inspirational sermons of Channing as the precursor of "the Emersonian synthesis of religion and art."[12]

Our fuller understanding of the aesthetic legacy of Unitarianism, however, threatens to overshadow the real urgency with which liberal Christians sought to retain a vivid, empowering belief in revelation. As a result, we inadequately appreciate the nature of Emerson's Transcendentalist concepts of inspiration, or intuition. Though they were "liberals," Unitarians still considered themselves "Christians," and they keenly recalled their common stand with the Calvinists against the threat of Deism at the turn of the century.[13] Whatever the difficulties posed by reading the Bible as an historical document, Unitarians insisted that they had not abandoned but only rediscovered revelation.

The preacher who most articulately sought to resolve the split between historicism and revelation was the man most responsible for introducing the Higher Criticism to America, Joseph Stevens Buckminster. For Buckminster the problem came down to which "evidence" was the best proof of God's will. This issue continued to exercise Unitarians of the next generation, conservatives like Andrews Norton arguing for the primacy of "historical evidence," Transcendentalists resting their case on inspiration. Buckminster charted a richer middle course, one familiar to Emerson by January

1825 as a divinity student. Buckminster's *Sermons* (1814) were included in Channing's "Course of Study for Students in Divinity," and Emerson noted reading "Buckminster's 1st Sermon On evidences" (*JMN* 3:354, 356).

Buckminster regarded "external" and "internal evidence" as related in much the same way that the Old Testament was related to the New in traditional Christian typology—as an historically valid foreshadowing that is not cancelled but fulfilled by the new dispensation. One had first to try to close with "the external evidence of the gospel, or, in other words, the credibility and authenticity of the historical testimony on which it rests." External evidence provided an objective, legal basis for belief and morality—comparable in Buckminster's scheme to the Covenant of Works in Reformed theology. Where the Puritan became terrified by a sense of the inadequacy of this lower stage in the order of salvation, Buckminster regards it simply as the base from which the Christian launches an ever-advancing inquiry into God's purpose:

> But when his conviction from this source is sufficiently established, and in this regular way, let the inquirer direct his attention to what is called its internal evidence, such as the character of Christ and his apostles, the nature of his instructions, and what we understand in general by the spirit of the gospel. In this way, if he is an inquirer of an ingenuous disposition, and of a heart warmed with the love of virtue, he will love the gospel too well to suffer any relicks of doubt to disturb him; he will be unable to reject what appears so divine, and what he finds so powerful, or to think it to be any thing else than what he wishes it to be,—the word of God.[14]

Internal evidence provided a new order of proof, sealing the truths of historical evidence and leading to both virtue and absolute assurance, while allowing Buckminster simply to dismiss the common fear that Higher Criticism would undermine the divine origin of Scripture.

Were the hypothetical "inquirer" not required to wrestle first with the external evidences, however, he would stand on the edge of Romantic narcissism as surely as earlier New Englanders who hungered too exclusively for the Covenant of Grace flirted with Antinomianism. There is more than a hint in Buckminster of strong imagination, of *willing* to believe that inspiration is divine. What makes his concept of evidences so distinctly Unitarian, however, and what is clearly reflected in Emerson's sermons, is the *meaning* of "internal evidences." According to Buckminster, they consist of a personal appreciation of, and identification with, Christ's "character" and "instructions."

Dramatically "transport[ing]" his audience "back to Judea," entering "history" *imaginatively*, Buckminster proclaims "four remarkable circumstances" in the gospel depiction of Jesus: "the *unexpectedness*, the *originality*, the *sublimity*, and the *consistency* of the character" (26). Contemplation of these traits reveals their divinity, leading us to want to "imitate" Jesus (40). Though, as we shall see later, "imitation" was an accepted part even of Puritan devotion, Buckminster's inference from this principle anticipates Channing's doctrine of "likeness to God" by about two decades: "[F]or the more like God, the perfection of all excellence, you become, the more will you feel all that is godlike in his Son" (40–41). Buckminster hopes through evidences to confirm the divinity of Christianity; his highest proof—anticipating Transcendentalism—is that one "feels" the sublimity of Jesus.

Throughout the late 1820s and early 1830s the *Christian Examiner* was filled with review essays of works dealing with the Christian evidences. Typically the reviewers welcomed *diversity* of evidences. In a relaxed, open-minded mood, Samuel Atkins Eliot offered that "[s]trong . . . as is the accumulated proof of revelation, men are always demanding more and stronger evidence," which was "very reasonable and proper" for "Rational beings."[15] Democratically, he suggested that in God's design there is "some kind of evidence or other adapted to the character of every mind." It was finally of little importance whether one preferred "historical, and internal critical evidence" or "moral internal evidence"; indeed, "[w]e rejoice in the power and the concurrence of both to establish the same truth." Though Eliot was uncommonly freewheeling in his judgment, his evidential theory rested on a doctrine shared by all Unitarians, conservative and radical, from Buckminster and Channing to men as unlike as Norton and Emerson: "The adaptation of Christianity to the nature of man, and its conformity with what we know of the character of God, is, unquestionably, to him who will reflect upon it, a very powerful evidence of its divine origin" (131–32. Buckminster had made the same point in *Sermons* [1814], 132).

Internal evidence, then, appealed to Unitarians for a variety of reasons: It overcame the emotional and logical dead end of historical evidence; it seemed an alternative to orthodox concepts of grace and revelation, stamping liberal Christianity with a seal of genuine piety; and it philosophically conformed the miraculous to the natural.

Underlying the general Unitarian concern for "more and stronger evidence," however, was the one great Christian promise that the early liberals had been especially anxious not to lose: the promise of immortality. In his Dudleian Lecture, "The Evidences of Revealed Religion" (1821)—a copy of which Emerson owned—Channing declared Christianity itself "a miraculous religion." And he clung to two "intellectual aids not given by nature. I refer to the doctrine of one God and Father, on which all piety rests; and to the doctrine of Immortality, which is the great spring of virtuous effort." Or, as he put it more bluntly, "The natural world contains no provisions or arrangements for reviving the dead." Channing concluded his lecture with brief reference to a kind of evidence "still more internal" than the essentially "internal *critical* evidence" (to use Eliot's phrase) that he had been stressing. Evidence based on "feeling" led to "a conviction more intimate and unwavering than mere argument ever produced." This kind of evidence (Eliot's "*moral* internal" variety) would be not an afterthought but the *essential* evidence for a young Channing admirer whose outspokenness on the issue would shake the Unitarian pulpit.[16]

II

For young Emerson, too, the questions of discernment, evidences, and immortality were intertwined. His reading on the Christian evidences was diverse, including Addison, Paley, and Channing. Paley, moreover, was one of several authors cited in his outline of his second-place Bowdoin Prize essay, "A General Plan for a Dissertation on the Present State of ethical Philosophy" (*JMN* 1:254). As an undergraduate, Emerson felt that the "Christian Fathers" had confused the issue of "the foundations of morals" by pitting "the laws of reason & revelation" against each other (*JMN* 1:258), and so he welcomed Paley among those philosophers who explained the purpose of the universe and the "grounds upon which [Christianity] rests" (*JMN* 2:34).

In his journals for October and November 1822, however, Emerson begins attempting to establish "evidences" in his own terms, speculating at length on "OMNISCIENCE" and ""OMNIPOTENCE." "All the attributes of the Deity," he noted, "are attributes of human nature ... extended to infinity" (*JMN* 2:24). (Channing had based "The Moral Argument Against Calvinism" [1820] on human ability to understand God by his "attributes.") He then writes that God is known either "*a priori*" or by rational study of nature (which includes "the internal and external evidences of Revelation"), and comments that while there is nothing new in these proofs, "the Conclusion grows irresistible by its accumulated weight" (*JMN* 2:26–28).

Yet Emerson probes the purpose of the universe for reasons that finally have little to do with logical proof: with "an Omniscient Governor" "[y]ou feel at once *secure*. . . . You feel that you are known" (*JMN* 2:33). Emerson's strikingly personal God (he would be condemned by Ware sixteen years later for *denying* the personality of God) is essential to his sense of well-being and of moral empowerment.

However scrupulously Emerson pondered the Christian evidences as keys to the source of all meaning, an unmistakable playfulness colors his speculation. In a particularly revealing journal entry for 2 November 1822, he deprecates the inability of his "adventurous and superficial pen" to add even "a straw to the weight of evidence." He formally nods to "Clarke, Butler, and Paley; to Sherlock, and to the incomparable Newton" for having "established the grounds" of Christianity. But with his "wayward imagination," he concludes with tongue in cheek, "For the present, I must be content to make myself wiser as I may, by the same loose speculations upon divine themes" (*JMN* 2:34). Even in his most soul-baring letters to Aunt Mary, the levity shows through. On 16 October 1823 he worries about "the Scotch Goliath, David Hume," and wonders, "Who is he that can stand up before him & prove the existence of the Universe, & of its Founder?" Significantly, he continued to read—and like— Hume, and though he professes to want "impregnable propositions" to answer skepticism, his own final solution is implied in what he offers to Mary as a dilemma, that "every one is daily referred to his own feelings as a triumphant confutation of the glozed lies of this Deciever [*sic*]" (*L* 1:138). Emerson's moral seriousness is real enough. But the expressed existential despair is largely a veil for a growing confidence about the true source of assurance.

III

Emerson's Sermon No. XLIII reveals in its contents and its history just how gradual was his evolution from Unitarianism to Transcendentalism, as Christian revelation and Romantic inspiration become indistinguishable. Unlike many of his earlier sermons, Sermon No. XLIII appears to have no specific sources in the journals, save for a few brief references, but rather to have been written out independently as a sermon. Beginning with a harsh warning of the moral dangers besetting liberal Christianity, Emerson goes on to stress that perception and the "development of the human mind" are the essence of all religion. He outlines three ways in which the soul is connected to God, calls for repentance, and proclaims the consolation and the joy derived from holy living. Delivered ten times between 12 July 1829 and 11 February 1838, Sermon No. XLIII suggests that Emerson was challenging formal religion at least from his earliest days as a minister at Second Church, and that he continued to hold these convictions during the most creative years of his Transcendentalist "revolt."

Readers accustomed to thinking of Emerson's brand of Unitarianism as the opposite of Calvinism, as an affirmation of divine benevolence and human goodness, will be surprised by his opening blast against liberal religion. The young minister warns his congregation that, in overturning doctrines of original sin and predestination, liberal Christians have left themselves open to a moral laxness with very real dangers. In priding themselves on perceiving the metaphorical nature of the Calvinist's angry God, Unitarians too often fail to regard the spiritual life seriously and drift into secular lethargy. Emerson draws on the rhetoric of the Puritan jeremiad, declaring that he would welcome the constraints of a bygone era, if need be, to chasten the human heart. Admittedly, his lax Unitarian turns out to be a straw man, for Emerson has the solution to this moral danger in redefinition: "[T]his laxity does not belong to true Christianity, but to bad men"; the burden of much of the sermon is to show just how demanding the religious life is. But his firm stance here is also in keeping with his long-held standards for being a true Christian. As early as November 1824 he had dedicated himself to a rigorous ministry: "Let me not be esteemed the prophet of lukewarm doctrines betraying my sacred cause to the desire of conciliating ease & worldliness" (*JMN* 2:292). In Sermon No. XLIII he argues that, lacking traditional doctrinal constraints, liberal religion must discover the "power" to inspire and guide moral behavior.

The sermon in part is an implicit response to recent criticism by Emerson's senior colleague at Second Church, Henry Ware, Jr. In a letter to Ware on 1 July 1829 Emerson expressed genuine concern that he had given the impression that he did not highly enough regard the Scriptures: "I shall certainly take great pains to remove any such impression. I consider them as the true record of the Revelation which established what was almost all we wanted to know, namely

the Immortality of the Soul—& then, what was of infinite importance after that was settled, the being & character of God. With the
revelation, we have very strong evidence of this immortality in Nat.
Religion but without it very insufficient" (*L* 1:273).[17] To an extent,
Emerson's staunch tone in Sermon No. XLIII certifies the legitimacy
of his religious views for friendly but worried critics like Ware. In
chastizing lax Christians, in arguing for the strenuous life, he is in
effect demonstrating his sincerity to Ware, but he is nonetheless
declaring heartfelt standards for a spartan life of the spirit.

Emerson's statement that "Christianity is only the Interpreter of
Natural Religion" partially addresses Ware's concern that he was not
adequately emphasizing revelation, while it also signals directions
in Emerson's concept of inspiration that would culminate in *Nature*
(1836). In October 1823 Emerson had been deeply impressed by William Ellery Channing: "He considered God's word to be the only
expounder of his works, & that Nature had always been found insufficient to teach men the great doctrines which Revelation inculcated" (*JMN* 2:161). In 1829—and in 1838, when he was still using
Sermon No. XLIII—Emerson continued to find unaided Nature insufficient to teach truth; but now revelation is conferred not by "external doctrines" but by direct experience. In making revelation a more
purely personal matter, Emerson was preaching an intense piety that,
on its face, Ware could hardly condemn, but that finally undermined
denominational authority. The "relation which the soul bears to
God" is so powerful, so immediate, that it levels sects. All religions—
including, significantly, Priestley's Unitarianism—are but the
lengthened shadows of individual encounters with God.

The notion that "the poor fences of human sects" fall before the
perception of God was a conviction of long standing for Emerson. As
early as March 1826 he had even speculated that the *universality* of
"moral truth" threatened "[t]he much admired argument that proves
the divine nature of Xty from its progressive adaptation to the advancing condition of humanity"; " 'Tis sublime," he declared, "to
see Unanimity, uniformity, one sect, one Creed, in morals or if you
please in the science of manners if in nothing else in the universe"
(*JMN* 3:14–15). Yet he continued to regard Christianity at its best as
an essence that *fostered* such "Unanimity," for the universality of
"Xn sentiment," he felt confident, was "an argument of my immortality" (*JMN* 3:144–45). Later in his ministry his criticism of sectarianism would become more incisive and caustic, lending itself to
aphorism: "A Sect or Party is an elegant incognito devised to save a
man from the vexation of thinking" (*JMN* 3:259); and in terms recall-

ing Sermon No. XLIII, he would declare that "[r]eligion is the relation of the Soul to God, & therefore the progress of Sectarianism marks the decline of religion" (*JMN* 3:260).

Emerson had always been inclined to believe in the universality of truth while, paradoxically, believing true Christianity to be most conducive to that insight. And like Channing he continued in the 1820s to regard revelation as the interpreter and confirmer of natural religion, though, as we have seen in his journals, he had begun to locate revelation in the moral sense itself. But as early as September 1826 he also sensed a fatal flaw in liberal theology. Though he interpreted "confederated evidence" of "design" in nature as proof of the existence of God and accepted natural religion as a synthesis of several kinds of proof, he had come to feel that "the best historical evidence" is weak: "But moral evidence, the evidence of final causes when it can be procured is unerring & eternal" (*JMN* 3:47). In Alexandria in May 1827 he was more explicit: "consciousness better evid[ence] than proof" (*JMN* 3:79).

Using Emerson's journals to "prove" the origin and development of his ideas is a risky venture. Journal entries must be read not only in their immediate context but also with the understanding that Emerson frequently gropes, tries out ideas, experiments with voices. Within a matter of days he can be found doubting the very existence of God and confidently proclaiming unshakable faith, worrying about the ministry as a vocation and declaring that it ideally suits his talents and temperament. The journals, in short, seldom reveal unambiguous linear development of ideas over time. But Sermon No. XLIII carries out the implications of a shift in Emerson's concept of the very grounds of religious belief, a shift that had been in the making for years. He was not rejecting science nor was he denying the importance of reason. He was simply and emphatically declaring what he had long held, that the personal experience of God "reveals" the meaning of life and all human endeavor.

Even Emerson's most graphic metaphor of the soul's drawing unto God, the attraction of "steel-filings" to a magnet,[18] suggests a dilemma in using natural facts to convey a spiritual fact. For while he declares that "[a]ll nature is full of symbols of its Author," he has cautioned that any natural sign is "but a faint type of the power of this idea upon the soul of man." Nature suggests the soul's relation to God, but that relation is not made real until the mind's "hidden virtue is called forth when God is revealed." Emerson's brand of revelation, however, is not orthodox. Subtly spurning the old Puritan emphasis on hearing the Word of God, he declares that "the soul becomes aware of the presence of God—not by the hearing of the ear but by its own belief." According to the letter to Ware already cited, immortality and the very existence of God were at stake in the question of revelation. How, then, beyond the individual's subjective assertion, is belief established?

God "manifests himself in the material world; . . . in the history of man; . . . in our own experience." All are proofs. But Emerson's sequence of ascending value suggests what he goes on to make explicit, that revelation is not inherent in the "material Creation," however glorious a sign of God nature may be. In early journal entries, we have seen, Emerson had approvingly cited William Paley's argument from design to prove the existence of God (*JMN* 2:416). Patterns and consistency in nature had seemed to reinforce Emerson's sense of the universality of truth, and reason and revelation had seemed compatible. Christianity does not "enjoin" upon us "the improvement of the mind," he had written on 9 January 1828; but it is implicit that when revelation removes the scales from our eyes we should use our new faculties (*JMN* 3:100–101).

But with his notion of revelation becoming less dogmatic, the argument from design became less satisfying. Emerson in this sermon confronts, as David Robinson points out, "the moral problem left by natural theology."[19] In the summer of 1829 he noted that a minister must be familiar with the "sciences" but that Paley and Newton now seemed shallow (*JMN* 3:152–53). Paley's watchmaker God is rejected because the concept separates "the laws of nature" from the active "power" of God. [20] Emerson's insight brings us full circle to the point in late-eighteenth-century apologetics when the "evidences" were no longer brought to bear primarily on the question of revelation but were expected to "prove" the *existence* of God. Short of a return to Christian dogma, Emerson was asking, how could religion interpret natural law with a power commensurate with the human need for inspiration and moral growth?

In a passage that anticipates the mystical "transparent eyeball" experience in *Nature*, Emerson declares that "when I look abroad I receive directly from him these impressions of earth and sea and sun and stars and man and beast." As the original draft of this passage makes explicit, Emerson found in the Ideal philosophy of Bishop Berkeley an impregnable solution to the otherness of the phenomenal world. True perception was not in the object, nor in human organs of sense, but in the inspired inner eye of the perceiver. The road to *Nature* lay not in exalting the material creation as a source of inspiration, but in defining perception itself as an experience of the divine.

Thus Emerson meshed the Idealism of Berkeley with inherited New England Puritanism. Emerson proclaimed the immediate perception of God in nature; but he went on to subordinate, or to subsume, nature (and even "the moral creation," which he skims over) under "the *individual experience*," much as he would distinguish the "NOT ME" from the soul in *Nature*. Much of the power of this sermon—and later the very moral force of Transcendentalism—lay in Emerson's redefinition and revitalization of revelation. ("Whenever a true theory appears," he would declare in *Nature*, "it will be its own evidence" [*CW* 1:8].) In silently abandoning scriptural revelation as an external proof, Emerson had lost the confirmation of natural religion that Channing had known; and by locating revelation in the individual's direct experience of God, he was opening himself up to charges of infidelity. But we have seen his growing tendency to identify "Christianity," in its universal, essential form, with revelation. He had come, indeed, to equate pure Christianity with Idealism. This stance was beginning to be seen by some Unitarian contemporaries as theological sleight of hand; after the Divinity School Address, when its implications were more fully realized, it would be seen as apostasy. But in 1829 direct experience, or intuition, provided Emerson with a version of assurance, a divine confirmation of natural religion that he demanded as strenuously as the most orthodox theologian.

Emerson's basing the emotional and moral evidences of religion on the immediate perception of God, on consciousness, may seem grounded on little more than the will to believe, even on hopelessly unverifiable subjectivism or narcissism. This was one of Ware's major concerns about Emerson's too loose regard for Scripture. But Emerson, no less concerned than Ware with certifying revelation as the basis for all knowledge, was aware of the problem, and his solution accounts for the powerful evangelical tone of much of this sermon.

Revelation, the experience of God, he asserts, is not merely abstract or ethereal; it is "a relation of the faculties and the affections, and so, of all the actions," changing one's perception of the most common and of the highest of human achievements. Emerson sees no antinomian dangers in the individual's encounter with the divine: "I do not think the man lives that comes up to this celestial mark," though all have "desires and glimpses of this beatitude." Indeed, this gap was to become a major intellectual problem for him after the 1830s. Because moral growth is a never-ending process, one can never wholly rest in assurance or self-satisfaction. Emerson acknowledges, moreover, that Jesus—though perhaps no more divine than man—was sent to reveal the truth. And most important, he declares that the source of man's greatest spiritual insight "is not man, it is God in the soul." This is Emerson's version of the "external" moral check he had found wanting and rejected in formal religion. He goes on to remind his listeners that life continues to offer misery, pain, and death. Living according to God's will leads not to transcendence of the world but to a blessed chastening in keeping with the human condition.

There is a tendency in Emerson, as Robinson points out, for the biblical text he purports to open to become merely a "literary epigraph."[21] Emerson's choice of Acts 17:28 seems remarkably well suited, however, to the vision expressed in Sermon No. XLIII. While finding orthodox grounds for belief unconvincing, he shows, with passion as well as reason, not only how we perceive the divine but how that perception alters our faculties, relationships, achievements, and ability to withstand adversity.

One senses that the "afflicted" man who faces "obscurity" and death with peace is a melodramatically inflated projection of Emerson's self, for the early journals are filled with lamentations about his poor health, lack of purpose, and failure to win renown. But on 23 September 1826 Emerson had pondered the theme of misery consoled, of the iron-clad strength of martyrs, and reflected that this "consolatory soliloquy" might later become a sermon (JMN 3:46). There is no direct borrowing from this entry in Sermon No. XLIII, yet Emerson does dramatize the consolations of religious perception when it becomes a way of life. The sermon is, we have seen, an extended redefinition of the vitality of revelation, and he returns at the end to his opening warning that liberal Christianity can be too easy. Having stressed not only the consolation and the joy of holy living but also its demand for self-denial, he asks: "Is this lax? Will this excuse our sins? He to whom these feelings are habitual is furnished for all duty, is armed against disaster. But it is high, it is hard of attainment" (cf. Psalm 139:6).

Emerson knew that his theological views were being scrutinized. And he was sensitive to suggestions that his brand of religion lacked strength and discipline; these were traits he valued highly, for moral law was central to his theology. His insistence that his version of revelation is even more strenuously demanding than what passed for Unitarianism is thus both a defense and an assertion of genuine conviction. It is also one of many suggestions in Sermon No. XLIII that Emerson in the late 1830s did not leave behind the major habits of thought formed during his ministry. For even in his most archetypally Transcendentalist essay, he is concerned that "Self-Reliance" not be misconstrued as self-indulgent and easy, echoing Sermon No. XLIII with a well-known challenge: "If any one imagines that this law is lax, let him keep its commandment one day" (*CW* 2:42).

Sermon No. XLIII was written and first delivered at a time when Emerson was courting Ellen Tucker, embarking on his only full-time ministry, and immersing himself in a variety of civic and charitable activities befitting his public role. Yet in 1837–38, after the publication of *Nature*, he began to use the sermon again—at a time when, besides temporarily supplying various pulpits, he was becoming increasingly active on the lecture circuit and delivering the Phi Beta Kappa address ("The American Scholar") at Harvard. Indeed, Sermon No. XLIII was preached for the last time just five months before the Divinity School Address would touch off a frequently bitter controversy in Unitarian circles, branding Emerson an infidel and thrusting him into unexpected (and unwanted) leadership of the Transcendentalist "party."

But as Robinson has argued convincingly, Emerson's "dissatisfaction" as a minister had been "essentially professional, or vocational," not "intellectual,"[22] and crucial ideas formulated in the sermons continued to inform his creative outpouring of the late 1830s. The editors of volume one of *The Early Lectures* observed that Emerson's "closest study" of science was "coincident with the intellectual crisis which led to his resignation as pastor of the Second Church (1832) and culminated in the publication of *Nature*"; but their suggestion that his study of science "was perhaps the principal agent in his shift from a theological to a secular base for his moral philosophy" (*EL* 1:1) does not fully account for this "shift." The issue, we have seen, was rather the personal appropriation of the concept of revelation, which for Emerson predated and verified what was of value in science. That is why Emerson in good conscience could still present Sermon No. XLIII to congregations after *Nature* had more firmly anchored insight in the "secular" world. The radical nature of the "inward revelation," the essential continuity from Emerson's Unitarianism to Transcendentalism, is epitomized in a subtle prepositional shift—Emerson's willful, telling revision of the Gospel definition of Emmanuel: Matthew's "God with us" (Mt 1:23) becomes, at the end of Sermon No. XLIII, "this literal Emmanuel *God within us.*"[23]

IV

The "God within," Emerson's version of the Christian evidences, is the definitive theme of the sermons, a theme that did not emerge from one moment of insight but that was treated in countless variations. In Sermon No. XXI he was already beyond Paley in arguing for innate knowledge. But in commending "Conscience" for "the very striking proof it furnishes, of the existence & government of God," he stressed the importance of *nurturing* this principle (he hesitated to call it a faculty). On a moral plane, Emerson's God here retained traces of Paley's removed watchmaker, for the principle of conscience he has instilled in us precludes the need for "the continual interference of the Deity." So compelling a guide is "the gravitation of the moral world" that Emerson found it inconceivable that it could be "uncaused" by God. And conventionally he found the moral order "seconded" and sealed by Christ.

By Sermon No. XXIII, however, he was already probing more boldly the implications of such insight. In our mundane pursuits, he argued, we often fail to appreciate how our innate "knowledge of God" raises us above "the level of the brutes." Despite our differences of opinion, "this redeeming faith" in "a superior intelligence" is found everywhere, even outside the Judeo-Christian world. "We put God away from us, by calling his operation, his *laws*," Emerson said, for we need look no farther than our own bodies and emotions to sense God's plan. And "although there is a perpetual flux & change, yet the same order lasts to the next moment, to the next day, for years, for centuries." Not voicing here concern about want of "consecutiveness" that would haunt the middle essays, Emerson declared that the "moral constitution of our minds" being ever the same, the best evidence of God "is from these simple observations, & not from abstruse reasonings." This is better evidence than "thunder," "earthquake," "comets." Evidence is not found "by painful study": "The Kingdom of God is within you. And there its evidence is best explored." Far from producing willful self-reliance, the principle of conscience recalling us to duty is as ever-present as the God in whom we have our being.

Emerson's sermons on moral truth *as* evidence explore the polar notions that truth is eternal and that all is mutable. Sermons XCVIII to C all enrich the theme that moral truth is never truly fixed but is organic: Truth is not relative; rather, as he argues in Sermon No. CLVIII, God presupposes that each moment is new. Truth is thus encountered in time and place, making religious insight and moral growth a process of continual self-reconstruction.

Nor did Emerson want his concept of looking within to entail asocial navel-gazing. He could be eclectic, for example, in recommending aids to reflection. In his published review of *A Collection of Psalms and Hymns for Christian Worship,* he praised "this poetry" for its "lively and affectionate conception of God"; indeed, "it is not the Bodies of Divinity, nor the ablest religious works, whether in prose or verse, that can ever hope to enter into the heart and faith of a nation, like the familiar religious song that is in their mouth every Sunday, aided in its effect by the reverence of the Bible, the power of music, the associations of the place, and the sympathy of a congregation."[24] As we shall see, Emerson's principle of the indwelling Spirit also carried inevitable aesthetic, social, and political implications.

Emerson brilliantly, decisively, and characteristically treats the relationship between truth, words, and acts—the whole range of issues contingent on the Christian evidences—in a pair of sermons preached in July 1831. His theme in Sermon No. CXX is reading— a topic he would return to in later lectures and essays, and which Thoreau, of course, would explore in *Walden* in strikingly similar terms. As a Unitarian minister, Emerson approaches reading in the context of Christian apologetics. The Scriptures, he grants, "afford a very valuable evidence of the truth of the facts they relate which tradition could never have afforded." Indeed, "this simple & consistent recorded account of miracles[,] this account of miracles sustained by a grandeur of sentiment in the miracle worker & communicated by him to the minds of his friends, & so animating every page of this wonderful book persuades me to believe."

But Emerson is *not* paying conventional lip service to the Scriptures as a record of miracles, as the revealed Word of God. For he goes on to *co-opt* the conservative grounds for belief in miracles by enlisting the Bible in support of *internal* evidences. "Our sacred books," he suggests, offer abundant proof of a distinctive "exalted spirituality." But he implies that even Scripture becomes a secondhand evidence: "We are so familiar with the language of the bible from our infancy, that we do not feel the immense force of this evidence until in our own hearts & consciences we verify the sentiments of Christ."

Scripture, then, is inefficacious *external* evidence until we personally close with its truth. How this is achieved Emerson portrays in a highly affective passage of mounting adverbial clauses:

> When in the progress of religion in the soul, the trite thread-
> bare texts which millions of mouths have repeated, become
> the expression of living truth to us, become descriptions of
> solemn realities that are taking place in our own conscious-
> ness; when every commandment seems to be an echo of a
> voice within us; when no saying of Jesus seems to us a hard
> saying, & none indifferent; but all are full of meaning & of
> truth, then our faith becomes perfect; faith becomes sight.

The cumulative power of this passage carries the evangelical message
that faith in the God Within is commensurate with our response to
Scripture. Emerson has thus seized the "orthodox" ground of Scripture and miracle by applying the test of consciousness, by showing
that in an *enlightened* reading of Scripture, *God* virtually reads
through *us.*

Emerson takes up the conventional terminology, explaining that
reading offers both "*historical* evidence" and "*internal* evidence" of
the "divine origin" of Scriptures, the latter too often neglected.[25] In
keeping with the Unitarian principle of moral growth, he defines
internal evidence not as an immediate, absolute conviction but—
as conservatives approached *external* proofs—as "an accumulating
evidence." And to foster the meditative frame of mind, he recommends works of Thomas à Kempis, Fenelon, Scougal, and Butler—
themselves "among the best evidences of ye truth of Xty." Indeed, as
Emerson saw it, Thomas à Kempis derived his "sentiments" *from*
the New Testament—not as second-hand testimony but as "a new
voice proclaiming the excellence & sufficiency of the doctrines of
the gospel, & so confirming me in the belief that they who wrote,
wrote as they were moved by the Holy Ghost[.]"

By conceiving of inspired writing and inspired reading as virtual
echoes, both reverberating to the Indwelling Spirit, Emerson solves
the contemporary dispute over the divine origin of Scripture. *Internal*
evidence, he insists, suggests that the Bible *was* inspired by God. But
by stressing a right *reading* of Scripture, by emphasizing ideas rather
than words, he demonstrates that the New Testament lives or it is
dead, and by implication he extends the realm of divine inspiration
into secular works. Thomas à Kempis, for example, uses language
specific to his own culture, but his devout approach transcends his
terminology. "Consider," Emerson argues, "that whenever he used
the word Jesus & worshipped—he presented to his mind precisely
the same infinite idea that is in your mind when you worship God;
& therefore there was no idolatry in his reverence." Emphasizing

right feeling over literalism and doctrine, Emerson seals his case in Sermon No. CXX by asserting that God designed the human constitution to use books as vehicles of truth.

Despite its obvious rhetorical power, Sermon No. CXX was preached only once, on 3 July. Emerson had now paid his ministerial dues by treating once and for all the scriptural aspect of the generations-old dispute over the nature of evidences. Having done so to his own satisfaction, he proceeded in his next sermon to celebrate the living, personal, internal evidence of God that he believed to be the heart of religion. Sermon No. CXXI, a more "Transcendental" declaration of the Pauline essence of spiritual perception, was preached first on 17 July, but it was reused fifteen times, as late as 3 April 1836 in East Lexington.

Examining the text of 1 Corinthians 2:14, Emerson posits a double consciousness: "A man is wonderfully placed in the possession of two worlds. By his body, he is joined to the earth. By his spirit, to the spiritual world. This is his natural condition but by his own choice he becomes more united to one or to the other." Expanding on his treatment of scriptural evidence in the previous sermon, he asserts that character and discernment together dictate whether or not we perceive "evidence of God's being"; the good do, the bad do not: "Is it strange that what he has ceased to see, he should cease to believe?" Evidence is acquired, however, not through passive contemplation alone but by moral activity.

In defining "the manner of spiritual discernment," Emerson reveals most fully his radically Pauline appropriation of Channing: "The whole secret is in one word, *Likeness*. The way to see a body is to draw near it with the eye. The way to perceive a spirit is *to become like it*. What is unlike us, we cannot perceive." This principle, he declares, "will show the *certainty* of Faith; that the legitimate objects of faith are not deficient in evidence, but are their own evidence." Implicitly responding to more traditional Unitarians, like Ware, who argued that internal evidence alone was the insufficient projection of one's own mind, he insists that spiritual perception is *not* the product of "imagination": "It is not hope, it is sight," the result of *surrendering* one's "will to God."

Anticipating his later Transcendental problem of want of consecutiveness of vision, he acknowledges that "nothing is more rare than consistent, distinct, steadfast views of [God's] character & providence," the result of "our sinfulness." But with "the cultivation of our moral & intellectual powers," our perception will become keener. Meanwhile, the "sensual state of the Church" perpetuates the error of depicting Heaven and Hell as "wholly a picture from the senses." This conception is "addressed to the natural man." But the "true heaven" is moral and spiritual likeness to God.

The spiritual view of things, Emerson contends, "corrects our false opinions respecting the manner in which the Judgment is passed & executed upon every mind. [In our natural state] We take the parable for a literal description of facts." Far from making us *disgusted* with this world, waiting for "release from the evils of life," spiritual discernment exposes the true source of discontent: "not in our peculiar circumstances, but in a querulous mind, which is not humble, or diligent, or kind enough to be at peace."

In the panorama of cultural history, Channing's concept of "likeness to God" is too often trivialized as a mere milestone in the progressively democratic march away from Calvinist views of human depravity, as a bald assertion of the self-evident divinity of the common person. Emerson demonstrates in his sermons that more was implied. "Likeness" meant far more than a liberating claim of co-sovereignty with a former dictator. "Likeness" for Emerson was the highest form of Christian evidence, carrying with it the personal security of being "known" by God (discerning his omniscience), moral empowerment (being permeated by his omnipotence), and a conviction of immortality.

Emerson knew, of course, that he was no rigorous logician. But even during his early period of self-doubt, we have seen, he had *felt* stirrings of divinity within: "I *feel* immortal. And the evidence of immortality comes better from consciousness than from reason" (28 May 1826. *JMN* 3:25). Significantly, liberal Christians, for all their professed differences from orthodox Congregationalists, continued to regard the promise of eternal life as the great and unique dispensation of Christianity. Though Emerson, typical of many, came to define Heaven less as an abode of the Resurrected and more as a continuation of moral development, he considered "evidence" literally as revelation, even redemption.[26]

The circumstances surrounding the writing of Sermon No. CXXI, moreover, reveal how much was at stake in Emerson's bold declarations about internal evidence and likeness. On 14 July, three days before he first preached this oft-used sermon, he reflected on the death of Ellen (8 February) and on the impermanence of all friends. Desperately, he looked to solitude itself as our best evidence of immortality (*JMN* 3:272). The next day he meditated at length on the text of Sermon No. CXXI (1 Cor 2:14: "The natural man receiveth not the things of the Spirit of God: for they are foolishness unto him;

neither can he know them because they are spiritually discerned"). Rejecting materialism as the basis of true understanding, he works out several Pauline truisms: "God in us worships God"; "No man but a spiritual man can know what heaven means, or see the evidence there is for its being" (*JMN* 3:273); "Miracles cannot convince a devil" (*JMN* 3:274). These passages, with Sermon No. CXXI, confirm Rusk's belief that Emerson's disaffection with Gospel historicity grew after Ellen's death (*Life* 151).

Having once felt *all* forms of evidence valuable, Emerson finally wearied of Unitarian hairsplitting, abruptly cutting the knot of evidential argument thus: "All is miracle, & the mind revolts at representations of 2 kinds of miracle" (*JMN* 3:242). Having suffered the greatest personal loss of which he could conceive, he craved stronger assurance and consolation than logical constructs could offer. Emerson's radical views of the grounds of faith, emerging from long-held convictions about the nature of Christian belief, were honed on grief.

V

Emerson's version of "internal evidence," according to Stephen Whicher's interpretation, was nothing more than a desperate attempt to get around the embarrassing problem of Unitarian miracles. To shore up his faith in Christianity, Whicher argued, Emerson turned to the Swedenborgian Sampson Reed, yet was always haunted by the awareness "that internal evidence was sandy ground for faith," that this had been a doomed strategy to cling to institutional religion.[27] In hindsight, we can, of course, see that viewing all life as miracle, as Emerson does in the great essays, would render belief in specific Christian miracles redundant. Yet Emerson's stronger ground of faith, on the one hand, was built on Unitarian categories of thought at least a generation old, and the sermons, on the other hand, present a far more "Transcendental" vision than generally has been thought. It is an added irony, given the critical charges of narcissism, that Emerson was acutely aware of the dangers of living too deeply within the realm of pure mind. Although he admired Swedenborg, for example, he would argue that mysticism is often accompanied by "disease" that "drives the man mad" or "taints his judgment"; Swedenborg's philosophy lacked "central spontaneity" and the "power to generate life" (*CW* 4:55, 74).

Too much can be made, moreover, of the unilaterally rational thrust of Unitarian Higher Criticism as it related to the question of evidences. Scholars like Andrews Norton unwittingly did much, with their emphasis on historical proof, to undermine the emotional basis of liberal religion. Even Henry Ware, Jr., urged "a wholesome rule—*Make the plain portions of Scripture the interpreters of the obscure*"; "there is indefinite room for difference of judgment and variety of opinion," he went on, for the aim of Christianity, after all, is not to make skilled apologists but "to make man better."[28] Emerson's father had believed literally enough in the Resurrection yet had complained in 1801 that the "age of miracles has passed away," leaving the liberal minister without supernatural gifts but with his reasoning power and moral character intact. Waldo exploited the implications of this natural ability, redefining the very notion of "miracles." Emerson's reliance on "internal evidence" to confirm spiritual truth aimed to restore a warmth and pietistic fervor to religion that appealed to a wide range of Unitarians. True, it was conducive of a subjectivity that came, in the eyes of some, to verge on infidelity. But "to internalize God's kingdom," as Andrew Delbanco has written of Channing, "is to restore its meaning," which is in the Augustinian tradition.[29]

Emerson's radically simple epistemology did not, of course, carry the day with all Unitarians, not even in his own congregation. Andrews Norton fought a dogged rearguard battle to authenticate the historical continuity, authorship, and consistency of the Gospels, taking aim at those who subscribe to "the principle, expressed in the perverted language of St. Paul, that *spiritual things are spiritually discerned*, and have, of course confined this unerring spiritual discernment to themselves."[30] Norton concluded his case for the "evidence" of "the genuineness of the Gospels" by suggesting a final test that bears an uncanny resemblance to the Buckminster/Channing/Emerson concept of "likeness"—"the evidence founded on the intrinsic character of the Gospels themselves." Assessing their "genuineness" and "truth," Norton offered that "the Gospels are of such a character, that they could have been written only by individuals of such a character, and so circumstanced, as those to whom they are ascribed."[31] Norton failed to see the irony that, as Emerson knew, "intrinsic" tests based on "truth" and "character" could be measured only, in a Pauline/Channingesque sense, by the inner lights of the perceiver.

Not all were as rigid as Norton in demanding historical proofs of the Gospels or of miracles. James Walker, Unitarian minister at Charlestown and later president of Harvard, sidestepped the issue, observing that belief in miracles often *follows* conversion, but noting sensibly that miracles "belong to the history of Christianity, and to one branch of its evidences, but do not constitute Christianity itself." The heavy burden of evidence, Walker knew, could smother belief. Anxious to stabilize the church, he further loosened Unitarian doctrine without the uncompromising vision or courage of Emerson. "Now, what we want to do," Walker maintained, "is not to convince persons of the truth of Christianity by this or that particular evidence, but simply to convince them of the truth of Christianity itself. Let every one be fully persuaded in his own mind, and it matters not on what evidence."[32]

Orville Dewey labored mightily to reconcile "the supreme value of the original intuitions, of the inward light, of the teachings of the Infinite Spirit in the human soul . . . without [which] we could have no religion," with the divinity of Christ and the reality of miracles. The latter, Dewey believed, *sealed* internal evidence and confirmed "God's paternal care for me and . . . my own immortality."[33] Emerson had no less sincerely dedicated his ministry to preaching what Joseph Henry Allen later called "a better ground of Christian faith."[34] He could have known only dimly that his insistence on the integrity of consciousness as the final proof of God's presence would split the denomination he had believed to be religion's best hope. Still, his single most important article of faith remained intact even in the darker essay "Experience": "[T]he definition of *spiritual* should be, *that which is its own evidence*" (*CW* 3:31).

In light of the furor Emerson stirred among the devout with his sermon on the Lord's Supper and the Address at the Divinity School, it is ironic that his ultimate test for confirming the internal evidences was the Buckminster/Channing concept of "likeness." Perception and evidence mirrored one another; indeed, since one could love only what one was, this self-reinforcing spiritual capacity was one with assurance of spiritual regeneration. Channing told Elizabeth Palmer Peabody that he understood God's love "[b]ecause in the last analysis I find I have a degree of it in myself." He stressed, moreover, that Jesus' love is essentially moral, "command[ing] our reverence as soon as we really see it"; indeed, "moral implies personal, because I understand conscience to be personality; which is not arbitrariness, but 'God working in us to will and to do.' "[35]

For Emerson even more than for Channing, perception was the heart of religion, and morality, far from being simply obedience to a code of behavior, was a dynamic response to knowing God. "Morality" meant an entire reorientation of one's life. The implications not only for religion but for the *res publica* were enormous. Though following a path clearly pioneered by Buckminster and Channing, Emerson in the eye of the Unitarian establishment had blurred the distinction between God and man. Juxtaposed in the November 1838 *Christian Examiner* with a review critical of the Divinity School Address was a review praising Ware's *The Personality of the Deity,* commending in particular the view that God is *not the same* as "the principles and the attributes." This was tantamount to a rejection of a key tenet of Channing's "likeness to God" as much as a denial of Emerson's radical form of Christian evidence. "Give us such writing and such preaching as [Ware's]," continued the review, "and defend us from the wordiness and mysticism, which are pretending to be a better literature, a higher theology, and almost a new revelation."[36]

Even in the essays, there is, nevertheless, a distinctly "orthodox" tone to Emerson's reformulation of the active, and hence moral, nature of "Intellect": "Nature shows all things formed and bound. The intellect pierces the form, overleaps the wall, detects intrinsic likeness between remote things, and reduces all things into a few principles" (*CW* 2:194). Though couched in "secular" terms, this essay continues to posit the perceiving mind as the means of establishing belief. This ultimately moral faculty finds analogy between what is felt to be true and what, based on that perception, can be concluded about the nature of the universe.

A striking passage in "The Over-Soul" stands as perhaps Emerson's definitive word on what had begun as a theological dispute over the grounds of belief. Now he speaks of "teachers sacred or literary," distinguishing in sharp, polar terms between poets as well as philosophers on the basis of the source of their authority: "[O]ne class speak *from within,* or from experience, as parties and possessors of the fact; and the other class, *from without,* as spectators merely, or perhaps as acquainted with the fact, on the evidence of third persons." Emphatically rejecting Paley as one of the latter "class," Emerson deliberately blurs the lines between secular and divine, pronouncing his judgment on all expressions of truth.

Despite the fervently Transcendentalist vision of the essay, Emerson's discourse remains classically balanced (a legacy of his sermonizing) as he weighs antithetical values. Yet he concludes the passage with a dramatically first-person declaration of allegiance, both appropriating the mantle of Christ from its orthodox context once again, and making his final comment on the "miracles controversy" by inverting the very terms of the argument: "It is of no use to preach to me from without. I can do that too easily myself. Jesus speaks always from within, and in a degree that transcends all others. In that, is the miracle" (*CW* 2:170).

What had been a distinctly liberal-Christian stance toward knowing God continued to emerge throughout Emerson's writings as a raw, undeniable will to believe. Contemplating Sleepy Hollow cemetery in 1855 he asserted that "[t]he blazing evidence of immortality is our dissatisfaction with any other solution" (*JMN* 14:17). This striking declaration sounds less purely willful, less desperate, when we recall the stakes Emerson had always placed on the internal evidences and on faith in the divine constitution of human nature. Twenty-five years earlier, confident hope in the ultimate Christian promise had been one with a sense of empowerment grounded on the God Within.

4

The "stifled voice":
Scripture, Language, and Expression

Emerson's sense of God's presence led him not only in the privacy of his journals but even in his sermons to explore the aesthetic dilemma of how to express the ineffable. The unreliability of language occasionally distressed Emerson, raised in a tradition that valued rationality in sermon form and content. More often, however, he relished stripping away the facade of accepted notions of words, metaphors, and doctrines. Believing deeply in the Spirit that eluded codification, Emerson through such preaching established his own prophetic voice even as he distanced himself from theological and vocational assumptions of moderate Unitarians like Henry Ware, Jr.

From Emerson's conviction that God is within us, it was a short step to the potentially Transcendentalist assertion of 1 Corinthians 6:19: "[Y]our body is the temple of the Holy Ghost." Emerson preached confidently on this text in Sermon No. LXXXVIII, first delivered on 12 September 1830, and as late as 5 March 1837. Yet toward the end of the sermon, following an eloquent appeal for holy living, he demurred:

> My friends, I have no hope of giving any thing like accuracy or great distinctness to this tho't. In our ignorance & sin we must dimly see it. I cannot find out the Almighty unto perfection. I cannot tell *how* he is present to me, & yet I can

feel that he is present—that in him I live & move, & have my being.

Giving form to religious experience, describing and explaining the divine, presented no less a challenge to Emerson than to the Old Testament prophets, Catholic mystics, or his Puritan ancestors. He affirmed, as had Fenelon, the reality that God is in the soul and the soul in the body, yet ultimately this was a fact "not to be defined, but every where present."

Coloring not only Emerson's duty to *explicate* Scripture but also his desire to recreate *his own* sense of the Spirit was his awareness of the lively scholarship and debate about the "Higher Criticism" in Europe.[1] His brother William, studying in Germany from 1823 to 1825, had sent fresh reports from the front; the *Christian Examiner* was alive with responses to these developments, both cautious and enthusiastic; and Waldo, by the time he entered the ministry, was already familiar with Eichhorn, Herder, and others who were subjecting Scripture to scientific, historical, and literary analysis. The ferment was both liberating and unsettling. The impact of Higher Criticism on New England theology turned out to be Janus-faced. As we have seen, it provided a useful tool for Unitarians systematically to refute Calvinist doctrine, even as it undermined the emotional grounds of belief and authority. A less traumatic but perhaps more far-reaching mixed legacy of Higher Criticism was the unmooring of basic assumptions about language itself. Sensitive to the cultural contexts of words and meaning, and eager to embrace the poetic and mythical dimensions of Scripture, the most progressive Unitarians unwittingly cast doubt on the very reliability of words to convey fixed, universally agreed upon meaning, a plight, Philip F. Gura has shown, that charged the darker literary masterpieces of the American Renaissance.[2]

Emerson was coming to believe that religious assumptions are tied inevitably to our use of words. His growing impatience with institutional modes of expression—sermon as well as ritual—derives in large part from his understanding of how language can entomb as well as express the felt experience of the Spirit. Emerson deals in the sermons with three major issues of language: right understanding of Scripture, the relationship of words and symbolic representation to character, and how these affect the larger concerns of eloquence, particularly the rhetorical stance—the voice—appropriate to the vision and role of a minister. His thinking on these issues, though not

especially original, was pivotal in the emergence of a "Transcendentalist" aesthetic from Unitarian culture.

What is remarkable is that Emerson chose to work out the relatively arcane problems raised by biblical scholarship not in critical
essays for the *Christian Examiner* but in the more immediately
public forum of sermons. This suggests not simply that Emerson's
thinking on such matters was derivative, that he was popularizing
scholarly topics, but also that he had a great deal of respect for
his audience's ability to grasp the implications of new ideas that
fundamentally challenged comfortable religious assumptions. It suggests also that he needed to try out these provocative notions conceptually before he could tap the *expressive* potential of the liberal-
Christian ministry. Emerson's sensitivity to questions of language,
moreover, compels reevaluation of the sermons not simply as intellectual constructs and formal exercises but as rewarding literary
performances as well.

I

On 31 August 1827, less than a year after he had begun to preach and
almost two years before his ordination by Second Church, Emerson
complained to his brother William about the trials of writing sermons: "Prithee, dear William send me some topics for sermons or if
it please you better the whole model 'wrought to the nail.' For much
of my time is lost in choosing a subject & much more in wishing to
write. . . . I aspire always to the production of present effect. . . . For
a strong present effect is a permanent impression" (*L* 1:211). Even
allowing a measure of unguarded fraternal playfulness, we find Emerson revealing not only a callow attitude toward eloquence, an egotistical striving for "impression," but also an uninspired notion of
sermons as artifacts contrived "about" some external topic, not as
inherently powerful vehicles for transmitting insight.

What amounts to a self-consciously mimetic approach to imagery
in the early sermons is evident also in the journals. As early as
1823 Emerson had found Buckminster "remarkable for a 'philosophic
imagination,' " a talent crucial to popularity. Though employing
"beautiful images" is not so high as philosophy, "[i]ts advantage is
owing to the circumstance that moral reflections are vague & fugitive
whereas the most vulgar mind can readily retain a striking image
from the material world" (*JMN* 2:365). To convey the sense of our
"horrid social profligacy," he wondered as a preacher, "Shall I draw

the picture of these horrid impending misfortunes?" (*JMN* 3:122–23). The result is a stirring but rhetorically conventional jeremiad (Sermon No. XVII) aiming with graphic detail and lurid imagery to awaken the audience to a vivid sense of sin (see chap. 5).

Another early sermon, No. VI, conceptually anticipates Emerson's "Transcendental" emphasis on spiritual discernment, but it makes its case through a combination of stale Puritan images of terror and an unnaturally dramatic speaking voice. Though the world appears "fair," it is "unsubstantial"; "Decay, decay," Emerson intones in an attempt to turn his auditors from this vain show. Building the sermon's affective power on the discrepancy between appearance and reality, he warns that focusing on the changing face of the world distracts us from "our design." Our only relief, he offers unsurprisingly, is "in the idea of God, in the belief of an overruling Providence," a vision "founded on the study of the works & the word of God." Expressing another belief he would always hold, he claims that God is not removed from his creation but is "at hand," supporting our very lives. He admits that *how* we believe is problematic in a world where "sophistry" often prevails. His partial solution is to proclaim a vision of dualism (body and mind are distinct). But instead of exploring this dichotomy through the highly poetic images and parables of the mind's encounter with nature that mark his familiar essays, he is content in Sermon No. VI to clinch his point by appeal to authority: " 'Choose you this day whom you will serve.' " Emerson would learn to appropriate biblical allusions to his own voice in other sermons and in his essays. But in Sermon No. VI he uncritically hitches his vision to conventional rhetorical and scriptural wagons.

Were we to read only such early performances as these, we would assume all the sermons to be a wholly different mode of discourse from the familiar Transcendental essays. Indeed, this is the scholarly consensus, based primarily on the evidence of "The Lord's Supper." Sheldon Liebman, in his pioneering studies of Emerson's rhetorical background, demonstrated Emerson's debt to Hugh Blair and the Scottish Realists, who viewed language as abstract and denotative, distrusted metaphor, and valued structural balance and unity. Similarly, Philip F. Gura suggests that in "The Lord's Supper" Emerson "regarded speech in an almost Lockean, commonsensical way." And Julie Ellison, diagnosing young Emerson as suffering from "a severe case of literary overinfluence," notes that "he expressed his own literary ambitions mimetically," resulting in sermons that are "[f]orceful and clear. . . . cogently argued and logically constructed." Lacking the rage essential to Romantic expression, the sermons are, in Ellison's view, unauthentic Emerson. Gura and Ellison, moreover, rightly explain Emerson's fundamental disaffection with the ministry in terms of his changing conception of language.[3]

Though the sermons indeed retain logical coherence, Emerson rather early in his preaching began moving away from the almost theatrical imagery and voice he had once thought so compelling. Even before he was licensed to preach, he sensed that eloquence was not a bag of affective tricks but an emanation of character. "A man's *style*," he wrote in May 1826, "is his intellectual Voice only in part under his controul. It has its own proper tone & manner which when he is not thinking of it, it will always assume. He can mimic the voices of others, he can modulate it with the occasion & the passion, but it has its own individual nature" (*JMN* 3:26). This conviction is not immediately or wholly reflected in sermonic style, yet Emerson began to think strongly pictorial imagery "materialistic" in that it seized and exploited the audience's imagination, thwarting the true aim of preaching—to induce a right perception of the Spirit. Emerson's frequent attack on Calvinist literalism is essentially a rejection of his own adolescent sense of imagery and metaphor.

As early as Sermon No. XVI, Emerson understood the connection between theology and language, suggesting that "*Pride*, pride is the universal & unsharing distemper"—the cause of both "that melancholy creed" of original sin and vitiated language and "contention." Redefining the Christian notion of pride, Emerson points to the true source of eloquence by distinguishing two men: the one who "rushes to his mark" unconscious of self, aware only of his goal and breaking "down the cobweb fences of artificial politeness," and the one who restrains his language in "an elegant decorum," worried about "slovenly" language and his "reputation."

Even in the pre-ordination Sermon No. XVIII, Emerson's *vision* of Christianity carried certain inherent attitudes toward symbolism and verbal expression without which, Emerson thought, we can never truly close with the meaning of the New Testament revelation. Opening the text of Matthew 11:30 ("My yoke is easy, & my burden is light") in the context of "the burdensome practice of the Mosaic ritual," he observed that "the language of the Saviour as was usual with him had a wider application than those who heard it could conceive"; he spoke to "the human race." Indeed, the very "simplicity" of Jesus' message has been the greatest "stumblingblock" to the spread of Christianity: "He insisted on *principles*: But men all over the world insist on *opinions*." Despite their pride and narrow vision, men crave "expiation," yet they look everywhere for it except in "obedience to this true Religion." Religion, Emerson explained, is "a choice between a temptation & a duty," and by practice "a holy life ceases to be an effort and becomes a habit of happiness."

To illustrate his point, Emerson invites us to consider the "substance" of the story of Naaman, a Syrian officer stricken with leprosy who proudly resists the advice of Elisha's messenger to bathe in the Jordan (2 Kg 5:1–14). A "former age," Emerson notes, would have read this parable as an Old Testament "type" of "that more perfect system of moral government which is revealed in the new." Puritan typology had been decidedly historical. But at this early stage of his career Emerson already denies "any superstitious value" in the tale of Naaman, seeing "in this story an useful mirror of our own disposition." Emerson is moving toward an ahistorical interpretation of typology, but in relating this "type" to universal human experience, he is far from a modernist version of symbolism.[4] The tale yields a valuable *moral* lesson: Although the West is not plagued by leprosy, "the taint of sin the leprosy of the mind—we share in common with the Syrian & the Jew."

Emerson then makes more explicit the problem of communication that so often veils human insight: We do not listen to God, he explains, because "he doth not burst the silence of his heavens & speak to us in thunder & by miracle." Similarly, "external observances" are not conducive to true religion. God speaks not in external shows or in literally audible pronouncements; he chooses to reveal himself through a gradual process of self-discipline, spiritual perception arising from refinement of moral character.

Human imagination, Emerson stressed in Sermon No. XXXVII, is fallen. Our true home, the spiritual world to which our minds are windows, can be approached by natural signs properly used: "Outward things are thine instructors, thy school, & not thine home." Pictorial depictions of heaven are "but the types—the outward representatives whereby to mortal ears the secrets of spiritual joy are faintly shadowed forth. Heaven is not a place, but a state of the mind. *Hell* is vice, the rebellion of the passions. . . . *Heaven* is the well ordered informed benevolent self devoted mind when it adopts God's will for its own." Emerson's attitude toward figurative language was permanently colored by his preacher's assessment—that picture language, useful as a rough reflection of the "material" world, pales with the appearance of "character" and of inspired, authentic speech.

Like many of his Unitarian colleagues, Emerson used Higher Critical tools to deconstruct what they deemed the dangerously "materialistic" scriptural reading of the Calvinists. In point of fact, the

Calvinists, in their conception of scriptural language, were not the literalist dolts painted by liberals like Emerson.[5] Over a generation before Emerson's ministry, Calvinist Samuel Hopkins explained the Old Testament figurally: "[T]hese words of David, are a prediction of the reign of Christ on earth"; "By Zion here is meant . . . the church of Christ, of which Mount Zion was a type."[6] Hopkins, moreover, understood the notion of "figure" not only in the medieval/Puritan sense of the Old Testament as historical anticipation of the New, but as metaphor. So he explicated the spiritual sense beneath the graphic images in Revelation 20:7–9: "This prophecy is figurative. It is not to be supposed that all this great multitude will be gathered together into one place; or that the church will be encamped together in one spot on earth, or collected in one city: But the gathering of the wicked, means their being abandoned to infidelity" (155). Emerson's sense of the partiality of language was not as radically different from Hopkins' as one might expect. Accepting the biblical notion of a prelapsarian universal language (Gen 11:1, 6), Hopkins trusted that "[i]n the Millennium, all will probably speak *one language*," a restoration premised on men becoming "universally pious, virtuous and benevolent." Remove the literal belief in original sin and in Scripture as the revealed Word of God, and emphasize the role of character, and the sentiment sounds remarkably Emersonian, especially when Hopkins goes on to envision harmony and unification as within human grasp, "without a miracle" (75).

European Higher Criticism, we often imagine, was received in New England by young liberals starved by provincial orthodoxy; more accurately, though its techniques could be used to bludgeon the establishment, it found on these shores a religious culture steeped in reading the Bible on many levels, with a sense of the slipperiness of language. If Hopkins granted the metaphorical nature of scriptural language, Joseph Stevens Buckminster, who introduced the Higher Criticism to America, taught his congregation how to approach critically not only the Bible but the *minister's* words as well:

> Repose not implicit reliance on our representations, on the one hand; nor accuse us, on the other, of departing from the word of God, when we give you an illustration of a passage, which may not coincide with your previous opinions, or even with the first impressions, which the words suggest. For it is not always true in the scriptures, any more than many other works written in a foreign language, and in a mode of thinking so different from our own, that the first and most natural

> meaning, which the words convey, is certainly the true mean-
> ing; but the history of God's will, as it stands in the scriptures,
> requires to be diligently and impartially explored, that our
> faith may not stand on the assumptions of men, but on the
> word of God.

Significantly, Buckminster was not appealing for relativistic critical
reading and listening; he was convinced that words *do* "convey" a
"true meaning." Higher Criticism was not a threat to belief, but an
aid to uncovering God's will beneath human words. Not conscious
of the irony that critical intelligence is also fallibly human, Buckminster continued to place high value on *preaching* the Word of God.
The congregation's "most important duty" as informed listeners, he
insisted, is to "convert the general language of the preacher into
personal admonitions and directions."[7]

Emerson was even more insistent than Buckminster that we must
grasp the cultural context of theological language. One of several
sermons focusing on the theme of language first preached in the fall
of 1830, Sermon No. LXXXIX shows that Higher Criticism could be
more than a deconstructive tool; it could also be pressed into the
service of liberal theodicy. Orthodox language, Emerson suggests,
has tried to account for the ways of God to man (that is, to account
for mortality) by recourse to an image of an angry God. But how,
Emerson wonders, can we reconcile God's wrath with his mercy (Is
54:8)? The answer, he argues, lies not in paradox and mystery but in
a proper understanding of how language is used. His own rhetorical
strategy, moreover, is designed to make his auditors feel that this is
hardly a revolutionary insight, that they have known it all along.

He opens with the assertion that Christianity has led to "a gradual
but decided improvement in the views that are entertained of God."
The audience thus shares pride in belonging to the progressive wing
of a religion that, while renouncing Calvinist concepts of election,
enjoys a special understanding of the divine. Today, Emerson declares, more people "search for God in the true heaven that he inhab-
its—in the soul & not in the body. They understand that they were
made in his moral image not in his natural[.] The truth is dawning
on the world that Jesus Christ was the express image of his person
only inasmuch [as] he was a better man than any other[.]"

Emerson has denied the need for supernatural mediation while
maintaining that death is not thus rendered incomprehensible. Having asserted the major obstacle to understanding God's plan—that
we look for God in the wrong place—Emerson goes on to explicate

the difficulties posed by language. God "is dishonoured," he insists, "by ascribing to him the passions of men." Indeed, "popular language respecting God recognizes" this fact, as in "the abundance of flippant objection & ridicule that is aimed at the unphilosophical language applied to God in the Old Testament." His audience now implicated in this bandwagon derision of Old Testament language, Emerson stresses that such language actually *undercuts* God's divinity; it is "faulty" and, as construed by nineteenth-century Americans, is "injurious to the character of God." What must be seen, Emerson argues, is that "all [Old Testament] speech is a bold allegory":

> [T]hose who used in a barbarous age to barbarous men a barbarous imagery, did convey truth by its means. The sentiments which they uttered in this coarse allegory, were true & sublime, & would constantly tend to purify & exalt the human soul, & to enable it to throw off these husks as fast as was good, & save the precious truth that was inside.[8]

The historicity of language, then, presents an interpretive challenge not only to subsequent generations and other cultures; it is implicit in the *contemporaneous* act of communication. So expendable is the artifact, the vehicle of insight, that it must be "husked" immediately (in this case by Isaiah's as well as Emerson's audience) to prevent spoilage of the "precious truth" it contains.

Emerson's iconoclastic message, of course, is that truth is absolute, form relative. But he immediately defuses any fear of the disruptive implications of *his* vision by taking the offensive, conflating the stance of biblical literalists with the foes of religion: "On the contrary, the evil disposition which leads men nowadays to sneer at every thing connected with the spiritual world is false in heart whilst it is true in words[.]" And he attacks the modern "disposition which despises or opposes any sincere religious sentiment" and which manifests itself in "hyperbolical expressions" about "yᵉ wrath of God." Unitarians were charged by Calvinists with being rationalists, Arminians, non-Christians. But Emerson turns the rhetorical tables, suggesting that progress, inimical to religion, has spawned not thinkers of his stamp but the very formalists who cloak themselves in the husks of orthodoxy.

All this, Emerson explains, is not to diminish the importance of words: "The Wrath of God is not just language. Christ has taught us better. Take the words in their fulness of meaning & the human mind would be confounded. The Hebrew poets . . . magnify the anger of a man & arm it with the powers over nature with which God is armed[.]" In terms that foreshadow his own reappropriation of Jesus as a "great man," Emerson suggests that words *are* crucial as mediators: They help us to grasp the ineffable; but once their job of mediation is accomplished, they become artifacts, relics that can *impede* spiritual understanding. For if God actually felt "human indignation," he would have better means of wreaking havoc: "Let him loosen one moment the invisible link which binds atom to atom which we call *cohesion*," or let him suspend the law of gravity! After a paean to the natural law of God, Emerson proclaims that

> the whole notion of Gods anger & its outward manifestation is unsuitable. Wrath is unreasonable. It is in application to man a temporary want of wisdom. Anger is called madness, and can never be applied therefore to God the all Wise who is Wisdom & Love and who dwells passionless & pure in all his works & not so much dwells in them as ever makes them. He is that by which they are, soul of our souls & safe guard of the world.

Emerson's concern with scriptural language is both negative (a polemical attack on erroneous descriptions of God) and positive (a declaration of his own view of God's ways to man). Emerson's God is both an authoritative protector and a perpetually active re-Creator. In this light, a merely literal reading of scriptural metaphor diminishes God, for "the judgments which we call his wrath are only the reflection of our timorous & sinful selves." There is no mistaking Emerson's own zeal. Yet as a controversialist he has deftly turned back on his Calvinist straw man the charge of impiety. And as if to erect a principle of divine justice as inexorable as the discredited Calvinist angry God, he observes that nature corrects its own "deviation" and "always vindicates Gods wisdom" in the end; we cannot evade self-reproach, for we see judgment in natural disaster "because we know that we deserve punishment."

Having disposed of the major theological stumblingblock imposed by language, Emerson proceeds to show in positive terms what God's judgment *is*: "Thus we have considered the meaning of the word *wrath*[.] It means, the sufferings of man. Let us now consider the word *mercy*, or, the relief of those sufferings." Ironically, though the burden of the first half of Sermon No. LXXXIX is to deflate the false image of the Calvinist angry God in order to assert his mercy, Emerson's strategy betrays its debt to a classic New England preaching model. We too often forget that even Jonathan Edwards, in his notorious Enfield sermon "Sinners in the Hands of an Angry God" (the luridness of which is actually atypical of Edwards) used terror primarily as an incentive to turn to the mercies of an ultimately loving God.[9] Seldom using terror as a converting technique after his early sermons, Emerson in Sermon No. LXXXIX quarrels with the Edwardsean metaphor only to stress spiritual growth and comfort.

What follows in the sermon is hardly the bland effusion of watered-down theology. Having explained away human wrath as a divine motive, Emerson proposes nothing less than to reconcile the fact of human suffering with faith in a loving God. In terms suggesting the concept of "compensation" (which would become a matter of urgency less than six months later with the death of Ellen), Emerson declares that "mans happiness must come from his character not from his condition." The explication of Old Testament allegory has prepared the congregation for a discussion of the *true* nature of God's dealings with humankind. Emerson now declares a version of his notorious doctrine that evil is merely apparent ("Suffering is occasional, local, limited"); and in a catalogue proclaiming all experience a builder of character, he goes on:

> The sources of happiness—why here they are, & every where. Life is a source of happiness; the light of day; the faces of men; the aspect of nature; the power of speech; the bodily functions; the memory; the imagination; the reason; the affections[.]

Emerson devotes most of the rest of the sermon to proclaiming the innate sources of happiness, which derives not from ourselves but from God. Toward the end, however, he forces us to consider "the more literal meaning of the text" ("In a little wrath I hid my face from thee for a moment, but in everlasting kindness will I have mercy on thee.")—a meaning "which Revelation disclosed."

The text, Emerson argues, was not intended to be crystallized as doctrine but was offered by God in the specific context of a people "under some overwhelming calamity" who for the moment "cannot understand the kindness of his Providence." God, he declares, is "hid" from us only in the sense that our own sinfulness obscures our perception of him. Emerson concludes by urging "worthy contemplations of the character of God of his dealings toward us." Contemplation in this sense entails distinguishing the contextual meaning of words from their essential referent. In the process, one achieves receptiveness to, and perception of, the Spirit, an experience that transcends words. Emerson's own "liberal" doctrinal assumptions underlie his critique of scriptural language. What is significant about his treating this subject in the sermons is that Emerson as a preacher was already concerned not simply with a formalistic assertion of the existence of authoritative, transcendent being, but with pointing toward *how* that reality is apprehended.

II

Ostensibly setting out to review a discourse by C. J. Ingersoll in what would turn out to be a wide-ranging critique of our "National Literature," William Ellery Channing quipped: "We shall use the work prefixed to this article, as ministers are sometimes said to use their texts. We shall make it a point to start from, not the subject of our remarks."[10] However creatively Unitarians used the Bible, most took it seriously, and Emerson was no exception. The ambiguity of human nature, the presence of God, and his distinct sense of eloquence crystallized for him around the words of Jesus. Indeed, the dominant theme of a cluster of sermons first preached in the fall of 1830 is the right understanding of Scripture—not as a doctrinal exercise or formalistic bow to authority but as as means of spiritual growth.

Understanding the Gospel of Jesus, Emerson contends in Sermon No. XCIII, is complicated by the paradox that human nature is only partially capable of responding to the divine message:

> The prominent fact presented in the New Testament is this; that, man hath a spiritual nature superior to his animal life and superior to his intellectual powers & comprehending them ... & which Jesus came to establish in its rights. ... The distinction he constantly draws is between the flesh & the spirit[.]

In this sense, the polar distinctions Jesus constantly makes—Rome versus Judea, and so on—are to be taken metaphorically. Yet man cannot comprehend the full import of these contrasts merely by logical translation. "It is the nature of the human mind to receive knowledge slowly," Emerson explains, "not to pass suddenly from ignorance to wisdom, but to intermix the first rays of truth which it receives with its own familiar errors. And Jesus seems always to have felt that what he said was very imperfectly comprehended by most of those who heard him." On the one hand, Jesus' plight is shared by modern preachers like Emerson, anxious to be understood. On the other hand, Emerson was fond of announcing that Christianity is ideally suited to human nature's potential for continual growth. In this context Jesus was a good Unitarian when he told his disciples that "a fuller understanding of his sayings awaits them, when a longer career of sincere devotion shall open their minds to the use of the truth."

The nineteenth-century mind, by implication, is no better pre-pared than that of the disciples to understand Christ, yet the modern church is under the ancient "command": "to preach the glad tidings of redemption of salvation of eternal life." Emerson clings to the ultimate test of orthodoxy—belief in the gospel promise of eternal life—as had his father, refusing to reduce liberal Christianity to a moral code. But he confronts a difficulty dating back to Jesus' own utterances, a dilemma ineluctably tied to the limits of human under-standing and of language itself: how to establish Christianity's "main distinction, that of being a *spiritual* faith."

Emerson's discussion of the limits of metaphor strikingly antici-pates the argument of his infamous "The Lord's Supper," suggesting that all outward forms are but finite shadows of spiritual truth, signs whose efficacy is constrained by historical and cultural context. The "common idea of heaven," for example, is a distortion; "it is the imagination instead of the heart that describes it to us. . . . [H]e that receives the account of the vision of St John in the Apocalypse as a literal description of heaven has been betrayed into the same error as the Jews who surrounded Jesus & whom he so often cautioned that his Kingdom was not of this world." This is not to say that the Kingdom cannot be *received* in this world, but rather that it does not partake of worldly form.

We deceive ourselves, Emerson goes on, when we flatter ourselves that our metaphors capture the divine spark: "[T]hough we call it *spiritual*, because we refer it to the soul after death, yet it is substan-tially *carnal*, because it is an image of external goods, an image of thorns, & splendor, of bodily rest, & freedom from inconvenience & want." Our attempt to come to grips with ancient truths symboli-cally is thwarted by the fact that metaphors, instead of transcending human limitation, actually *reflect* human prejudice and misconcep-tions of divinity.

Some are able partially to see the error of this carnal perception. Granting too much to the immateriality of the spiritual world, how-ever, such people proceed to a different self-delusion: that because the world is so encumbered with "external goods," God "will give them what they shall enjoy." Responsive to this human blindness, the Gospel recorded what for Emerson was Jesus' fundamental pronouncement:

> [T]he Kingdom of God is within you. He teaches us that it is not something God shall give us but something God has given us power to do for ourselves. He teaches us that the Kingdom of God is not meat & drink, but righteousness & peace & joy of the holy Ghost.

Emerson's favorite scriptural passage (Lk 17:21) is here combined with Romans 14:17—the text with which he would begin "The Lord's Supper"—suggesting that the grounds of his eventual resignation of the Second Church pulpit was less a rationalization of vocational discomfort than the outcome of years of contemplating the meaning of the Christian dispensation. Carnal interpretation of the sacraments was as destructive, in Emerson's view, as literal belief in an "angry God." We cannot understand how he perceived the problem of discourse and metaphor without seeing that he regarded a *genuine* acceptance of the text as tantamount to conversion, literally a turning, a reorientation of one's life.[11]

The *"love of God"* and *"virtue* . . . are heaven,"* Emerson declares, and "a man's improvement is by the development of his own mind. Our improvement is from within not from without. Each mind has its own laws & agrees with itself." According to this law, the stamp of a man's "character" pervades all his "views," opinions, and "motives of action," as "the light that shines on one object illuminates all parts of the room." Using a more organic (and vaguely biblical) metaphor, he stresses that though a seed receives nourishment from the earth, "the seed [must] have life in itself" or it will not grow. The growth of each mind is regulated by the principle named, in other sermons, "compensation," and the operation of this principle is described—again, in dynamic terms:

> [T]he state of mind is always agreeable or painful according to the moral character of the feelings we indulge. . . . [E]very vice hath its sting. An ungovernable ambition is a raging fever. An army of mortifications attends it. . . . If we are selfish, envious, suspicious, revengeful, we are inevitably unhappy & all external luxuries, the sweetest meats, the softest couch, the rarest music will be only poison & thorns & strife to our depraved &

sick perceptions[.] But courage & benevolence & magnanimity are happiness.

Emerson has difficulty depicting the pain and misery of the bad man, though ironically he must do so by recourse to "carnal" imagery. Significantly, he is at a complete loss for imagery that adequately portrays the state of blessedness. He is left merely *asserting* the abstract qualities that comprise "happiness." Yet his vision of the highest state is typically conveyed by declaring that when we act in accordance with our inner law, we fulfill the spirit of the Gospel.

The closest Emerson comes in Sermon No. XCIII to graphically describing "happiness" is to declare it a wholeness, a connectedness:

> [A]ll our intellectual powers are joined together, part with part, & all our moral powers, so that the whole man advances or recedes together; & . . . every good feeling is connected with its own joy, & every bad one with its pain.

Even the image of advancing and receding is problematic, since one is blessed, according to Emerson, not by accumulated actions but by an innate capacity, by principle. Indeed, he anticipates his Transcendental notion that travel is a fool's paradise: "It is not to go abroad & seek God; God will come & dwell with those who truly do his will. Blessed are the poor in spirit for theirs is the Kingdom of heaven."

The ultimate failure of metaphor is that it cannot transcend carnality to convey immortality. Admitting that we have no precise knowledge of death, Emerson can say only that we will "lose the incumbrance of the flesh. But this circumstance," he goes on, "ought not diminish our confidence in the eternity of spiritual distinctions & in the fact that our condition will always be determined by our character." Heaven, in short, can be conceived only as an extension of earthly happiness.

The profound simplicity of this doctrine for Emerson redeemed the essential problems of inspiration and communication:

> The true doctrine as Christ taught it can only be received by each mind in proportion as it becomes virtuous, in proportion as the great work of regeneration goes on within it.—Only as far as we are good, can we know what heaven is. It is spiritual & must be spiritually discerned. . . . If heaven was a place, bad men might go there; but since heaven is goodness & the

> inseparable effects of goodness there can be no hope but for
> repentance & reformation & justice & self denial & love.

Though he rejected authoritarian revealed religion, Emerson was hardly reducing religion to morals, as is often charged. Being and knowledge, he believed with St. Paul, are one—the most severe of religious tests. Revelation had its own inexorable logic. It could be received only on its own terms, by turning from the flesh and truly accepting the divine impulse within. An angry God, by this logic, was a carnal metaphor capable of frightening but powerless really to convert. And so, as he often did to clinch his arguments for the God Within, Emerson celebrated the frame of mind in which we truly close with the meaning of Scripture: "I wish brethren we might all be induced to read the gospel of St John, where our Saviours discourses are most fully recorded, with a constant effort to apply the phrase *'Kingdom of God,' & 'K. of heaven,'* to the state of the soul." "[S]ince we live by the spirit," he concludes, "let us walk by the spirit," making hourly "progress therein . . . that every day we enter by the force of good purpose & good habit into interior mansions of the spiritual house of God."

Here is the voice of a preacher quietly enraptured by his vision of truth, convinced that he is purely opening Scripture. He has used the best techniques of argument and persuasion he knows to share his vision: analogy, comparison and contrast, biblical paraphrase, simple assertion. But he is left with a communication dilemma that becomes the greatest challenge for his hearers: Since being and knowledge are one and since God resides in all persons, the sermon cannot finally replicate or engender vision; and the preacher, even as sayer, can only proclaim the way. Hearer (and reader) must complete the circuit. As Emerson knew, even the words of Jesus were so constrained. His sense of the limitations of expository discourse contributed to his gradual disaffection with the ministry and informed his evolving practice of eloquence.

III

Emerson's growing conviction that "[t]he best part of wisdom can never be communicated" (*JMN* 3:260) is a paradoxical symptom both of his pietism and of what Barbara Packer has called his "deep skepticism about the capacity of language to embody truth."[12] He never lost his faith, however, that truth existed. The initially liberating notion he entertained of one-to-one "correspondences" between Nature and Spirit might ultimately have proved a wooden, stultifying scheme. But Emerson was always essentially a spiritualist, not a platonist, and his very distrust of metaphors as fixed indexes to meaning saved him from a deeper metaphysical skepticism. The mature Emerson, as several excellent studies have demonstrated, embraced a theory of experience as dynamic, organic, fluid. The notion of continual transformation and recreation became his model of God, the Mind, Nature, and Art. In the sermons this vital, synthesizing force was called "character."

A broader sense of scripture and life is already evident in the middle sermons, where Emerson explicitly describes the *experience* of God as a form of "language." Explaining in Sermon No. LXXVIII the eternal nowness of the scriptural offer of salvation, he emphasizes that "this Salvation is not definite partial good, but vast as intelligent being & without end." To think of salvation in temporal terms only delays individual reform, for experience shows that we are essentially the same from month to month: "O, let not this experience plead in vain. This experience is another tongue by which God speaks to you." We intuitively "read" our own experiences as direct, though subtle, messages from God.

Reading the Bible critically enabled Emerson to connect revelation to voice and character. Like most Unitarians, he regarded such an enlightened approach not as an assault on legitimate authority, but as a reaffirmation of the divine "constitution of our minds." Aiming in Sermon No. CX to naturalize revelation and miracle, he musters his Higher Critical skill: "The word signifying *Spirit* is used in the Scriptures in as many as <twelve> ↑eighteen↓ different senses. . . . This variety of senses makes it necessary in order to learn what it means in any one passage to make a careful examination of the context." He cautions that "[t]he custom of all Eastern writers to *personify* abstract ideas, that is, to speak of love as a person, of wisdom as a person may be seen in every page of the Scriptures." Uncritical reading of such personification, he argues, has led to such wrongheaded and dangerous formulations as the doctrine of the Trinity.

The "evidence of miracles I look upon as altogether secondary to that of the conscience," he explains; indeed, "miraculous power is only more power not different power." So with prophecy;

> And so I understand the *inspiration of the Scriptures*. I believe
> when a man wholly opens his heart to the love of God & has

> no self love, no motive but from on high, that man speaks
> with authority, & not as the Scribes, he becomes passive to
> the influence of God, & speaks his words.

This echo of Matthew 7:29 (which was also the text of his Sermon
No. LXXVI on the "authority" of Jesus) dramatizes how a right
appropriation of Scripture makes us Christlike, empowering heart
and voice alike. Toward the end of Sermon No. CX Emerson makes
clear the context of his emphasis on moral law: "Far be it from me
to bring into question the reality of spiritual influences. I believe in
them with my whole mind but not in local, capricious, anomalous
influences. God, God is always near." Scrutinizing Scripture for its
true sense does not "lower" our idea of the Spirit but makes it "more
sacred."

Corresponding to Emerson's belief in access to divine "authority,"
a sense of "artistic" responsibility dawned during his ministry as
he became dissatisfied with inherited rhetorical models and rote
performances. "Every composition in prose or verse," he wrote in
his journal on 16 August 1831, "should contain in itself the reason
of its appearance" (JMN 3:280). He stressed the moral stakes implicit
in natural expression in an entry on 4 November of the same year:
"Your understanding of religion is that it is doing right from a right
motive. Stick to that mighty sense. Don't affect the use of an adverb
or an epithet more than belongs to the feeling you have" (JMN 3:304).
And two days later he was preaching, in Sermon No. CXXXIV, about
the integrity of words themselves.

In part, Emerson's aesthetic theory carries on that of his father's
generation, with its high regard for balance and control in feeling and
expression. But Waldo's aesthetic is something less studious, less
"refined." As countless journal entries reveal, Emerson had come
to respect the honesty, the directness of everyday speech, and his
knowledge of Higher Criticism had alerted him to the many senses—
and uses—of words. "To name Truth is to praise it," he declares
aphoristically to open Sermon No. CXXXIV. His text ("Thou desirest
truth in the inward parts." Ps 51:6) suggests "the larger sense of truth
which is called *truth of character*." But we are constrained by "bad
customs." "You are expected to say smooth things first," he complains, "& true things no longer than they are pleasant." We feign
interest in drivel and mistakenly think "civility" requires "a compli-
ance with deceitful forms of speech."

Nowhere is this "heartless talk" more obnoxious than when it
"intrude[s] in the chambers of sickness, in the desolate house of

mourning." Familiar with grief, Emerson demolishes the bearer of false consolation:

> He is thinking only of himself, & how he shall come off. Let him be silent. There are words that are things and words that are words. The mourner is suffering now under a privation of the affections & this insincerity adds a privation of the whole spiritual world.

Emerson's "words that are things," a paraphrase of Sampson Reed,[13] aims not, of course, to reduce words to artifacts; it demands integrity, a genuine relationship between feeling and expression. "The source of all these falsehoods," Emerson makes clear, is no simple lack of social grace; it is "the want of a reverence for truth itself."[14] The truly good person does not feel compelled to speak words for words' sake. "In all conversation therefore he seeks not to *say* what he can, but to learn what he can."

Emerson is here defining a linguistic version of Christian meekness, a state manifested not only socially and verbally but also in a desire to know God's will, and to be—and speak—like Christ. In this spirit, "We are not angrily to take sides upon questions, but to find what is true." Thus, we "approach to truth": "Truth in things is skill; seeing truth is wisdom; speaking truth is eloquence; loving truth is holiness; acting truth is power." The intermediary role of eloquence is significant. Orator, statesman, all are governed by the same immutable law: "As Jesus saith 'it is not I that speak but my Father.' It is not I that speak, but Truth thro' my lips."

"[T]ruth in the inward parts," then, is not egotistical; by aspiring to likeness to God, it "would be the perfection of the human character." Honest words, moreover, "are felt to be as forcible as actions," and on occasion "[s]ilence, says the old maxim, is the candidate for truth." To live up to this demanding, Christlike "unity of character" would involve constant vigilance. But Emerson leaves us with "a practical application of its doctrine": "that we ought to set out with the sublime purpose never to violate the truth."

Carrying out this agenda, which requires "sacrifices" in overcoming the vices of character cited earlier, has enormous ramifications for Emerson's own rhetorical stance:

> ↑ You must be careful when you dispute. Be careful with those whom you wd. please ↓ It will cost you many self denials & possibly some unjust reproaches to hold your tongue when a

talker looks in your face for assent, or a flatterer expects his payment in praise. Let it cost something[.] It is worth all.

Here are the theological roots of what is perhaps Emerson's most exasperating trait: his utter refusal to engage in polemics. Following the Divinity School Address, Emerson's former senior co-pastor, Henry Ware, Jr., tried to engage him in further debate about the nature of Jesus. Emerson's famous response has been read variously as obtuse, naive, sanctimonious, obsequious, coy, or spineless:

> I could not give account of myself if challenged I could not possibly give you one of the "arguments" on which as you cruelly hint any position of mine stands. For I do not know, I confess, what arguments mean in reference to any expression of a thought. I delight in telling what I think but if you ask me how I dare say so or why it is so I am the most helpless of mortal men; I see not even that either of these questions admit of an answer.
>
> (L 2:167)

Emerson seems less peculiar in this regard when we realize that, throughout his ministry, theological controversy had itself been a matter of controversy. Unitarians thought of themselves as benevolent, progressive, above partisan acrimony. James Walker traced the very decline of Congregationalism to contentious internal debates over separatist purity, a squabble he dated back to the founding of the Bay Colony.[15] Remembering the bitterness that marked the Unitarian emergence from Congregationalism, Walker elsewhere tried to levitate his denomination above the fray: "[I]t is a question not of doctrines and theories, but of character and life." Cleverly setting the terms of their distinctness from the Calvinists, he asked, "Whose principles and measures are most conducive to free inquiry, religious liberty, and Christian charity?" He patronizingly answered his own question: "[W]e commit its issues to the providence of Him who judgeth righteously."[16] Emerson too thought that Christian "doctrines, like every thing in dispute, have been strained a great way, yea, out of all shape, but they are originally solemn verities" (JMN 3:226; January 1831); and in Sermon No. CXI he probed beneath the "perversions" of dogma: "Now though this *language* is incorrect the doctrine is bottomed in eternal truth." George Ripley, who after the Divinity School Address would take up the polemical cudgels in defense of his fellow member of the Transcendental Club, was already broadening his critique of what Emerson would later call the "corpse cold" origin and nature of Unitarianism:

> As it began with the work of demolition, Rationalism must have remained, for a long time, a merely negative system. But so long it could not pretend to constitute a religion. A religion cannot be established on negations. It must maintain positive truths.[17]

An antiformalist like Emerson, W. B. O. Peabody insisted that truth "is not something arbitrary, changing, and capricious; it is not formed by invention, nor does it depend on argument." Accordingly, truth is "spread" not by attacking the falsehood of another's beliefs, but "by awakening a spirit of inquiry."[18] A more vigorous soul, F. W. P. Greenwood accepted "the necessity of controversy." Debate was inherent, he thought, in any pursuit of truth: "We were made to differ." Without such a spirit, human nature would never have achieved such advances as American Independence or abolition of the British slave trade. More frankly than Walker or Peabody, Greenwood felt debate "has exceedingly softened down the most rigid and repulsive features of Calvinism, at the same time that it has exposed them." In keeping with the dynamic nature of ideas and reform, "controversy" actually "promotes both peace and truth."[19]

Controversy was inherent, of course, in the Higher Criticism. What was needed, suggested Orville Dewey, was a "good translation of the Scriptures." "Controversy enough we have had," he had declared, and it all boiled down to language. He thought "simple exposition" appropriate for "general reading" and worried that most were not up to the "abstruse discussion upon the meaning of language, which is the ultimate resort of all Christian controversy." Dewey was broad-minded, a reformer, an eloquent preacher. His theory of language finally owed more than Emerson's, however, to the Common Sense philosophers. "Our minds," he explained, "converse much with their objects through images, through symbols. The universe in which we are placed is one vast system of representation. All truth, though not originated in us, yet is mainly impressed upon us by emblems. The senses are thus indispensable helpers of the soul. Now, the chief signs of thought are words."[20] This sounds almost Swedenborgian, seems even to anticipate the language theory of *Nature.* But Emerson, even during his ministry, was already impatient with a correspondential theory of words, proclaiming more uncompromisingly than his friend Dewey the primacy of Spirit in shaping character and speech.

Emerson's stance toward controversy was so unequivocal that he expressed it aphoristically. In his journal on 28 August 1830, he wrote: "Alii disputent, ego mirabor, said Augustin. It shall be my speech to the Calvinist & the Unitarian" (*JMN* 3:193. The editors note that in Sermon No. 169, not preached until 7 September 1834, Emerson translated the Latin, "Let others wrangle, I will wonder.")[21] In his journal called "Encyclopedia," he wrote under "Christianity": "Jesus simply affirmed, never argued" (*JMN* 6:183). Truth, he believed, preexists its utterance and is superior to the speaker, even if that be Jesus. This conviction was at the root of his charge in the Divinity School Address that the Church has corrupted the message of Jesus: "The idioms of his language, and the figures of his rhetoric, have usurped the place of his truth; and churches are not built on his principles, but on his tropes" (*CW* 1:81).

Emerson's suspicion that language is an inadequate vessel to convey true vision is reflected in his style, which F. O. Matthiessen found not "dramatic" but "simply ejaculatory."[22] In vision and style, Emerson has much in common with John Cotton and the first American Antinomians, who depreciated the efficacy of preaching, the surprising nature of the Holy Spirit rendering verbal effort futile.[23] Despite his thoroughgoing spiritualism, and despite the unforeseen effect of Unitarian scriptural exegesis in disrupting fixed notions of language, Emerson could not hold a genuinely antinomian view of expression. He was convinced, as he declared in Sermon No. LII, that language is "made after one model," sustained by God himself. Were this not so, "the faculty of speech would only be the organ of hopeless contradiction & perplexity. But we find there is a certain *standard idea of man* which we all have in our thoughts in our conversation."

As Emerson contemplated the rare gift of "Godtaught teachers" in his journal, he found that "voice & rhetorick" are inconsequential before "truth." A distinctive "tone" emerges, and "[i]t is impossible to mimick it" (*JMN* 3:185). Did the pulpit constrain such genuine expression? At the head of Sermon No. LXXXI Emerson jotted "[I would write as a man who writes for his own eye only.]" (Emerson's brackets.) But his real quarrel was not with the genre but with integrity. "Adhere to nature never to accepted opinion," he reminded himself. "The sermon which I write inquisitive of truth is good a year after, but that which is written because a sermon must be writ is musty the next day" (*JMN* 3:326–27).

Whatever the vagaries of experience, character, we have seen, provided continuity and unity. Emerson was too much the heir to early-republican concepts of oratory ever fully to embrace a notion of eloquence as sheer afflatus. Even in his most Romantic period, he admired Milton as a model of balance, his power of eloquence yoked to character: Milton knew "that this mastery of language was a secondary power, and he respected the mysterious source whence it had its spring; namely, clear conceptions, and a devoted heart."[24] "Character is higher than intellect," he maintained in "The American Scholar"(CW 1:61). Against this backdrop, even Emerson's well-known complaint in "History" ("it is the fault of our rhetoric that we cannot strongly state one fact without seeming to belie some other"—CW 2:22) seems less a gesture of personal inadequacy than a matter-of-fact assessment of "normal" discourse, a flaw overcome by oracular, affirmative, Christlike utterance.

Emerson may have cut the Gordian knot of religious controversy in a way that helped him achieve a clearer sense of voice and expression. But to say that he simply adopted the tone of Jesus raises a new set of problems. Unitarians could not agree on what exactly it meant to speak with "authority" like Jesus. Preaching at the ordination of Chandler Robbins as successor to Emerson at Second Church, Henry Ware, Jr., came full circle to the polemical tangle Emerson had sought to transcend. Ware granted that religion has suffered from "scholastics" and "pedantry," and he sought to move the heart. But "[t]he most powerful preaching," he thought, "will be that of argument; not of subtilties and refinements, of formal technicalities, and metaphysical abstractions," but the sort used by Jesus and the apostles![25] Ware was not recommending contention; he wanted, as much as Emerson, to rid preaching of pompous "declamation," literariness, and unbridled emotionalism. But he and his young colleague had come to different understandings about preaching, authority, argument, and eloquence.

Emerson's aversion to argument, we shall see in the next chapter, was politically problematic. Broadly, his stance was respectably Unitarian. But it was more than an attitude of innocuousness. Refusal to engage in controversy was a sign of hard-won spiritual and rhetorical integrity which, as he was careful to point out, must "cost" something. Speaking like Christ, with "authority," was to subordinate the self, to become representative, transparent, aphoristic, oracular, before the truth.[26] That such a style and vision could provoke the storm that followed the Divinity School Address is one of the ironies of the liberal-Christian legacy.

IV

Emerson's conviction that language is local, partial, culturally conditioned, mediatory, transferred to every aspect of religious formalism—rites, institutions, professional roles. Correspondingly, as Gura and Ellison have demonstrated, mimetic and oracular linguistic impulses exist in tension in the landmark sermon on "The Lord's Supper." Emerson indeed undercuts his own careful Higher Critical analysis of his disaffection with the rite: "That is the end of my opposition, that I am not interested in it" (*W* 11:24). In a sense, this sermon is, as Jerome Loving has argued, a public rationalization, an afterthought masking deeper roots of discontent.[27]

To the extent that Emerson defined his theology, his vocation, his voice, around Scripture and eloquence, his *definitive* sermon is perhaps No. CLX. First preached on 2 September 1832, one week before "The Lord's Supper" would explain his impending resignation from Second Church in doctrinal terms, Sermon No. CLX reveals more succinctly than its more famous successor the convictions pushing Emerson toward a broader conception of the pulpit. These convictions, centering around the relationship between spiritual insight and language, are expressed in a tone aspiring to Christlike affirmation, Emerson's ideal of utterance.

In hindsight, the first presentation of Sermon No. CLX is laced with irony; the occasion for Emerson's latest attack on formal religion is his first sermon in the old "New Brick Church" after an absence for repairs to the edifice. Basing the sermon on Colossians 1:9–10, Emerson recommends St. Paul's "best prayer for his friends . . . that they may increase in the knowledge of God." But this text is pretext. "It is pertinent surely to our recent return to this ancient house," he coyly proposes, "to consider the purpose for which churches are erected & worship is instituted." It is soon apparent that the sermon is an occasion publicly to subordinate institution to insight.

Emerson's premise is that "God is unknown in the world." He does not specifically explain this cryptic claim but instead sets up a series of rhetorical questions that invite assent:

> What avails it to collect all knowledge of the origin & progress of states, if we see not & ask not why men exist at all? What avails it to penetrate the motives, admire the characters, imitate the manners of our fellow men—to understand human

nature, as it is called,—if the master spring which moves them all, lies unobserved?

The questions mount. "And such it is," declares Emerson, "to him who has not yet learned to see God manifested in his works." Clearly this is a straw man enabling Emerson to assume a voice of authority. He presents the alternative case—conceptually general but rhetorically effective—that "every man who looks beyond the present moment to a continued being" should strive "to increase in the knowledge of God" and to take strength from the ensuing "settled convictions respecting his nature & laws."

How do we accomplish this feat? Emerson explains in a simple, familiar assertion: "This has God provided for in the constitution of the human mind." He anchors this spiritual insight morally and theologically: "[E]very step taken in the knowledge of God," he stresses, "is also a step gained in real humanity, that the more just are your views of God, the better is your ability to discharge well all the duties of a man"; and men "ascend to the knowledge of God" in clear steps. Emerson denies both the liberal belief that we are "born" to this knowledge, and the conservative belief that it seizes us unexpectedly. A rigorous "process" is required, for "[o]nly by his own reflexion, only by his own virtue, can a man grow in the knowledge of God."

The substance of the sermon is five "successive steps" that comprise the "process" of spiritual growth. Listeners familiar with Scripture and with the long battle with Calvinism would have been inclined to interpret Emerson's outline historically, as either a typological progression from the Old to the New Testament dispensation, or as an account of Unitarianism's victory over orthodoxy. But the "process" points ultimately toward a highly personal realm of experience in which religion is subordinated to life, in which the role of language—including that of the pulpit—has become problematic.

In Emerson's sequence, the "first great hint" from God to men was "to forbid the worship of images." Emerson musters not only the God of Exodus and Deuteronomy but also his own straw man of Calvinist "materialism" when he invokes God's injunction to "cease to look in every thing that shines or to listen in all that thunders for the Invisible & Omnipresent. He is the Soul within all nature." After this mixture of argument and assertion comes the second step in human progress, "the disuse of sacrifices." This old token of "the childish mind," motivated by "the senses," was truly directed not to God but to men's "imagination of God." As a modern Higher Critic and comparative culturist, Emerson finds sacrifice repulsive; viewed symbolically, however, it was "a most valuable exemplification & introduction to the great moral truth that all high attainments, all true heroism, can only exist by self denial & self sacrifice."

In the third step, the mind has left behind the literalism of ancient usage to discover "the truth, that, not power, but benevolence is the basis of the Divine character; that God is not a tyrant." Emerson rejects the Greek and Roman concept of "a Fate, a Destiny, which even the gods cannot move"—as well as the later notion of "natural evils" as divine punishment—to explain the existence of evil. Emerson offers his version of the common Unitarian doctrine of "retribution":

> [W]hen a more extended observation has been taken of events, & it is seen how inseparably good & ill are mixed, it begins to be seen, that out of all evil issues good; that our misfortunes are our best friends; & the obvious inference is that there is one Governor, & that Want, Difficulty, Affliction, are the rough but needful masters which he has provided for the teaching of man.

From this plateau one takes "a divine courage & cheer into the heart in face of every danger," achieving that Stoic/Christian sense of equilibrium Emerson elsewhere calls "compensation": "It removes the terror of death & the dread of the future. We see that we belong to a system in which every error is repaired every loss is compensated & the happiness of the meanest member is not too low for the care of the Infinite Mind."

Having established both a "system" and a stance for the religious life, Emerson proceeds to the decidedly temporal fourth step in the soul's spiritual unfolding, "the discovery that God is not to be worshipped by specific acts but by the conformity of the whole character to his laws. This is a very high point & very slowly reached." Only a projection of puny human vanity imagines a God "pleased with honors & deceived by forms." "Specific acts" and "forms" recede before a sense of the Spirit in which experience and explanation merge, as we "perceive that God does not look at us from afar, but literally animates us."

We are now prepared for the fifth step: "the greatest truth—greatest in mystery & greatest in practical effect,—this namely, that God is within us." Declaring that we become "more & more sensible that the brightest revelation of the Godhead is made in the depths of our own soul," Emerson makes a careful distinction: "It is not our soul that is God, but God is *in* our soul." By not *obliterating* human autonomy, Emerson emphasizes the importance of *response* to God, of growth. Undermining the reliability of a logical construct, moreover, becomes a characteristic Emersonian rhetorical strategy that places even greater responsibility on his audience. "Truth" must be pursued individually, internally—outside the tenuous framework of the sermon. The sermon can only provoke, unsettle, point the way.

"I <will not endeavour> ↑ know not how ↓ to set this great & blessed truth before you in precise statements," he admits. In the revised phrase is the difference between what Emerson would attempt one week later in "The Lord's Supper"—to justify himself through doctrinal exposition—and what truly represented his sense of the Spirit. The progress of the soul could be *suggested* in images of steps, growth, enlarged vision. But in the end, the reality of the indwelling God could not be explained. It could only be *felt*. As language fails before the ineffable, one can only "feel," for example, "that there is a sense in which the language of the Apostle is true, that, 'we are temples of the Holy Ghost, & that the Spirit of God dwelleth in us.' "

In a sentiment Emerson could have found in Sampson Reed, or Coleridge, or the New Testament, he declares that "[t]here is something in us which is higher & better than we." Precise terminology again fails Emerson (or, perhaps more accurately, fails to *interest* him): "This pure & holy inmate of every human breast, this Conscience, this Reason,—by whatever name it is honored,—is the Presence of God to man." This "Presence" transcends language, but its impact is real enough. "By renouncing all other laws & by a devout listening to this oracle, a man shall be guided to truth & duty <to power> & to heaven." The cancellation might make the sentiment more pious, but it hardly conceals Emerson's feeling of empowerment.

The importance of Sermon No. CLX lies not in any new ideas but in its synthesis of very familiar Emersonian ideas. We have seen how in earlier sermons he explored the nature of religious forms, truth, language, and the voice of Christ. All of these issues are brought to bear here as a de facto credo of a minister about to resign his pulpit. Yet how can Emerson square his concessions about the ultimate shortcomings of language with his personal *feeling* of certainty of the Spirit? What prevents consigning experience to utter subjectivity, rendering *any* "communication," including this sermon, an exercise in futility?

Emerson's conceptual solution is based on an inherited sense of the scope and duties of the liberal pulpit. The clue is to be found in his notion of "compensation" and its corollary in shaping "character"—the third and fourth "steps" in the soul's growing "knowledge of God." Emerson makes a leap of faith over the insight/language gulf to announce the ethical implications of knowing God: "Every man knows that the most absolute obedience to the inward law is the greatest height of virtue, & something very distinct from selfishness." Compared to the inner "rewards" of having done "a good action, . . . the eloquence of angels would be cold." Still describing his sense of the glory of the "inward Teacher & Sovereign" in metaphors of sight and words, Emerson finds "the good man" "attended always by the resplendent image of perfect goodness." God is perceived *above* words and is manifested in character. Yet

> If this mode of acknowledging God's presence be strongly conceived, it will help us to understand the remarkable language in which Jesus Christ always spoke to men of God. He worshipped the Father as he appeared to him in his own heart. He felt that his own being was derived from one Source with the sun & moon with man & beast.

But *how* did Jesus speak to men of God? Emerson occasionally speaks of Jesus' use of figurative language, of parable. However, we are disappointed if we seek in Emerson an aesthetic or rhetorical model derived from the example of Jesus, for Emerson conceives of language as a *process* of expressing truth, not as a material structure. Frustratingly too for assessing *Emerson's* rhetoric, he is not, in citing Jesus, advocating a particular *style*. The most we can conclude about Jesus' "remarkable language" is that, because he acknowledges the unity of being with "a faithful an affectionate obedience," "the whole of his instruction down to the last sublime act of sacrifice, was to make men submit the outward to the inward, the flesh to the spirit." Exactly what shape such a submission ought to take we cannot be entirely sure, though Emerson suggests that it entails an "earnest endeavour to seek the eye of God within ourselves," in the process discovering "the only real happiness."

Sermon No. CLX continued for years to epitomize Emerson's sense of spiritual authority and personal empowerment, for he drew on it nearly a score of times for preaching engagements as late as 25 September 1836. Some time after he wrote the sermon, however, he wrote a new concluding paragraph to dramatize its radical import.

The original ending began with rather orthodox piety: "My friends, let it be our prayer & endeavour to increase in the knowledge of God." Despite the conventionality of the sentiment, the passage metaphorically mimics the sermon's theme of words and vision: "The good man is the best picture or shadow of God"; scriptural images of insight are offered, and Jesus in this context is cited as the " 'express image' " of God. This ending concluded with an image of an image: When we are truly open to God, "our whole soul becomes one refulgent mirror of the presence & power & love of God."

The new six-sentence ending lacks not only the tone of piety but also the self-consciously literary quality of the first, moving from a potentially contentious opening charge to the serenely confident and generous tone of a benediction—and valediction:

> My friends the world runs after an external religion an external God but let all whose affections & understandings are so far cultivated open their hearts to the unspeakable gift of an inward revelation of the Divinity. Every man that has been born has been born with this privilege of access to the Eternal. The reason why so few men have found the Father is that so few men watch their own minds. But if a man will reverently watch his own thoughts he will find that a verdict which is indeed divine is there rendered upon every act, & that God is inviting him to renounce a wretched dependance upon human censure & human praise, by writing his own sentence there in letters of light. This is the gospel of glad tidings which Jesus Christ brot to men It is glad tidings of great joy to him who hath ears to hear.

The first sentence is argumentative. The second proclaims a universal law of God's presence, the third, a crisp diagnosis of the human predicament. The fourth, a lengthy, conditional sentence, offers a simple solution (self-trust) driven home by an almost angry challenge ("to renounce a wretched dependance") and a glowing image of self-possession.

The paragraph exhibits, moreover, at least three major rhetorical qualities that together show the difficulty of making rigid distinctions between the preacher's voice and the Transcendentalist's. First, as each sentence opening clearly signals, the paragraph seems relentlessly logical. Second, it is more declamatory than the original ending. Emerson's assertive, self-confident tone, while suggesting his rhetorical ideal of Christlike affirmation, arises from a refusal to consider that matters could be construed any other way. Finally, the assertions of the first four sentences are interwoven with subtle yet necessarily carnal images of insight—the promise of "inward revelation" pursued by human "watch[ing]," the religious nature of self-reliance captured by a striking image conflating words and vision: "writing his own sentence . . . in letters of light."

The final two sentences, grammatically parallel, invoke Jesus' "glad tidings" to clinch the sermon. The timing of the sermon notwithstanding, this is hardly hypocritical, since the prime article of Emerson's faith was that in discovering the God Within we become Christlike. The fifth sentence announces simply that Emerson's gospel *is* the "glad tidings" of Jesus. The last sentence echoes the fifth, resulting not in redundancy but in tones of prophetic, oracular power—and a deliberate note of incompleteness. Playing with the metaphor of hearing, Emerson neatly balances the simple affirmation of self-reliance with the paradox that not all *use* their God-given faculties. This insight draws strength from metaphors of hearing, familiar to the congregation, that are abundant in the Old Testament (especially in Isaiah) and in the parables recounted in the synoptic Gospels. Much as Thoreau does in the famous conclusion to *Walden*, with its images of dawn and light, Emerson in the last sentence of Sermon No. CLX opens spiritual prospects while challenging his listeners with the continually transitional nature of human experience.

V

Emerson's conceptual concern with Scripture and language in the sermons is increasingly matched by an Orphic style that seeks not to obfuscate his views of doctrine, but, in a rhetorical leap of faith, to avoid the trap of theological controversy even as it aspires to Christlike affirmation. Emerson's ideal of transparency in speaking voice anticipates the Romantic style of the great essays and lectures, in which discursive logic is superseded by metaphorical brilliance and aphoristic pronouncements.

It is a mistake, however, to look for a single authentically "Emersonian" voice or style emerging in the sermons. He continued throughout his life to write for a variety of audiences and occasions. And though we may continue to cherish the challenge of *Nature*, the ebullience of "The American Scholar," or the complexity of "Experience," we cannot dismiss as un-Emersonian the *Historical*

Discourse for Concord's bicentennial because it is antiquarian, *English Traits* because it is discursive, the papers on slavery and John Brown because they are polemical, or *The Conduct of Life* because it lacks youthful intensity. A mystical, "Transcendental" voice emerges in the sermons, but it coexists with the voices of pastor, teacher, Jeremiah. And in the great essays, sermonic form persists in what Lawrence Buell has called a "buried outline," a sense of cohesion and progression, even as the reader must assume responsibility for husking the form of words to confront the living truth within.[28]

The coexistence of logical and Orphic modes enables Emerson, in "Prudence," to classify men according to their ability to convert language into character: Men commonly see "the utility of the symbol"; poets, artists, naturalists, and scientists see "the beauty of the symbol"; and the "wise men" see through the carnal trappings of the symbol "to the beauty of the thing signified." Since, as Emerson believed, life and art are fluid, all partake at some moments in each of these three levels of perception. But those who deal in words must yield to the currents of Universal Being so that the artifact will become a transparent vehicle for the Spirit. The poet "should not chide and insult," for "[t]he natural motions of the soul are so much better than the voluntary ones, that you will never do yourself justice in dispute" (*CW* 2:132, 136, 141).

Emerson's primary "audience" became himself. Yet he continued to regard the orator as representative and mediatory, declaring in "The American Scholar": "[T]he deeper he dives into his privatest secretest presentiment,—to his wonder he finds, this is the most acceptable, most public, and universally true" (*CW* 1:63). Through the lesson of having ministered to real people, he had also come to conceive of his audience as co-equals in a divine transaction: "Each man whilst he hears," he announced in his 1839 lecture "Genius," "thinks he too can speak; and in the pauses of the orator bursts forth the splendid voice of four or five thousand men in full cry, the grandest sound in nature" (*EL* 3:83).

Having outgrown the overblown rhetoric of Everett and having sought to uncover the true revelation behind honest words, he became increasingly convinced, as he wrote in "Spiritual Laws," that "a public oration is an escapade, a non-committal, an apology, a gag, and not a communication, not a speech, not a man" (*CW* 2:88). A paragraph in this essay will suffice to show how Emerson continued to enfold Orphic assertions about ineffableness of Spirit within a rhetoric that convinces without recourse to "argument." He has just suggested that a "little consideration" will show that "by contenting ourselves with obedience we become divine" (81). What has conscious reflection and logic to do with transcendence? Emerson takes up this seeming contradiction:

> I say, *do not choose;* but that is a figure of speech by which I would distinguish what is commonly called *choice* among men, and which is a partial act, the choice of the hands, of the eyes, of the appetites, and not a whole act of the man. But that which I call right or goodness, is the choice of my constitution; and that which I call heaven, and inwardly aspire after, is the state or circumstance desirable to my constitution; and the action which I in all my years tend to do, is the work for my faculties. We must hold a man amenable to reason for the choice of his daily craft or profession. It is not an excuse any longer for his deeds that they are the custom of his trade. What business has he with an evil trade? Has he not a *calling* in his character. (82)

Several trademarks of Emerson's sermon style mark this paragraph. No communication is possible without a right understanding of words, and Emerson immediately distinguishes between carnal and spiritual senses of *choice.* There seems to be an intellectual decision to be made. And yet, typical of his strategy in the sermons, he proposes a logical construct only to assert that Spirit knows no reason or logic. "Choice" here is Pauline: One chooses not a specific act or course; one is already *chosen* by one's *character.* Emerson sounds militant in attacking the notion of vocational identity. But his questions are rhetorical, nonthreatening, because his authority derives from the classic Christian notion that we are free to choose, but only to choose what is right. The tone of the paragraph thus has the edge of argument, but the thrust is to invite agreement. The man who participates in an "evil trade" is externalized, and the reader is empowered to reflect on the "calling" within.

As a minister Emerson had sought to redeem the experience of the Spirit from formalism. Growth of character, he thought, not words, rites, and doctrines, connect us to God. As he declared at the end of Sermon No. LXXXVIII, "our ignorance & sins are clouds & obstructions thro' which he speaks in a stifled voice but every effort to do his will to obey this voice does something to remove these obstructions." A continuing sense of the inadequacy of language to contain the Spirit made it impossible for Emerson to codify his own doctrine or ever to sustain a purely belletristic conception of literary vocation.

Yet belief in the mystery that transcends words never deserted him. "There is power over and behind us," he wrote in "New England Reformers," "and we are the channels of its communications." No matter, ultimately, that our articulation falls short of the reality:

> What is the operation we call Providence? There lies the unspoken thing, present, omnipresent. Every time we converse, we seek to translate it into speech, but whether we hit, or whether we miss, we have the fact. Every discourse is an approximate answer: but it is of small consequence, that we do not get it into verbs and nouns, whilst it abides for contemplation forever. (*CW* 3:165–66)

Neither this pietistic stance nor distaste for polemics kept the political world from increasingly occupying Emerson. Having valued "words that are things" above all else, he believed the source of corruption of human affairs to be the corruption of words. Indeed, his angry pronouncements about the political and military debasement of language are worthy of the classic twentieth-century critiques by George Orwell and Ezra Pound. Emerson was deeply disturbed by the extension of slavery and by the euphemisms with which politicians justified the slave trade and imperialism. In a masterfully controlled tirade, he declares that "[l]anguage has lost its meaning in the universal cant. . . . *Manifest Destiny, Democracy, Freedom*, fine names for an ugly thing. They call it otto of rose and lavender,—I call it bilge-water. . . ." "But this is Union, and this is Democracy," he sarcastically observes. Slavery is made possible not merely by brute force, but because the people are "led by the nose by these fine words," which are concocted by "the plotters in the Capitol" ("Speech on Affairs in Kansas," *W* 11:259–60).

That Emerson's political activity stopped at trying to restore the sanctity of the word testifies not to his hypocrisy but to his integrity. (Though, as we shall see in the next chapter, this was both his limitation and a source of idealist extremism as social prophet.) To engage in debate and argument attacks only the surface of a problem, he believed; indeed, it forces participation in the very process by which language becomes finite, corrupt, fallen. Emerson continued to believe, in the late essay "Inspiration," that "[w]hat is best in literature is the affirming, prophesying, spermatic words of men-making poets. Only that is poetry which cleanses and mans me" (W 8:294). Emerson's mission to cleanse and man his contemporaries could be accomplished only by steadfastly downplaying the word-as-artifact. Sermon, lecture, essay, poem must be a fluid bridge for Spirit to cross over and uplift his audience.

5

To "speak & act . . . as a freeman & a Christian": True Virtue and the Fortune of the Republic

I

Emerson preached with conviction and passion about the nature of belief and its expression. Spiritual insight and the devotional attitude were not, however, the exclusive themes of his sermons. Like his father, he assumed the mantle of commentator and prophet on the Christian as social being, as citizen of the Republic. Jeremiads, election sermons, and July Fourth orations had long since institutionalized this impulse within the clergy.

As his sermons reveal, however, Waldo Emerson faced an untenable paradox. The ministry in his day was looked to as a source of refinement, taste, cultivation, moral uplifting, even as its authority was becoming increasingly precarious in an age of widening democracy, economic growth, and geographical expansion. Further, given the favored status of the typical Unitarian congregation, pressure to endorse the emerging secular order was as great as the call for moral prophecy. Emerson's image of the minister, his emotional tone, his rhetorical stances when preaching on civic issues, are carefully modulated to extend the influence of a pulpit whose power had been eroding for decades. Even as he defined the minister as a kind of ideal republican hero who addresses "universal" principles instead of concrete issues, Emerson, in seeking to be "representative," ran the risk of relegating the pulpit to the very sphere of effete deference against which Orville Dewey railed. Moral anger and prescriptive cautiousness stand in uneasy balance in Emerson's sermons.

The ethical and political equivocations of Emerson's ministry anticipate his later relation to "action," which has been a matter of constant critical dispute. Faulting himself for a lack of "animal spirits," he often expressed distrust of sense experience and social engagement. In turn, critics have charged him from various standpoints with betraying a broken circuit between visions of the ideal and the actual.[1] Emphases on individuality or society are indeed discernible at various stages of Emerson's career. But throughout his writings runs a consistent awareness of the duality of human nature, of the need for ideals to be practiced in the world. What Edmund S. Morgan has called the "Puritan dilemma"[2] had been recast in the early republic as a challenge for the clergy to yoke the affections and the spiritual life to the demands of a politically and economically dynamic society. Emerson had no distaste for "action"; he *insisted* on it. But what did he *mean* by action? The ethical convictions and rhetorical stance he assumed as a Unitarian prophet/orator are the source of his later bifurcated, ambivalent views on virtue and politics.

Emerson is often charged with waiting for the armchair security of the sage who had won "acceptance" for his earlier Romanticism, before offering sustained moral commentary on life in America. He was early convinced, however, that "the Genius of America" was advanced by intellectual treasures "struck out from the mines of religion & morality" and embodied in politics by the election of Webster to Congress (*JMN* 2:39). And in his journal for 1823, he proclaimed the traditional Christian view of "*love*" as a manifestation of religion: A Christian is "prolific in benevolent deeds," thereby transforming "Chaos" into "a beautiful & useful order" (*JMN* 2:168). Despite America's apparently favored condition, Emerson knew that the "passions" were among the weaknesses weighing down buoyant expectancy for the progress of the nation, though he believed also that human nature had "lost no virtue" (*JMN* 3:121–23).

Emerson's political outlook, moreover, is closely related in the early years to his psychological landscape. Six months after Ellen's death and the serious illnesses of his brothers, for example, he gave vent to one of his bleakest utterances on the state of the political soul of Jacksonian America: "Sad political disclosures every day brings. Wo is me my dishonored country that such poor wretches should sit in the chairs of Washington Franklin & Adams" (To Edward, 15 August 1831; *L* 1:330). Political vision for Emerson was not mere rhetoric but felt experience.

Emerson's response in the pulpit to social issues reveals, nevertheless, how he was shaped by his culture even as he challenged it. Unitarianism in his day was tending to settle comfortably into the mode of commercial, cultivated, polite Greater Boston. The image of complacent, unevangelical homogeneity was not lost on the denomination's critics. "When the American Unitarian Association was formed in 1825 it numbered one hundred and twenty-five churches, one hundred of them in Massachusetts and most of them within forty miles of Boston, a fact," notes church historian Winthrop Hudson, "which led the irreverent to quip that the Unitarians believed in the fatherhood of God, the brotherhood of man, and the neighborhood of Boston."[3]

Emerson's sermons reflect the values of an emerging middle class, with its conventional forms of sentimentality and domesticity, a distaste for theological doctrine, and a concern with self-culture. But beneath this stereotype of bland conformity and complacency lurked threats and tensions that complicated the liberal minister's role as social commentator. Emerson's assimilation of his culture's economic and political concerns determined both the rhetoric of his prophetic voice and his response to specific instances of injustice and evil.

Emerson proclaimed uncompromising self-reliance and was reluctant to lend his name to particular causes, yet in the middle and late essays and addresses he was increasingly concerned with the national character and, specifically, with slavery.[4] This apparent contradiction has provoked apologies for his integrity of vision and attacks on his hypocrisy and lack of will. Recently David Leverenz has argued provocatively that Emerson's distaste for the masses and his *internalizing* of power, while seemingly the height of democratic Romanticism, is really a strategy of self-protection. Offspring of a declining Boston social order, according to Leverenz, Emerson shaped an ostensibly "representative" vision that in fact "veil[ed] a politics that divides people into a new elite and the mob."[5]

How can Emersonian Transcendentalism appear both democratic (even radical) and reactionary? The roots of Emerson's problematic view of the form and exercise of power indeed lie in the social position and self-image of the liberal ministry. Conrad Wright has demonstrated that Unitarianism in America flourished in the Federalist, mercantile northeast during a time of growing "tendencies towards democracy and secularism," the rise of liberal Christianity being in a sense the *product* of professional anxiety: "The continued prestige of the ministry depended, not only on the survival of Christianity, but also on the preservation of a social structure in which the role of the minister was a significant one."[6] O. B. Frothingham long ago observed that "[t]he Unitarians were conservative, believers in providential arrangements of society, believers in respectability, in class distinctions."[7] Reacting to the "horrours and crimes" and the "atheistical rebellious philosophy" of the French Revolution, Arthur Maynard Walter spoke in 1805 for all Federalists when he declared it "the duty of every one to exert his talents for the preservation of what exists, and the renewal of what is past. This can be effected only by a steady, sober, and religious application of our minds to the development and settling of first principles in morals and politicks."[8]

By the 1820s the conservative sensibility of Boston Unitarians was beset by new challenges to stability on political, economic, and denominational fronts. Each colored Emerson's own sense of identity and mission. The success of Andrew Jackson in 1828 refueled a clerical rhetoric that "recalled the antipartyism of the early republic," notes Ronald P. Formisano citing Channing's Election Sermon for 1830. Political parties, however, were slow to evolve in Massachusetts. Federalists and Republicans alike worshipped their Revolutionary heritage, the former identifying themselves as "the constitutional party," the latter as " 'the party of the revolution' "; but "the struggle for legitimacy promoted centrist appeals." For many of the clergy, Jackson was the incarnation of disorder, yet the antiparty rhetoric veiled a deeper worry about more immediate social and economic signs of disintegration.[9] Federalism might be dead as a political party. But Channing showed how fear of democracy, "party spirit," and restless capitalism could elicit powerful nostalgia. "National Union," he declared, is "of transcendent and universal interest." Critical of John Quincy Adams' contentious spirit, Channing idealized Federalist rule as a golden age of unity, and faulted that party only for yielding to a spirit of "despair of the republic," the final unforgivable republican sin.[10] If the Federalist rhetoric of William Emerson's generation referred to political realities that were receding into history, more tangible new social strains were emerging that had yet to be named or fully assessed.[11]

II

During Emerson's tenure at Second Church the connection between virtue, social order, and commerce took on new significance. A center of trade and banking, Boston saw its population swell by forty percent in the 1820s, from 43,928 to 61,392. Yet during this decade foreign shipping declined, New York threatened to intercept much of Boston's trade, and a panic in 1825 was followed in 1828 by a recession. These ominous developments frightened a city whose personal, family, and civic values were shaped by the values not of Jeffersonian agrarianism but of urban commerce—investment, corporate business, entrepreneurship. Hard times were not soon forgotten. "Anticipating growth through most of the 1830s," write William and Jane Pease, Bostonians "also remembered the late 1820s when, wherever one looked, to whomever one spoke, times were bad, money was tight, interest rates high, dividends low, businesses failing, and unemployment pressing hard on the poor."[12]

Early republican anxiety about foreign threats and party strife largely was supplanted by the more tangible fear that a weak economy could not keep step with the pressures of a growing city. Social tension was increased by a widening salary gap between merchants and artisans, yet the new-money families, though they introduced an element of instability as troublesome in its own way as the rise of Jackson, seemed to offer the best hope for renewed prosperity. The liberal clergy had somehow to acknowledge the need, even desirability, of these entrepreneurs while reminding them of the implicit connection between wealth, virtue, and social cohesion.[13]

Henry Ware, Jr., looking to the "political, moral, and religious destinies of this country," worried about "certain hazards to which our prosperity and character are exposed." American democracy already was tainted by a crudeness—a loss of "outward forms of courtesy" and "deference." Many of our leaders, Ware admitted, were undeserving of admiration. Social order, however, demanded character, which is exhibited in legitimate respect for "real greatness" and "true wisdom."[14] Ware refused, however, to cloak himself in nostalgia or hide behind tradition. He knew that " 'Onward' is the watchword of the times," and he sought, by instilling in young people a love of knowledge and taste, to keep pace with the spirit of the age. For "the danger is, that the progress of the mind will lag tardily behind the growth of the outward prosperity." Yet Ware did turn to a New England tradition of moral and intellectual cultivation: Thirty years before, Buckminster had bought a collection of great books in Europe, and his positive example should "warn [our young men] against the effeminacy of soul to which this feeding on the popular literature of the day will inevitably lead."[15]

Money, as the biographies have documented, had been a constant worry in the Emerson household. Waldo's sermons express a longing for the benefits of economic growth and prosperity, along with a chastened awareness of the ephemeral nature of economic success and the moral responsibility of business. Several preordination sermons in particular aim to establish moral principles of stewardship by locating the source of true virtue. In Sermon No. XII, a Thanksgiving sermon preached first in Waltham in November 1827, he cautions that our "success" is not "safe"; "we were put hither to be disciplined," "educated." The purpose of religion is to "teach us how to enjoy." Our response to divine blessings is, in turn, essential to spiritual well-being: "[G]ratitude is a free will effort, on the part of a moral agent, which God is pleased to regard, as an equivalent for his goodness." While this "equivalent" of human moral effort and God's grace points toward a Channingesque doctrine of *likeness*, Emerson subsumes the moral individual within a vision of the United States "favoured of heaven" and insists that our "reverend & sovereign laws" are "higher than any citizen." Prophesying the transience of a nation conceived only in secular terms, he imagines art and industry destroyed by "profligacy," by the return of "the bloodhounds of domestic anarchy," with New England reverting to the Indians, swept again by revolution, covered by the sea. Against this apocalyptic vision, he warns that even the "warm thrill of patriotism" pales "before more deep & solemn feelings," "for we are citizens of another country."

This other "country" could become not only a source of moral rectitude but a haven from the corruptions of *this* country. Yet Emerson goes on in Sermon No. XII to celebrate the rising nation. "It seems almost superfluous," he remarks, "to point you to those shining advantages of our condition which have given such lustre to this country in the view of all mankind." He nevertheless offers up a verbal iconography of the new republic's achievements in images of progress, equality, navigation, agricultural and manufacturing abundance, learning, the arts. (Emerson's vision evokes the popular allegorical prints of the day depicting the Genius of America.)

But lest his audience be seduced by secular prosperity, he declares again that all earthly distinctions are obliterated by religion. "[T]he superior moral condition of the civilized man," he notes, "is not to be forgotten. The savage state is not the virtuous state." Such extreme alternatives were surely calculated to reassure listeners that they were in the proper camp. But the proper view enfolds economic activity within the message of the Resurrection. And in a remarkable concluding metaphor, Emerson envisions the Christian as a customer of the Ultimate Insurance Agent. "*Insure* these blessings," he proclaims. "Secure them now so that if they be taken from you, you also may receive an equivalent. . . . Hold them as a steward & not as a proprietor." Emerson's economic scruples are not simply the priggishness of the intellectual/cleric who stands above the din of the marketplace. He worried, like others in the Unitarian pulpit, that the nation's moral sensibility might lag behind its bounding commercial energy. But he also feared that economic security, which had eluded his family and which he fervently desired, might rest on a sandy foundation.

The centrality of religious principle as the basis for *all* endeavor is the theme of a cluster of preordination sermons. Preaching on Matthew 11:30 ("My yoke is easy, & my burden is light") in Sermon No. XVIII, Emerson cites three yokes that enslave us: "bad passions . . . the dominion of human opinions . . . the yoke of false religion." He graphically depicts the end of "notorious malefactors" who labored under such yokes, declaring that their energies, properly directed, "would surely have given them honest wealth & respectability & high standing in the community." What was lacking in such cases, he goes on citing Jesus, was "*principles.*" We crave "expiation," looking for it everywhere except in "obedience to this true Religion," which is eternal. Religion is not a matter of obedience to "external observances" nor cumulative good deeds. Rather, to do "one single duty in one single moment" "is to be a Christian."

Emerson specifically urges honesty in "affairs of trade" and moderation in personal gratification (do not, he cautions, "pamper the palate"). Religion is an enduring barometer of behavior, domestic and civic, "a choice between a temptation & a duty," and "Conscience will always point with her silent finger." But by practice, "a holy life ceases to be an effort and becomes a habit of happiness."

In Sermon No. XIX, expressing optimism that "a more just idea of the Christian religion" is yearly being realized as "a more spiritual faith," Emerson presses the importance of the deeply personal source of virtue. "[N]ot the actions but the principles" are the key. Particular evil acts are done not "to the world . . . but to yourself." Yet "[h]onesty . . . is nothing but Truth applied to affairs, instead of words." Transcendentalists, of course, subordinated artifacts to truth, preferring a vital, organic principle in both art and living. So too had the Ciceronian tradition in the early republic viewed rhetoric as pointing beyond itself to character. As he does more often in the early sermons, Emerson tends to tedious prescription (one episode of drunkenness, he suggests, may not damage your body, but it represents "[t]he shameful slavery of your moral being to your animal being"). But on a grander scale he points to the colonial protest of the tea tax as an example of "the *principle* of *Freedom.*" Specific actions are important "only as they are expressions of principles, & not for themselves & their effects on the world."

Emerson does not see the *tragic* potential for two people making different decisions based on the same principle, expecting that this stance applied purely will lead to consensus. He is convinced that God permits our "little agency" for our "own happiness [and] education to moral greatness." For when we live with "a habitual regard to the great relations we bear to God & to Eternity," "the events of this life cease to appear important." This habit of Christian humility applies to wealth, career, residence—all limited and inconsequential in light of the images of astronomy that follow. Included in Emerson's list of pursuits and possessions subject to "vanity" are "all that your hands performed; the house that you built; the money that you earned; the honours which you attained; the pages which you wrote [an autobiographical check]; your extensive influence, your charitable acts." Not our acts but the principles "are immortal," and conscience is "more persuasive than any language."

Though he is bent on instilling a sense of habitual piety in his audience, Emerson has no intention of inducing a state of passive contemplation. Sermon No. XX makes clear that, though acts must derive from principle, our public selves *do* matter. Taking the text of Titus 3:2, "Speak evil of no man," Emerson distinguishes the "vice" of "calumny" from slander, which "can be publicly refuted." But "this evil propensity" poisons both the perpetrator and the wider community. Only "*Character,*" "the great engine by which the world is moved," can check its spread. And character has value not only "in the eye of the possessor" but "to others" as well.

Mingling images of success with injunctions to be good, Emerson cites one who, in obeying the biblical Commandments, has "prospered": "He vindicates, by this simple logic, the ways of providence to man"; the law offers "encouragement to . . . virtues," a "pillar" of faith, a "powerful motive" to goodness, and "consolation." The pestilence of gossip, however, spreads even among the "well bred." The "temptation to evil speaking" must be met with "the merit of resistance." At our best, when we achieve "elevation of mind," we incline to attribute good motives to others, thus spreading good will essential to the community.

Though "resistance" is an active moral state, Emerson pulls up short of recommending *outward* condemnation of corruption in the affairs of state. Character, he has insisted, is the source of virtue, which in turn is the cement of society. But a curious tension surfaces when he discusses opportunities for engaging in specific civic acts. He offers a hypothetical case, in Sermon No. XX, that you are the only person who could expose a corrupt politician. You would, he grants, have a duty to do so. But this "can hardly ever occur," he goes on. "In the present imperfect state of the world you may safely leave the office of stigmatizing bad men to the public eye & tongue." Almost conflating legitimate civic involvement with calumny, he declares, "[T]here is little danger that injury will arise from the want of your activity in aspersing the character of any man." Quite the contrary, we run the "danger" even in this extreme case of self-deception, to "magnify venial faults into grave charges, & serve your own evil passions." Suggesting a stance toward political rhetoric that parallels the extreme aesthetic implication of the God Within, he warns that "[t]here are times when the silence of a good man is more impressive than any harangue." A greater danger than political corruption is destroying our character.

Emerson's reluctance to draw out the full political implications of his moral vision reflects the tenor of Boston culture in the 1820s. As William and Jane Pease explain, "Boston politics . . . were, especially on economic issues, pragmatic. The Revolution was venerated, but revolutionary rhetoric was not. . . . Economics should not be politicized. . . . And politics should remain subservient to the community's economic well-being."[16] Making heavy investments in public education and developing an efficient new approach to city services, Bostonians nevertheless "feared social upheaval."[17] And though lay power was emerging to dominate clerical influence, Unitarian liberalism "encouraged innovative responses to new economic forces without at the same time threatening social or political stability."[18]

From the pulpit Emerson too sought to morally shepherd the economic and political energies of his audiences without essentially questioning the status quo. Was this strategy a spineless evasion of fundamental social problems? Or was it a carefully modulated stance to assure some measure of continuing moral influence in a dynamic age when the clergy was clearly losing to secular forces whatever "power" it still held in economic and political life?

The evidence of the sermons suggests that Emerson shared his contemporaries' material aspirations even as he witnessed the growing tenuousness of the pulpit in an entrepreneurial culture. Emerson's sermons would soon change emphasis. The cluster of early sermons that cautiously advanced themes of the public ramifications of private character were given frequently before his ordination, but rarely afterward. Emerson's attention turned increasingly to bolder affirmations about the reality of the God Within, and implications of this fact for social life. But he remained committed to consensus and to a sober sense of the necessity for (and precarious state of) the political and economic order. Even as he became more confident about addressing *specific* issues from the pulpit, he retained the habit of calling for an uncompromising, militant moral stance, only to pull back from the concrete implications of his vision.[19]

But it is a mistake to regard Emerson's early sermons as merely salving Brahmin consciences or pandering to big money. Sermon No. XXII, which begins as a conventional account of religion as living to "the God of Truth," recommends his stock virtues of moderation— of rising "above passion & error," of recognizing that "all falsehood of opinion is injurious to the intellect, & all falsehood of action is injurious to the morals." But his more specific criticisms and his model man resemble less a construct of Hamilton or of Jefferson than Franklin's ideal of "mediocrity." On the one hand, Emerson warns that "haughty manners" and "parade of wealth" are evanescent, opposed to his principle that "the power & value of truth is not particular & local, but absolute & universal." On the other hand, he observes that habitual regard to truth also stands in opposition to "the fickle public." Emerson's sense of moral discrimination may itself be elite, but his view of the virtuous individual embodies a balance that transcends marketplace pressures: "This is a man whose theory of duty & whose practice are the same; whose manners are the simple expressions of his feelings."

Emerson's moral strictures, however, are compatible with both the Puritan sense of stewardship and the Revolutionary generation's Lockean notion of property as a foundation of the republic.[20] Indeed, in Sermon No. XXII he revised his criticism of the vanity of money, changing "property" to "wealth." Sermon No. XXV ("We shd live righteously in this present world." Ti 2:12) is Emerson's most direct statement of economic stewardship as an essential social aspect of religion. "The Gospel," he argues, "is not a contemplative but a practical system & would be of little value to us if it overlooked our social condition." This view carries an explicit ethical component: "To live righteously, is to live in a manner not to violate the rights of others," key to which is "respect to the property of others." Christianity dictates that "this life is a state of discipline" under which "things [are] valuable . . . only in their *utility to our character.*" Anticipating the "ubi sunt" theme of "Hamatreya," he observes that ownership is relative, "temporary." Yet stewardship is obligatory. Emerson doubts that there are thieves in his audience but he declares that there are other "modes of dishonesty," including delaying a debt payment to the poor. The ripple effect of "the commercial embarrassment of one man," moreover, can destroy twenty other families. Some such crises are caused by natural disaster, but most, he insists, are brought on by indulgence.

Far from being "a lover of parsimony," Emerson celebrates the dynamic mercantile economy. He applauds the prosperity and grandeur of maritime towns as "evidence of the triumph of industry & art." What he condemns is the "ostentation of wealth . . . by one man" at the expense of others. "[W]e ought to feel," he announces, "that too great importance cannot be attached to an exact fidelity in the discharge of pecuniary obligations." Charity, however, can be "mean spirited," and the worthiest cause must not be given money that "is not your own." The virtuous circuit of stewardship is completed, then, only as we recognize "other rights" besides "Property," especially "personal liberty." Righteousness embraces "conversation, the manners, the whole life; it does not stop short with justice but adds mercy." In an added passage Emerson specifically endorses charity to the poor and to "useful" and "elegant institutions."

Republican and Christian virtues merge, toward the end of Sermon No. XXV, in a vision of selfless character. The "greatest perfection to which humanity attains, [is] when it ceases to live for itself that it may live for others." Self-forgetfulness—a trait of Jesus, the medium for perceiving the God Within, and the aesthetic imperative of that vision—became also the basis of social action. "[S]ome of the best men," Emerson explains, "appeared to lose themselves in the great actions they performed; they put their whole being into them." An occasional good deed, "an occasional elevation of sentiment," is not enough. Virtue demands "habitual righteousness," whether in politics or the marketplace.

Commodity would play an important, if subordinate, role in *Nature.* At his most exuberant, Emerson could be confident, in "Art," that "the railroad, the insurance office, the joint stock company," and all the products of science can be put "to a divine use" if they proceed "from a religious heart" (*CW* 2:218). The qualification is crucial. This was no sudden shift of Transcendental vision but a continuity of Emerson's view from the pulpit that commerce, like politics, *is* subject to the rule of virtue. Emerson's effusive remark that money is "in its effects and laws, as beautiful as roses" (*CW* 3:136) was labeled "staggeringly innocent" by F. O. Matthiessen.[21]

Yet Emerson's view had been an article of faith among the Boston merchant class in the 1820s. And as a Unitarian minister, he had been expected to address the full range of human activity, including the morality of commerce. If the minister was thus overextended, vulnerable to naivete, the aim, at least, had been not just to flatter but to channel the nation's rising economic order.

III

The role of emotion was problematic not only in the pietistic life of liberal Christianity but also in the minister's appeal for social and political engagement. Emerson was not the first to brand Unitarianism "corpse-cold," nor is the charge entirely fair. Unitarians, attempting to distance themselves from Calvinist doctrine, felt obliged also to distance themselves from Calvinist sensibility. Too often Unitarianism had been defined primarily by what it was not, and, as Emerson grew to know, often sounded bloodless in trying to define what it *was*. But Unitarians could display their own brand of fervor, however unsuccessful they may have been in conveying it to common folk. Henry Ware, Jr., believed religion to be "so much a matter of sentiment and sympathy" that he urged ministers to eschew rational, "scholastic" preaching, for "the most efficient speaker is he who most throws his own soul into his eloquence." This was his reason for urging pastoral care, which establishes ties of affection, and for recommending "extemporaneous" preaching, which gives vent to the heart.[22]

As early as 1825, a contributor to the *Christian Examiner* was writing that "religious feeling" is not "a supernatural excitement of the heart" but "a sense of duty." Aware that this definition might not kindle a fire in the heart of the devout, the writer hastened to qualify this vision of duty: "Not the cold and uninspiring thing, that too often bears the name,—not the dead letter that measures and weighs our obligations, and tells us we need not go any further. Religious feeling is the sense of duty in its living force, urging us onward in the narrow way with pleasure instead of unwillingness, and making our labour light."[23]

As a minister Emerson too felt the grandeur of duty, of a faithful pursuit of truth that uplifts the Christian even as it cements the community. His concept of conscience was an attempt not to measure and weigh our obligations but to charge human life, from the commonest domestic scene to the grandest political event, with purpose and joy. In his inaugural address as Harvard's Boylston Professor of Rhetoric and Oratory on 8 December 1819, Edward T. Channing noted that ancient civilizations were not "split . . . into parties," oratory serving to channel the "warlike" impulses of simpler societies. The ancient rhetoricians understood human motivation, however, and their "rules" remain applicable to our "altered condition of society," though oratory, rhetoric, and eloquence, he believed, were in decline.[24]

"The object of eloquence," he declared, "is always the same,—to bring men, by whatever modes of address, to our way of thinking, and thus make them act according to our wishes." Yet the modern orator must also accommodate himself to changing circumstances. For Channing, a Federalist and a Unitarian, modern times were not conducive to individual, heroic effort, for today's society is based on "the very improvements of the age, the stable foundation and ample protection of government, the general diffusion of knowledge and of a spirit of inquiry," and "modern eloquence" must be tailored to an age not of despotism but of the rule of "laws and institutions" (13).

Pulpit eloquence, moreover, aims not at "striking change in . . . opinions or conduct" but at "a growing and permanent influence over the character and opinions" (18, 19). To do so is not to ignore the "affections" but to use all "language . . . beauty . . . imagery that could delight or refine our taste, and make our conception of [liberal religion's] truths distinct and glowing" (22).[25] Emerson aimed in his sermons both to quicken in his audience a sense of virtue as felt experience and to channel this impulse in the interest of the public good. His notion of self-reliance was based largely on the conviction that "society rightly considered [is] but a number of persons of very fickle judgements governed for the most part by their passions." Yet he believed that "so strong is yet the natural sense of virtue, that they will heartily applaud you when a heroic act takes them by surprise" (*JMN* 3:140). The minister mediated between human nature that was socially decadent yet, potentially, individually divine. His rhetorical dilemma as prophet was to find a voice, a stance, that would engage a diverse, sophisticated audience, stir their feelings, engender a lively sense of moral righteousness, and establish a climate of communal dedication to high purpose.

IV

Early in his ministry Emerson held a rather Jeffersonian optimism that, in an open marketplace of ideas, truth would prevail over falsehood. This sense was crucial to his regarding the pulpit as a legitimate platform for political commentary. Men, he noted in Sermon No. XIV, are "divided into parties in government, & sects in religion." This division leads not only to the "*evil*" of "bad passions" but also to "*good*" in "the development of truth which is always the result of free discussion." "It is the order of Providence in this world," he observes, "that every good thing should be bought with a price." "[T]he progress of religious opinion," accordingly, is of necessity a dialectical process, with religious controversy the "price" of advancement.

Paradoxically, Emerson, like most of his colleagues in the liberal pulpit, was troubled by the disruption of denominational bickering that lay behind their emergence from Calvinism. Such strife, forcing Unitarians to devote excessive energy to negative defenses, inhibited development of anything like a positive evangelical spirit within Unitarianism and prevented the denomination from ever achieving the kind of consensus essential to their own self-imposed mission of transmitting the legacy of the Founding Fathers. Emerson's familiar antisectarianism is echoed by W. B. O. Peabody, who declared in the *Christian Examiner*, "The narrow boundaries of sect,—the warlike liveries of party,—the uncouth names of Catholic and Protestant, Episcopal and Congregational, are nothing to Him. He knows but one church,—the Christian, which is not divided by these differences among men."[26]

Emerson continued to believe that error and injustice demanded a response. But the *Christian* response must avoid becoming tainted by the very evils it would redress. He put it most succinctly near the end of Sermon No. LXXV:

> Every man ought carefully to ponder the evils of party spirit, that he may be a partisan, when he must be, without them. I do not think it is possible entirely to keep aloof from these communities of opinion. When a persecution arises against an opinion which you hold, you must avow your sentiment, & join the weaker party in their defence. We are to use all our means to spread the knowledge of true religion, & we must unite with others to make our efforts of any avail.
>
> But let us cleave, in the midst of parties, to an independence of party.

Emerson's stance toward sectarian strife is thus a version of the Puritan dictum that we should live in the world but be not of it.

Emerson would take part in legitimate, unavoidable "party" clashes while somehow not being contaminated by "party spirit."

As Sermon No. LXXV reveals, Emerson, in his vision of republican order, conjured up the ecclesiastical and the political together, using interchangeably the terms "party" and "sect," labels that since the early days of the republic reflected an anxious search for elusive cultural unity. Emerson expressed confidence that the course of religious "progress" was sure, but like many other Unitarians he worried about realizing the fruits of spiritual culture against the backdrop of denominational and party warfare, economic problems, and rapid social change—all captured in the menacing image of Andrew Jackson, from whom Emerson instinctively recoiled.

Emerson conflated the religious and political most fully in his July Fourth sermons, which express the civil millennialism of the Revolutionary heritage. Waldo's own father had preached a popular Independence Day oration in Harvard, Massachusetts, and a similar sermon before the Ancient and Honourable Artillery Company led directly to his selection as minister of Boston's First Church.[27] Expressing the popular fear of the corrupting influence of Deism and the excesses of the French Revolution, Emerson had declared that Christianity and liberty are alike anathema to despotism, that a universal tendency to misuse power required a strong militia. Embracing republican ideals and anxieties helped the post-Revolutionary clergy broaden its influence, even if, in retrospect, its power was becoming more shallow.[28]

As a young man Waldo found the July Fourth oration reduced to rote by "complacent orators," and he feared that this rhetorical rot was matched by decay in the body politic. On 3 July 1822 he wrote to John Boynton Hill: "In this merry time, & with real substantial happiness above any known nation, I think we Yankees have marched on since the Revolution, to strength, to honour, & at last to ennui." He saw declension implicit in the narrow victories accorded such great men as Daniel Webster, and he worried that a scandalous Court Martial might presage "that power may even in this country, triumph & trample over right." Yet he still believed in the prophetic potential of the jeremiad, suggesting that this "dismal foreboding" "warrant[s] a croak on the fourth of July" (L 1:120–21).

By 1829, when Waldo rose to preach his July Fourth sermon on the text of 2 Corinthians 3:17 ("Where the spirit of the Lord is, there is liberty"), the American jeremiad had evolved into a highly formulaic "ritual of consensus" by which an increasingly diverse and secular nation reasserted its sense of providential destiny.[29]

Emerson presented Sermon No. XLII only once. It is representative, however, of his view of national mission, and it has important implications for his understanding of the nature of ethical action. "It has pleased God in his providence," he declares, "to distinguish our country in great & important respects." In this we are superior to the "barbaric magnificence" of the East and the "gross superstition" and "fawning adulation" of Europe. As the nation celebrates "the memorial of virtue of a self devoted Christian struggle . . . *for a principle,*" "let us be careful that we have right views of the blessing & sure conviction that we partake in it." No less than his father's, Emerson's "ritual of consensus" is designed both to give vent to anxieties about republican permanency and to reestablish the legitimacy of a democracy facing new social and economic strains. "For the forms of a free government," he goes on, "do not make a free state." Rather, "to exist in the community [i]t must exist in the heart of the citizen." Moral vigilance is the cornerstone of democracy, which is heaven-bestowed only to the worthy: "Freedom," like all God's "best gifts [is] offered to our exertions, not dropped into idle hands."

With a sense of representative moral heroism worthy of a Cicero or a John Adams, Emerson qualifies his enthusiasm for mere democracy: It is easy "to shout with a crowd"; "[b]ut a few men always do understand the worth of this birthright & hold it with religious awe." The crowd is fickle but truth is eternal, providing a theoretical and practical base for republicanism. Indeed, "the truly wise in all times, in all cases, have common ends. The moral energy that rises anywhere in man to sublime thought & action must always rest on sublime motive," "on truth & goodness."

Emerson's aphorisms on private virtue—particularly in the late essays—are often cited as evidence of his sentimentalizing the domestic, the genteel. But in Sermon No. XLII his probing of character undergirding the republic has a Puritan's staunchness, a Federalist's wariness of human nature's ability to govern itself. In a remarkable fantasy, Emerson imagines following home "a patriot" and finding him "the prisoner of his own avarice," another who "is the servant of his belly," yet another who is a slave to "venomous party spirit." The strength of the republic is based in countless patriot homes. And while "the proud American" is indignant if told he is a "slave," the bedrock of liberty is embodied in Jesus' words: "[T]he truth shall make you free." Pursuing truth and abiding by God's law, the truly free man is one "who is placed by his love of God & of Christ out of the reach of earthly motive who is incapable of fear cold to pleasure deaf to flattery master of himself." Never absolute in his political optimism or celebration of self-reliance, Emerson cautions that "[n]o man is perfect; no man is wholly free."

Just as his father had proclaimed, Emerson warns that the "freedom" signified by July Fourth "is local & temporary." But the rhetoric of the American jeremiad celebrates even as it laments. Emerson's "ritual of consensus" steers his audience between the extremes of anarchy and despotism. Personal independence is held in check by the old Puritan—and Republican—stricture that the true individual is representative of the chosen community. The anchor of democracy, Emerson announces in familiar terms, is Christ, who confers freedom that is "perfect, & infinite, & everlasting." When this is realized in the individual, "[t]he habit of holy action, the spirit of God in your spirit, shall be your charter."

The rhetorical (and even moral) corollary to Emerson's desire for consensus is an aversion to "controversy." This quality has been admired by his champions as an emanation of lofty idealism; detractors who would have had him more engaged in the political issues of his day regard it as a stance of spineless innocuousness. Whatever our verdict, Emerson's preference of assertion to argument was hardly idiosyncratic. Professor E. T. Channing regarded the church service as a respite marked by "the seriousness, the silence, the heartfelt or the habitual respect for the speaker" which contrasted "with the turbulence and rancor which are often seen in other assemblies." Controversy is inappropriate in the church not because the preacher is perfect but because the occasion dictates that dispute be deferred.[30] William Henry Channing, himself an ardent reformer, would later commend the same quality in his uncle: "Controversy was utterly uncongenial to Mr. Channing; his temper, tastes, desires, habits, all conspired to make it repugnant. . . . He was chiefly desirous to forget the things behind and to press on. . . . He was seeking to reverence and love God, to respect and sympathize with man, to form himself and his fellows anew in Christ's image, to mould society upon the pattern of Divine justice."[31] For William Ellery Channing, moreover, this benign attitude was compatible with increasingly direct criticism of the evils of slavery.

As with Channing, Emerson's cultivation of serenity in demeanor, purpose, and expression derives from many sources. By nature he was deferential, self-effacing. The verbal imperative of his vision of the God Within, furthermore, was a preference for assertion and proclamation instead of argument. A uniquely Unitarian issue is also implicit. After years of doctrinal battle with Calvinists, Unitarians by

1830 had developed a virtual code discouraging internecine rhetoric. Intradenominational debates, it was understood, should follow the high road, seeking truth in the spirit of Christian benevolence. Contributing significantly to this rhetorical posture was the liberal clergy's long-standing, self-imposed role of upholding fragile republican virtues, which by the late 1820s had been complicated by the added strains of economic hard times, Jacksonian democracy, and sectional strife and abolitionism. To maintain the increasingly tenuous connection between the secular and the sacred, the clergy would have to proceed in a spirit not of confrontation but of conciliation.[32] Emerson's commitment to a policy of militant rhetorical neutrality derives less from a simple distaste for the world of affairs than from adherence to the liberal-Christian concept of the orator/minister.

Not that Emerson opts in the sermons for blandness. As in Sermon No. XVI, he often catalogues natural disasters as tactics for breaking down human pride in self-sufficiency. He declares in an early Fast Day sermon (No. XVII) that penitence suits the human condition, that American society is on the edge of collective peril because of its own prosperity. In spite of the society's tendency to self-congratulation, it partakes of timeless flaws. "Human passions," the root of war, are still corrupt; indeed, "human nature does not change with change of place & change of circumstances," and man in the nineteenth century is the same as he was "in the garden." And in Edwardsean images of storms, floods, and worms, Emerson suggests that nature is a metaphor for moral conditions. Here is a "hint of Eternal Providence, this expression of omnipotence"; seeming to echo the Enfield Sermon, he warns that God can still unleash calamities, and we should derive no false security from the fact that he "has forborne to use them."

Like Edwards he releases some of the tension created by his angry vision lest his audience become paralyzed with fear and despair. He grants that both individuals and community in America are *relatively* virtuous but that we must heed warning signs: "the malignity of our parties . . . license of our press . . . fury of religious controversy . . . intemperance . . . uncharity . . . fraud." Ceremonies of penitence are not enough, for the "foundation of all patriotism" is individual "virtue." Still bedevilled by the vision of a corrupt republic that had haunted his father's generation, he declares that we must not "lament" public evil: "It is we ourselves & we alone who can cure that evil which we bewail." Not wishing to induce a frightened passivity, he then allows his chastened audience an opportunity for moral action. All share in "guilt"; what is needed is genuine

"contrition," that we may "go sternly to the work of reformation."
"[R]eform yourself," he urges, for though man has not lost his vices,
neither has he lost "one virtuous disposition." We have, moreover,
encouragement from the "Revelation" and in the thought that
Christ's virtuous acts redound through history.

Emerson's classic sermon on republican virtue and the state is No.
LXX, a Fast Day sermon preached first on 8 April 1830. (Though a
certain dutifulness inheres in such occasional pieces, Emerson
thought enough of the piece to use it again as late as 13 November
1836.) Teaching our youth about the nation's institutions and constitution, he announces, is inadequate to maintain the soul of the
community. More important, every "individual should see the connexion between private & public duties; should be accustomed to
extend the dominion of his conscience over these as much as over
his secret actions."

Ever sensitive to the pitfall of controversy, Emerson explains his
stance toward using his office to address political issues:

> I am very sensible brethren that it would be a violation of
> the plainest decorum, if the pulpit were made the vehicle of
> proclaiming or of insinuating opinions upon men & measures.
> In so doing the Christian preacher quits his true & dignified
> place & just as surely forfeits the confidence of those to whom
> he speaks. But it *is* the office of the pulpit to warn men unceas-
> ingly of the universality of the law of duty, & to charge them
> that [t]he state can never be in much danger as long as men
> vote for laws & for law makers according to their conscience
> & introduce into their political action the same regard to
> rectitude which they feel bound to exercise in dealing with
> their families & friends.

Emerson is not reluctant to make the case for the connection between conscience and politics. But to define a prophetic role for
the ministry requires an amazingly nimble rhetoric. This lengthy
passage consists of a pattern of disavowal and assertion, the ministerial persona alternately claiming the high ground above party strife
and insisting on a voice in the affairs of the world. Yet Emerson is
not simply dodging responsibility. In finding it inappropriate for
ministers to offer specific solutions to social problems he mirrors to
a degree the growing gentility of the Unitarian pulpit as a source
primarily of reflection and consolation; he also understands the daily
realities of parish politics that test the minister's pastoral skill. In

the context of Unitarian history, however, Emerson is shrewdly aware of the difficulty of *sustaining* pulpit influence in a liberal, secular society. Clerical authority, especially in liberal ranks, had become precarious. Emerson's "true & dignified place" is conceived less as an effete realm protected from turmoil than as a vantage point from which legitimate influence can continue to be exerted. For after this passage of seeming inconsistency in which the Christian minister seems loath to raise his voice, Emerson raises the old republican specter of the "violent grasping" after selfish, short-term, "expedient" ends that is "a dangerous symptom not only for the permanence of our civil institutions but for our own moral health as individual men." And though his tone remains unassuming, Emerson makes it clear that "[i]n this season of ferment & expectation, I shall not hesitate to ask your attention to the source of our social evils."

Though Emerson's minister declines to make specific pronouncements, he sustains at least a *tone* of moral commentary. He gives the *impression* of prophecy. "All gov'ts are mutable," he says, "& each man wields a portion of influence in determining their form." But while mutability suggests the possibility of reform, it suggests also the instability of *good* government. And, reverting to his youthful despairing view of history, he finds government predominantly "a tragic tale of the pernicious connexion between the ruler & the ruled," offering the Jeffersonian hope that "[i]n a well constituted state, the government itself will be out of sight." Our own republican government, which he traces to the English model, has evolved into "the most perfect" yet realized on earth. Government at its best, however, is "negative." It cannot make its citizens better people; it can only protect "property" and "rights."

The most specific contemporary evils Emerson cites are "a licentious press" and a "strong tendency to disunion" in politics. The former, conducive to "the madness of party spirit," produces a Babel-like confusion and chaos, the latter a pride that sees error only in others. "Consider," Emerson declares, "whilst we so readily repeat & deplore the fact of the increasing profligacy in the public morals if we ought not rather to lay our hands on our own breasts, & say, *We are the men*." Politics is an "index" of private morality. And again, Emerson's hope lies in the unsettling but dynamic truth of mutability: "that this average public virtue is never a fixed amount but always fluctuating; that it depends not on masses, but on individuals; & that each of us every day does somewhat to raise or to depress it." The moral life of community, moreover, is based upon imitation.

If slanderous newspapers and selfish parties sow discord, virtue commands "deep respect." The "virtue in the world . . . is always the average of the virtue of individuals." Ultimately, "[w]e are citizens of the heavenly country." Yet "God has so harmoniously joined together the good of this temporal & of that eternal world, that every effort which we make with a pure heart to deserve his favor, every struggle with temptation is so much done to purify & so to perpetuate the civil institutions of our land."

Emerson's concern with principle may seem on its face a hypocritical evasion of political engagement. Samuel Hopkins' early antislavery activity reminds us that Calvinists were not necessarily otherworldly or politically reactionary, that liberal Christianity did not necessarily mean liberal politics. Yet Theodore Parker is evidence that a Unitarian willing to become embroiled in controversy could make his mark in public affairs. For Emerson, however, raising the minister above the din of party strife was a means of ensuring, in a world of secularization and professional insecurity, that his voice would continue to be heard at all. The notion of public virtue as a "fluctuating" water table based on the sum of its parts is based on Emerson's honest and complex view of human nature. He distrusted external "power" yet knew that people never achieve perfection. The American Republic seemed man's best hope not because it was a perfect form but because, like all forms—physical, sacramental, verbal—it was transparent. American democracy was not solid, absolute, permanent, but a vehicle through which fluid, imperfect human nature could realize its power.

Truth, as Emerson always believed, is self-evident or it is not truly received. The democratic principle of imitation, properly viewed, meant not slavish copying but acceptance of worthy models, much as Christ was revered by Unitarians. Emerson's minister is meant to be representative in this high sense—above the need of controversy, not out of hypocrisy or fastidiousness but, in his prophetic role, as a model to which the goodness in all people might be drawn.[33]

V

How successful was the Unitarian model of eloquence in addressing moral and political issues threatening to rend the new republic? Classical oratory held that reason and a wide knowledge of the order of nature, accompanied by clarity and grace of expression, were the vital bond between the *res privata* and the *res publica*. Eloquence was ultimately not a system of mere formal, stylistic theory but a discipline indispensable to citizenship, to action. Filtered through traditions of English common law, Puritan church polity, and Enlightenment philosophy, the model of Cicero had special appeal to the Founding Fathers, revolutionaries in search of a more genuine yet stable republican order.[34]

Though the Ciceronian ideal is associated most fully in the United States with the law, the concept of rhetoric galvanizing private virtue and public conduct continued to serve the post-Revolutionary generations who, in the Unitarian context, expected the pulpit to both stimulate and channel the rising hopes of America.[35] For William Emerson's generation, to whom the success of the Revolution seemed by no means assured, the clergy was still expected, in tandem with elected officials, to embody and elicit civic responsibility on all fronts, domestic, commercial, political. Waldo was barely out of the Second Church pulpit when church and state were sundered in Massachusetts. But with the onslaught of Jackson, economic troubles, and a perceived failure of the law to address pressing moral issues, the pulpit, during his ministry and after, was still looked to not only for inspiration and consolation, but for order and direction as well.

Emerson was not blind to evil, whether personal or institutional. To perceive the wickedness of slavery, he noted in his journal, is evidence of "the progress of every soul" (*JMN* 3:209). His sermons, in fact, demanded more than perception achieved in tranquility. Sermon No. XCV, for example, specifically listed "War, Duelling, Assassination . . . [and] Intemperance" as evils judged by Christ; and among the most heinous, "[s]lavery has been judged by him & must be cut off root & branch. It is now threatening those who are engaged in it, & us for our share in the guilt with accumulated evil."

How, then, does the pulpit—and the liberal Christian—address actual *social* evil? The notion of the indwelling God potentially promoted radical individualism. After outlining the absolute moral implications of "likeness" in Sermon No. LXII, Emerson preached, in Sermon No. LXIII, on Romans 12:2—"Be not conformed to this world." The way is prepared for Thoreauvian self-righteousness when Emerson declares that a virtuous individual "can do no wrong," "that if he is a denier of him self he need never consult the consequences of his actions, but may leave them with God." Sermon No. CIX argues further that true virtue is not "self originated but all is derived" from God. Virtue, moreover, is no intellectual abstraction. Rather, "every truth brings a man nearer to goodness & every right feeling brings him nearer to truth"; "the best minds in the world have got most of their wisdom from the heart." Every aspect of human nature, then, conspires with God as "power." "[T]ruly considered," Emerson concludes, "there is nothing in the least arbitrary & capricious in the exercise of power by a good man." This has implications, he suggests, for our response to the government's mistreatment of the Indians. Action, then, is not partial but a healthy manifestation of the indwelling God.

In Sermon No. CXLV Emerson goes so far as to find yielding "the right of private judgment" to "the custom of society" in contradiction to the New Testament. The "voice of God" is heard only by "patient listening to your own conscience." Why, indeed, has slavery "passed for an innocent institution"? Why have drunkenness, capital punishment, and torture persisted? Not because the means do not exist for their eradication; "[i]t is only that eyes of love & understandings of discernment have scrutinized things which other men passed by without inquiry."

But Sermon No. CL, a Fast Day sermon first preached on 5 April 1832, reveals both the power and the limits of religious liberalism as a social and political force. Emerson's understanding of the Fast Day as a public gesture owes much to his theory of language as a bridge between privately received truth and others; and it looks ahead five months to the very terms in which he would be deprecating the efficacy of another outward observance, the Lord's Supper. The Fast Day, he notes, is no longer widely observed, but he defends the essential truth of the key elements—fasting, humiliation, and prayer. He grants that these are "forms." But contrary to his view of the Lord's Supper, "rightly considered, these venerable usages are of no local or accidental origin, but are as old as the world & have their roots in the nature of man." The "essence" of these "practices . . . is *the subjection of the body to the soul.*" Specific ancient procedures and acts "were signs & may be dispensed with, but the thing they symbolized is as needful for us as for them, namely the acknowledgment of unworthiness; of sin; of being less than we ought. And this certainly is a sentiment that eminently belongs to our dependant & erring nature."

Emerson carefully outlines the moral stance of continual vigilance that marks virtue:

> The true office of every good mind is a jealousy of itself a constant comparison of its performance with its duty and an anxious penitence for every wrong step. This is real humilia-

tion, and it should be not a rare not an annual act, but a permanent principle.

The contrast between spirituality and carnality that characterizes all of Emerson's definitions of true vision versus delusion, of self-reliance versus self-indulgence, gives shape also to his definition of prayer:

> [I]f any one considers what is real not what is apparent, & reflects upon the purely spiritual nature of God, he must perceive that the prayers of men are not the forms of words they address to the name of God in the church or their bedside; These are only vehicles of prayer. And if these are only strings of words; if they do not express one single real desire of their hearts, they are only so much wasted hypocritical breath; These are not prayers but the true prayers are the daily, hourly, momentary *desires*, that come continually into the soul flow from its permanent will & are welcomed the sincere habitual wishes that occupy our minds at morning & noon & night.

This lengthy passage expresses the crucial harmony of Emerson's thought with regard to insight and expression, private virtue and public manifestation. Forms are important chiefly as they give outward life to inly seen truth. Expression of truth cannot be dissembled but flows from a pure source; prayer is partial, and hence false, unless it proceeds from habit. And prayer is manifestly language, not merely as a collocation of words but as a "vehicle" for receiving, comprehending, and sharing the Spirit. As in Emerson's carefully wrought theory of language, rites and observances, like words, are essential not as outward acts or artifacts but as *signs* of spiritual truth. Once the Fast Day has fulfilled its purpose—to "awaken the recollection of these duties in our minds"—it becomes an expendable residue. But until human nature is perfected, Emerson recommends the validity of this "*social & political* commemoration."

What, then, are the implications of such an observance for the health of the republic and for the redress of tangible social evils? In a democracy, Emerson declares, the burden on the individual is greater than elsewhere to maintain a righteous government. In one of the great *tours de force* found anywhere in the sermons, he proclaims:

> [E]very man having by his vote & his influence a measured share in the government, is really responsible, in that propor-

tion, to God & to men for the acts of government. And since
this is so, if a great outrage is done to equity; if in the adminis-
tration of the government, the strong oppress the weak; if a
sanction is given in high places to licentious manners; and we
hold our peace or approve such government by our vote, we
have our part in that wrong as truly as if our tongues gave
the counsel, hands signed the instrument, or our feet ran to
execute it. Let every man say then to himself—the cause of
the Indian, it is mine; the cause of the slave, it is mine; the
cause of the union, it is mine; the cause of public honesty, of
education, of religion, they are mine; & speak & act thereupon
as a freeman & a Christian.

This was heady stuff in 1832 Boston in a congregation whose
individual members were benefitting at least indirectly from the
slave trade. An insistence on *true* virtue, an uncompromising exalting of moral law, it foreshadows Thoreau's resistance to civil government and Emerson's own support of John Brown. As a religious
liberal, Emerson was declaring that access to higher law, to the
indwelling Spirit, was innate in every person, citizen and victim of
injustice alike.

But as he worked toward his conclusion, Emerson curiously backed
off from his own implication that the individual has a moral obligation to take direct action to oppose social and political evil: "But at
the same time," he cautioned, "let him be also careful step by step
with his censure of the public vices, to censure & reform his own in
the conviction, as we have said, that the public wrongs are only
private wrongs magnified. This will temper his condemnation of the
public evils, & at the same time prove their most effectual remedy."

These qualifications embody the republican notion that the public
virtue is rooted in the private. While there is an undeniable integrity
to Emerson's vision of civic responsibility, like many other liberal
religious leaders of his day, he was caught in a temperamental and
theological dilemma. On the one hand, they believed in the unity of
Spirit—in the equality before God of all people. In theory, at least,
this implied not only potential spiritual growth for all, but also
economic and political justice. On the other hand, liberal theology
also meant self-culture—spiritual growth that was a gradual, lifelong,
even eternal process. Emerson's peers took pride in this as, in its own
way, a liberating doctrine, much more human than Calvinism with
its emphasis on depravity and sudden conversion. But this streak

also contributed to a form of gentility that made many religious liberals reluctant to engage in wholesale, active reform.

Emerson clearly was doing more than generalizing about social evil. The plight of the Indians, particularly the forced removal of the Cherokees by the government, had been discussed at length in the *Christian Examiner* and would later prompt Emerson's famous, lamented letter of protest to President Van Buren.[36] Emerson's sermons are sprinkled, moreover, with references to slavery, and he allowed the Second Church pulpit to be used as a forum for antislavery activity (*Life* 153). But while Sermon No. CL calls for militant alertness to injustice and is downright impassioned in its litany of "causes," the topics facing "a freeman & a Christian" move not from the general to the specific, but from particular abuses to fundamental questions of the stability of the "union" and republican institutions.

The moral tone of the Unitarian pulpit, particularly after 1830, ranges from decorous formality to authentic reformist fervor. The clergy participated in a broad cultural consensus—which they shared even with their Calvinist and Jacksonian rivals—that held republican virtue to be the fundamental test of the nation's health. Sharing this vision, they differed, of course, on diagnoses and remedies. The vehicle by which the essential vision was conveyed, the jeremiad, promoted progressiveness and vitality even as it fostered conformity. It could justify secular Manifest Destiny and what Tocqueville called the "tyranny of the majority," even as it fired the rhetoric of Transcendentalism, abolitionism, and feminism. In both cases, the impetus was broadly to fulfill, in Sacvan Bercovitch's phrase, the "meaning of America," which meant to transmit and control the nation's Revolutionary heritage.[37]

As Bercovitch explains, "the rhetoric of the jeremiad not only allowed for but actually elicited social criticism." But because the culture valued progress and inclusiveness, this rhetoric precluded the need for *truly* radical options in America. American political rhetoric typically "transform[s] what might have been a search for moral or social alternatives into a call for cultural revitalization."[38] A self-enclosed, self-defining rhetoric, the American jeremiad, as embodied in the Fourth of July oration/sermon, has contributed to our national arrogance as well as our idealism, enabling America to adapt to change even as the culture absorbs its critics.

If Sermon No. CL anticipates the radical individualism of "Civil Disobedience," it reveals also the essential conservatism of the roots of Transcendentalism. While Emerson does not diminish the horror of specific evils, his ultimate concern is with restoring the health of the body politic, calling forth individual responsibility to that end. He envisions a purer democracy. But his image of the freeman and Christian is one of balance. Heir to post-Revolutionary fears that the new republic would disintegrate, and facing the immediate uncertainties of Jacksonian politics, Emerson insisted that protest be channeled—on the principle, of course, that this was also the surest way to root out injustice. Citizenship in a democracy, Emerson believed, must recognize that political and social evil are the result finally not of external, institutional corruption, but of human frailty. In his sermons, he accommodated his innate conservatism and a growing awareness of the inevitability of change, to a vision and a rhetoric that shaped his later stance toward public issues and the "fortune of the republic."

In the great essays, Emerson scrupulously noted the ethical implications of vision. For the regenerate soul, he announced in "The Over-Soul," "the power to see is not separated from the will to do." As "the surges of everlasting nature enter into me, . . . I become public and human in my regards and actions" (CW 2:175). The world, he declared in "Character," is "a material basis for [one's] character, and a theatre for action." Because "men of character are the conscience of the society to which they belong," the children of the Puritans have a special obligation; indeed, "the west and south" wonder "whether the New Englander is a substantial man, or whether the hand can pass through him" (CW 3:57, 54).

Yet the translation of ethical "action" into politics remained problematic. Emerson always would be skeptical of the efficacy of politics to achieve genuine reform. In "Politics" he expresses a perfectionism worthy of Roger Williams: "Every actual State is corrupt. Good men must not obey the laws too well." Political parties "degenerate into personalities, or would inspire enthusiasm." Both of America's parties serve limited ends: Her "radicalism is destructive and aimless," her conservatism "timid, and merely defensive of property." The state should be simply a means to produce "character"; "and with the appearance of the wise man, the State expires" (CW 3:122, 123, 126).

Emerson's later political thinking in this regard may not have been pragmatic, but it was hardly cozy or safe. Though he never had sympathy with Thoreau's "resistance to civil government," he came to believe he saw signs of America's greatness in the moral fervor of the Civil War. Given the fear of social division that characterized the early-national period and his largely inherited professional identity, it took a remarkable act of will and imagination to raise a prophetic voice as the ultimate domestic cataclysm loomed. The bloodshed of civil war, which he regarded as inevitable and even desirable, is a haunting reminder, however, of an ultimate failure of Emersonian prophecy. Though the impulse remained to synthesize private virtue and the body politic, to carry out the mission of the early-republican liberal pulpit, the state proved intractable. Emerson did not fail to "engage." But his later lectures and essays emphasize an essentially personal and religious sense of virtue and heroism that stands as counterpoint to, rather than infusion of, his commentary on the republic.

Emerson's interest in "representative men," for example, may be traced to the fundamental connection he saw between speech and character, and the attempt of Emerson and his contemporary liberal theologians to define the Christian minister as a representative good man. This is why Emerson was so hurt when his lifelong hero Daniel Webster slipped from his pedestal. Grounding his opposition to the Fugitive Slave Law in republican theory, Emerson lists statesmen from Cicero to Jefferson in defense of the proposition that "immoral laws are void" (W 11:190). Only his minister's sense of the primacy of virtue internalized kept him from expressing his moral outrage more overtly. Civil millennialism had always encouraged Emerson's generation to regard the obligations of political oratory as similar to those of pulpit eloquence. In the latter sphere, Barzillai Frost had failed to let his congregation know he had ever lived; in the former, related, sphere, "[n]obody," Emerson wrote, "doubts that Daniel Webster could make a good speech. . . . But this is not a question of ingenuity, not a question of syllogisms, but of sides. *How came he there!*" (W 11:225).

And in his address on "Eloquence" first read at Chicago in 1867, Emerson still maintained that "[e]loquence shows the power and possibility of man" (W 8:112); the orator is "the benefactor that lifts men above themselves" (113). Though the Civil War posed the ultimate threat to Emerson's treasured vision of personal integrity and republican unity, he still held that each "true orator," including the preacher, is a hero whose "speech is not to be distinguished from action" (115). The crowning "special ingredient" of eloquence is "a grand will, which, when legitimate and abiding, we call *character*, the height of manhood" (117). Oratorical power is "only the exaggeration of a talent which is universal" (118), but clearly the "exaggeration" occupies the foreground as Emerson seeks to define the new hero.

In Sermon No. LXIX (4 April 1830) the young preacher had announced that from a "minister of Christ" "a good conversation good manners good actions shall proceed as naturally as clean water from a pure spring." The image of purity, of flowing, conceals distaste for the political niceties, haggling, and compromising necessary to republican government; representative *government*, in essence, would be transfigured in the image of the minister as the age's new representative *hero*, from whom perception of truth flowers in eloquence, deportment, and citizenship. Many in Emerson's congregation would have been shocked to hear him nearly forty years later now declare the likes of John Brown at Charlestown and Lincoln at Gettysburg "the two best specimens of eloquence we have had in this country" (*W* 8:125). But as Emerson's ideal minister inhabited a special "true & dignified place," so too the blood of Potawatomie, Harpers Ferry, and the Civil War had been Transcendentalized. The lineage of these new Emerson heroes can be traced back some seventy years, in a new and vulnerable republic, and in a vocation undergoing rapid change, to the liberal clergy's attempt to maintain true community through piety, character—and eloquence.

6

Emerson and Antinomianism:
The Legacy of the Sermons

I

Ever since Andrews Norton characterized Transcendentalism as "the latest form of infidelity," Ralph Waldo Emerson's place in American thought has been a matter of dispute. The prevailing opinion, usually supported by selective reading of the bold, exuberant addresses and essays of the 1830s and 1840s, is that Emerson's intensely mystical piety and his antiauthoritarianism are rooted in a native Antinomian tradition.[1] But some scholars posit a very different Emerson—temperate, balanced, even conservative—an image that stands uneasily beside the portrait of the Transcendental rebel against religious formalism and social evils.[2] Crucial for understanding the sources of these seemingly contradictory elements are Emerson's long-neglected sermons, which to a remarkable degree shaped his later thought. As a minister Emerson tried to evoke a total commitment to Spirit and grace; at the same time, he cultivated a complex view of the spiritual life that implicitly confronted the dangers of Antinomianism. Finally, the habits of thought that led Emerson to resign his pulpit owe less to Antinomian antiformalism than to orthodox Puritan concepts of the Spirit. The sermons and their legacy reveal that Emerson's place in the Puritan tradition is even more central than has been supposed.

Emerson was reared in the twilight of New England Puritanism.

His ancestor the Reverend Peter Bulkeley had founded Concord in 1635; his step-grandfather, the Reverend Ezra Ripley, and his Aunt Mary held to strict Reformed doctrine, for which young Waldo had respect and, later, occasional nostalgia. His father, William, was minister of First Church in Boston, church of John Winthrop and John Cotton. When from 1829 to 1832 Waldo served as minister to the church of the Mathers, Second Church in Boston, he was carrying on a family tradition. Undoubtedly he grew to chafe against the restrictions of duties and doctrine; but his ministry is all too often misconceived as a mere incubation period during which he outgrew the security of Aunt Mary's anachronistic notions and prepared to burst forth a full-blown Transcendentalist in the mid-1830s. In fact, Emerson took his sermons seriously and examined with great care both contemporary and perennial theological issues. Many of the sermons he continued to deliver as late as 1839; others, quickly abandoned, were crucial steps in his Puritan evolution toward Transcendentalism.

Recent Puritan scholarship has taught us the folly of viewing "the New England orthodoxy" or "Antinomianism" as a monolithic entity. But Larzer Ziff has given us a useful definition of Puritanism that transcends the historical period he speaks of: "[T]he Anglo-American Christian tradition . . . exists in a tension between legalism and antinomianism." Puritanism, he goes on, "is not the antinomian pole itself but the political movement which, in the late sixteenth and early seventeenth centuries, brought into being institutions which adjusted the tension in favor of that pole."[3] In New England, where those institutions were given freest rein and where the dangers of Antinomianism were most fully realized, Puritans had continually to readjust that tension to prevent their experiment from vaporizing into an Antinomian denial of all things temporal. Indeed, in terms of both the inner life and church polity, "New England Puritanism" became the process of tension itself, whereby the heart, thirsting for the Spirit, made its necessary accommodations with the world.

The Synod that tried the Antinomian heresies of 1636–38 arrived at firm doctrinal definitions—useful touchstones for the modern scholar—of just what Antinomianism is in terms of the nature of Spirit, human faculties, use of Scripture, and the relationship of individual to community. But the Puritans embraced many paradoxes. John Cotton, who came perilously close to being seduced into Anne Hutchinson's camp, went on to become the great apologist for the New England Way. Thomas Shepard, among the leading opponents of Hutchinson, hungered for assurance of salvation with an intensity that suggests emotional and spiritual needs in common with those who had drifted into heresy.

Such intensity and ambivalence became the trademark of subsequent Puritan revivals in New England. Jonathan Edwards, the champion of the Great Awakening of the 1730s and 1740s, took pains to warn his parishioners that conversion is not a wild, giddy liberation but a divine burden; indeed, genuine conversion had to be distinguished from mere emotional excitement or imagination. The saints, he declared, must not rest on their laurels, for conversion does not guarantee perpetual assurance. And in his Funeral Sermon for David Brainerd, Edwards praised his friend for decrying "enthusiasm" and "Antinomianism," and their attendant evil, Separatism. A century later Emerson grappled anew with traditional Puritan tensions. His entire career, from minister to sage, is a continual attempt to adjust and readjust inspiration to the demands of the world, to maintain a creative interplay between spiritual hunger and the constraints of the human constitution and social obligations.

II

Emerson brought to the ministry a conventional but genuine belief in original sin. His early journals and letters to Aunt Mary are filled with musings about the inadequacy of human nature and the problem of belief. Mere nature was no vehicle of divine insight at this stage of his life. Bothered by the problem of the "Origin of Evil" and skepticism, Emerson wrote to Aunt Mary on 16 October 1823, that he had found a solution in the sermons of Dr. Channing. Channing was preaching that "Revelation was as much a part of the order of things as any other event in the Universe" (L 1:137–39). Emerson added in his journal that Channing "considered God's word to be the only expounder of his works, & that Nature had always been found insufficient to teach men the great doctrines which Revelation inculcated" (JMN 2:160–61). Channing had naturalized Revelation while asserting the infinite superiority of Scripture over Nature. Emerson found Channing's example helpful in positing a tentative solution to his craving for spiritual assurance. But he continued to vacillate between doubt and certainty. He wrote in 1826: "It is not certain that God exists but that he does not is a most bewildering & improbable chimera" (JMN 2:340. The degree of Emerson's doubt is evidenced by the fact that he struck out "wild" as the third adjective modifying "chimera").

Young Emerson pondered the nature of the spiritual life as had Puritans before him. His desire for assurance is hedged about on all sides by Puritan fears that he might be misled by his own enthusiasm. In his College Theme Book he acknowledges the benefits of enthusiasm for scriptural promises; but it is another matter to be deceived by "false raptures." A person cannot be a vehicle for pure Spirit, but must accept "the necessity & finite nature of the human constitution, which will not admit of any expansion of ideas proportionate to the truth" (*JMN* 1:193). As a minister Emerson well understood the terror of finite man contemplating his inadequacy. His descriptions of anxiety resemble those of seventeenth-century divines: "First, he feels that an indefinable evil hangs over him. . . . [H]is soul is oppressed with *fear*. Its active powers are paralyzed, its affections cramped, & all its energy directed to an anxious exploring of ways of escape, a way of atonement. . . . Fear makes the spirit passive." He warns, however, that one must not take the "rigid" way out by fleeing to the easy security of an inscrutable authority any more than one should deny one's sin and turn to the "licentiousness" of liberalism. Emerson's middle way is not compromise; it is a classic New England Puritan's readjustment of the counterclaims of legalism and Antinomianism. For Emerson, as for those who opposed Antinomianism in the 1630s, the successful Christian learns to rejoice "with trembling," to acknowledge "the weight of his sins" and "his occasional backslidings," without being broken by them; "though he is cast down he is not destroyed" (Sermon No. LXXV).[4]

Instead of opting for the passivity of Antinomian assurance, Emerson suggests ways in which we can detect divine workings in the soul; but he condenses or eliminates the difficult steps by which earlier Puritans had measured growth in assurance of salvation. Throughout the sermons he proclaims the efficacy of reason. God does not reveal himself through extraordinary events. He operates through natural, reliable means that "the heart" can perceive immediately. Experience and observation become one with assurance, for to know God does not require "time & preparation" (Sermon No. XXIII). Like Jonathan Edwards, Emerson believes that the Book of Nature, read purely, unfolds and confirms the word of God. In Sermon No. XLIII, for example, he declares, "All that is beautiful is only a revelation . . . of that which is fairer"; and, "Thro every image of poetry of art of science" one "worships" the Source of all beauty. Not content with easy correspondences, he insists in Sermon No. CXXI that we are obligated to will, to choose between body and spirit. He anticipates his concept of "compensation" when he warns that, even though Heaven and Hell are not literal, Judgment is. We must therefore expand our spiritual capacity here and now: "The wants are spiritual, & so must the objects be."[5]

In Pauline terms he says that we can *know* only what we *are*. For the prepared and receptive person, "Faith"—"the perception of spiritual things"—is its own evidence of divinity. To have such insight does not put an individual above the Law. Living according to the Ten Commandments prepares us for "spiritual discernment," which confirms and fulfills the laws of the prophets. For Antinomians, faith had been an unnecessary preliminary to seizure; but for Emerson the preliminaries were themselves assurances. He did not need, as Anne Hutchinson did, sudden, absolute certainty effected without man's participation. Instead he found adequate comfort in the *growth* of "the spiritual faculty," which in transcending the natural senses transcended fear and death; for as he preached at Second Church on 27 October 1833, a year after resigning his pulpit, a "stronger & stronger word of assurance comes from the undeceiving inward Monitor" (Sermon No. 165 [Emerson's arabic numerals]).

We can see in Emerson's notion of innate assurance the budding of his familiar concept of self-reliance. As a minister, however, he was not attempting to inflate man's inherent worth; he was insisting, as had the first American Puritans, that longing for the Spirit must not obliterate the role of the soul's faculties in preparing for salvation.[6] Retaining his youthful sense of human finiteness, he reminded his parishioners in Sermon No. CXXIII (preached in East Lexington as late as 30 July 1837) of the moral and religious "limits of self-reliance." You can judge the truth, he said, of a "proposition the terms of which you understand"; but in trusting oneself "*the origin of self must be perceived*" lest one become a "bundle of errors & sins."[7] Yet God cannot make a man "perceive truth," he went on to say, "except by the use of his own faculties." New England Puritans from Hooker to Edwards confronted the Hutchinsonian argument that the influx of divine light destroys, or works above, human faculties. God *works through* the faculties, they countered; and they embraced the paradox that, although we must prepare for grace, it is Christ who is the worker in our salvation. So Emerson warns in Sermon No. XLIII that we should not misjudge the cause of our turning to God in adversity: "[I]t seems to me it is the triumph of man, it is not man, it is God in the soul." He could admit in Sermon No. LXXIII that there is an unsettling lack of precision in "the Christian Revelation whose greatest value must always be reckoned the assurance it gives of the immortality of the human soul." But he added that further knowledge of "the next life" is withheld because it would "probably unfit us for the duties of this." "We have in our own minds," he declared, "intimations sufficiently clear for the direction of our conduct." It was in keeping with Emerson's honest view of human nature that he could hold in balance and creative tension both his need for assurance and the means for achieving evidence thereof.

Emerson spelled out the limits of self-reliance for another reason. He knew that Antinomians had courted slothfulness because they denied the efficacy of human endeavor, but that Unitarians were often charged with a different kind of "laxity": By stressing the "mercy" of God, contemporary Calvinists thought, Unitarians had lost the constraint, the ballast, for "a godly life." Indeed, as we have seen Emerson declare in Sermon No. XLIII, it would be better to return to Calvinist doctrine, to "put a bridle on the heart," than to live loosely. He goes on to say, however, that "this laxity does not belong to true Christianity, but to bad men." He stresses that, although knowing God is sweet, Christianity is demanding and requires continual vigilance and obedience to a higher power. Ultimately, the efficacy of deeds is attributable to the indwelling God, who becomes "a principle of action."

By involving human faculties in the search for assurance, Emerson confronted the most threatening ethical implication of Antinomianism—that without the "witnesse of the Spirit," all of our "gifts and graces" and "contributions, &c. would prove but legall, and would vanish." To this extent, the "publick Ministery" had found Hutchinson on solid scriptural ground (Hall 263). But did it follow that we are absolved from obedience to law and from good behavior? Thomas Shepard spoke for all orthodox Puritans when he demanded that we must make an effort even though works are not inherently saving: "Thy good duties though they cannot save thee, yet thy bad workes will damne thee. Thou art therefore not to cast off the duties, but thy resting in these duties."[8] For the Puritans it followed that, if we are obliged to make an effort with our spiritual faculties, we must also, in a godly way, exert control over the material world. Culture and success, properly viewed, were both indexes of spiritual estate and social restraints upon unbridled "natural men" in Christian communities. In mercantile nineteenth-century Boston, Emerson found men grossly overevaluating one another's respectability by standards of "wealth & power." To do so, he charged, is to "judge . . . according to the flesh" (Sermon No. V). But he was not opposed in principle to nurturing and using the world. The savagery of primitive islanders encountered by explorers proves, he said in Sermon No. LVII, that "depravity was not the fruit of refinement, but was planted wherever the seed of man was sown." Just as the Puritans had permitted proper use of creatures for man's benefit, Emerson declares that "security of Property" and "dominion over the material world" are God-given imperatives to structure moral and godly societies.

Like a scrupulous Puritan, Emerson saw the danger of exalting the efficacy of human conduct. Always distrustful of reformers, he accuses liberal Unitarians of serving their egos rather than the needy with charity. The "overweening conceit" that often accompanies good deeds is futile; for God "explores the heart & the motive" that prompted the deed (Sermon No. XIX). Like Edwards, Emerson understood that some acts can be performed "alike by those who feel & by those who do not feel their obligation"; indeed, "[d]ecency & calculation may be proxies for self devotion & love" (Sermon No. XXVI).

Like Thomas Shepard, however, Emerson does not recoil from charity or recommend passivity. In Sermon No. XLVIII he interprets the history of Christianity as a continual debate between those who consider religion to be "a *system of belief*" and those who consider it "a *practical system*." Typically, Emerson settles for neither extreme. He argues that the only "index by which it is possible to determine your progress in goodness" is "good works." Like orthodox Puritans, he defines good works not simply as "any partial or outward or ostentatious activity" but also as inner movement by the "*will*" and "*conscience*." He implicitly criticizes the Antinomian attitude when he observes ironically: "If we are capable of a momentary glow of pious feeling, we think we are nothing less than martyrs. But our experience may show us that these feelings are very subject to ebb & to flow." We are creatures, he goes on to say, of both "Reason & Affection." As such, our works give continuity to our lives; they are a preparation completed by "Faith." We are therefore obliged to behave ethically. Though deeds are not intrinsically saving, as Emerson says in Sermon No. LXXXI, our "character" is manifested in deeds and so recognized by good men and by God. Our need to foster good works is not so much an Arminian assessment of human worth as a reminder that we cannot soar to spiritual perfection; we need earthly signs to measure our growth.[9]

As a minister Emerson developed a dialectic of Pauline grace and human effort that expressed in the nineteenth century much of the seventeenth-century frame of mind. Of paramount importance both for Emerson and the Puritans was divine light; nature and man were fallen and could be reborn only through the saving power of Spirit. But Emerson shared with those Puritans who resisted Antinomian helplessness before Spirit the conviction that man must use the world as a passage to heaven. A man could not save himself by his own acts; but he must be able to detect in the workings of his mind the seeds of regeneration; and society must for a principle of order be able to judge men by their conduct. Young Emerson was more conservative than many of his fellow Unitarians in calling for a renewed awareness of the need for conversion by spiritual means. He was more liberal than Calvinists of his day in reviving the Puritan paradox that grace must be earned.

III

Emerson's analysis of the private spiritual life and its ethical obligations is ineluctably linked with an intense patriotism, a conviction that redemption in America is a corporate concern. Enthusiasts and Antinomians had always concluded from the doctrines of original sin and free grace that only the assurance of election, privately received, could satisfy the soul's longing. Other people, the mere clay of an imperfect world, were of little account in the drama of the soul's redemption. But Antinomianism was anathema on these shores largely because it denied that New England could be New Jerusalem; it denied the significance of historical, communal destiny.

Visible sainthood was for seventeenth-century Puritan congregations a means both to maintain social structure and to guarantee that the churches of New England should be a reasonably accurate reflection of the invisible church of the elect, whose members were known only to God. The forging of strong bonds with other Christians was part of the godly person's work in the world. Thomas Hooker explained: "Mutuall subjection is as it were the sinewes of society, by which it is sustained and supported. . . . It is the highest law in all Policy Civill or Spirituall to preserve the good of the whole." Regenerate men, Hooker elsewhere declared, naturally seek out like-minded men for mutual strength and brotherhood. "Oh then get you to the Saints of God, and get them to your houses, and lay hold upon gracious Christians, and say, I will live and converse with you, for the Spirit of Christ is with you." The English Puritan William Ames had also kept strictly to the injunctions of St. Paul regarding the vigilance—indeed fastidiousness—necessary in choosing acquaintances. "No man capable of blessedness," Ames wrote, "ought to be removed from the embrace of our love"; but he cautioned that "[s]ome men are more to be loved than others, namely, those nearer to God and in God to ourselves. Gal. 6:10, *Let us do good to all, but especially to those who are of the household of faith.*"[10] Later Jonathan Edwards further defined the emotional grounds of "true virtue" as a "disposition to benevolence towards being in general"; but he continued to insist that the *truly* virtuous are drawn instinctively to those of a like disposition and that one cannot truly appreciate a benevolence one does not possess.

Standards for church membership had lost their rigor by Emerson's day. But he retains the impulse to search out and cleave to good people as a way of cultivating love of God and detecting through social involvement intimations of God himself. In true friendship, he says in Sermon No. XXVI, we love not the friend's body but his "spiritual properties." Our very expectation of perfection in friends is a holy sentiment: "Consider that every good man, every good thing, every good action, word, & thought that you love, is only a *fragment of the divine nature.* Thus does our Father make himself known to his children. This is the hourly revelation by which our minds are instructed in his goodness." He goes further, in Sermon No. CXXI, to declare that men save or damn themselves by the company they keep. Bad men "seek . . . companions who love the same things. They shun the society of good men precisely as the lustful, the glutton, the miser, the robber[,] the murderer here shuns the society of wise & pious men." Correspondingly, the good seek out the good: "It is a law of spirits, wholly independant of time & place, that *like shall be joined with like,* & it holds of the good, as of the evil." The responsible Christian attempts to discern goodness as a way of growing in assurance. Emerson could be speaking of the Antinomian when he complains, "We sit still & hope that our salvation will be wrought out for us, instead of working out our own." With patience, faith, obedience to the Law, and a willingness to use this world for good, we prepare for that perfect understanding which now belongs only to God but which one day will be accessible to the true Christian.

Intertwined with Emerson's concerns for friendship and society is his concept of the destiny of America. In his jeremiads he speaks of church and nation interchangeably, seemingly unaware that America's geographical, economic, and political expansion is evolving outside the sphere of influence of Boston Unitarianism. On the contrary, he often takes comfort in the conviction that his church is the saving remnant upholding the standards of the Puritan Fathers. The opening of Sermon No. LXXX, "Patriotism" (4 July 1830), resembles Bulkeley's reminder at the conclusion of *The Gospel-Covenant* that New England as "a City set upon an hill" is a beacon for the world. Because of this privilege, New England owes God special obligations, obligations met only by inspired communal effort. Of Independence Day, Emerson declares: "The return of this anniversary cannot fail to awaken in our minds the recollection of Gods peculiar favors to our country & to quicken our religious feeling . . . [to rejoice together] is in our eye more godlike, & what mysterious grandeur in the consciousness of sympathizing with vast numbers of men, in acting on the feeling that is shared by a nation in the same hour." In Emerson's fusion of spiritual and political mission, the American Revolution is held up as an inspiration not only in this land, but also "on both sides of the Andes, in France, in Greece & throughout Europe." To the fact of actual corruption in his New Jerusalem, he has a ready solution: redefinition. He simply makes a distinction between the *true* patriotism that "binds him to the best citizen" and "draws him to the purest action," and "[t]he America of the selfish & ambitious man," which by implication is not "real." Rather than bemoan or rail against evil, Emerson simply denies that evil is *inherent* in the *true* America.

We have only recently been made aware that the American jeremiad from the beginning was not merely a lamentation. Sacvan Bercovitch has demonstrated that the promise of America as a redemptive land rendered the thought of actual failure unthinkable. The New England Puritan imagination improves on reality, keeping the promises alive in the heart of the regenerate Christian.[11] For Emerson too the inbred conviction that the New Jerusalem is always still to be achieved feeds the myth that our corporate mission is ongoing, always vital. "[T]he present generation," he says in Sermon No. LXXX, must "determine for themselves the character of their country"; indeed, the *real* America is an "idea" in each person's mind, implicitly protected from adverse events.

That America's destiny is unfinished makes her, confident of past and future, able continually to respond to fresh challenges. Thus Emerson can make a cult of the Puritan Fathers while at the same time updating the myth to encompass the ideals of the American Revolution. He warns of the danger of America being loved for "convenience" and "calculation": "O my friends [let] not this low corrupt unhonoured America be the image in our hearts[.] It was not such an one that fiftyfour years ago was declared free. It was not such an one that the Puritans sought to build the cities of their Zion in its untrampled snows." Although one side of the nineteenth-century mind stereotyped the Puritans as sour-faced, hypocritical witchhunters, Emerson appeals to that other side of the nineteenth-century imagination that sentimentalized America as "that hallowed asylum of religious liberty which heroic men persecuted in their own country sought & found." That legacy still informs Emerson's "America": "Let it be the country consecrated by the unaffected piety of our fathers by their anxious desire of the spiritual good of their posterity[.]"

In order to make his Puritan heroes palatable to liberal Unitarians, Emerson often scrubbed them of their sterner Calvinistic colors, in effect making them suitable progenitors of Thomas Jefferson (a process Perry Miller blamed on Vernon L. Parrington and James Truslow Adams). But in Sermon No. CXIII, "Fasting, Humiliation, and Prayer," which Emerson notes was written for "FAST DAY, 1831," he makes no excuses for Puritan severity but lambastes his contemporaries for falling short of Puritan standards. He admits that many criticize the continuation of the Fast Day custom "as a relic of an ancient race, which has outlived its day." But he cajoles his parishioners: "There are, it may be hoped, a great number yet remaining who hold in honour the memory of that old people, that self-denying race, who redeemed England, & planted America" ("self-denying" is inserted over a scratched-out "generous"; Emerson seems to have felt that to humanize the Puritans too lavishly was either sentimental or condescending). "It has become fashionable to praise them," he goes on. "Our self-love leads us to extol our ancestors. But far better would it be that we should praise them with understanding,—that we should value what they valued."

He explains away the Puritan's reputation for fearsome sternness: "He that thinks so profoundly, he that acts so habitually in reference to the principles of the first class as to give all his life & manners the expression of simple gravity, may be excused if he have little playfulness in his conversation, & little elegance in his circumstances[.]" The Puritans had "faults as a party," he admits; but "they had *enthusiasm.*" Emerson is not advocating the *heresy* of "enthusiasm"; he is recommending a cure for nineteenth-century ennui and the craving for purposive action in the religious community during a brawling, materialistic, democratic era. The Puritans "tho't life had something worth contending for. They lived & died for sentiments & not for bread only. To these apostolical men, the cross was a dear emblem, who knew how to suffer themselves, their idea of Jesus was an indwelling thot, which manifested itself in every action—in the house; & in Church & in State."

For Emerson the Fast Day is no hollow relic; it grows from the human propensity to sin. "Penitence," he suggests, is "needed for our public & our personal safety." The strenuous life is both appropriate to the human condition and a guarantee of social order. In terms Emerson seldom rivalled for severity, he declares, "The house of mourning is better than the house of feasting. The hair cloth, solitude, & bread & water, are safer courses for tempted man, than much company, & rich clothes, & easy living." He expresses the fear that America's greed may lead to civil war in terms that resemble both the first American Puritans' quest for self-contained uniformity and Jefferson's principles of military and political self-sufficiency: "It needs no strange or impossible foreign influence or marvellous series of external events. It needs only certain change in the speculative principles which we ourselves entertain." The American dream can be destroyed only by negligent Americans. He goes on to list the symptoms of the national malady: the government's mistreatment of the Indians, "a barefaced trespass of power upon weakness" which is sanctioned by law and is met with a distressing "general indifference" by the American people; the "ferocity of party spirit," which contaminates even the courts; a love of quick money and vain "display"; the "hunger for excitement" and willingness to "sacrifice the holiest principles to any popular cry." All this Emerson sees as both a declension from Puritan ideals and a betrayal of public purpose. Citing Jeremiah, he suggests that "[t]hese are bad tokens for the permanence of our institutions."

Quentin Anderson has shown that Emerson spoke for a generation that in the wake of Jacksonian levelling was profoundly insecure with respect to its institutions. Anxiety about the disintegration of the social order served to throw Americans back upon the isolate self as the only reliable source of value, the last refuge from anarchy. While Anderson admits that Emerson was aware "of our incapacity for a final absorption into being," he is critical of the stance of Emerson's audience: "It was a creation of the age, antinomian man, gathered into the antinomian congregation." Anderson explains the danger of Emerson's posture: "Secular incarnation involves a denial of history, membership in a generation, charity, reform, institutional means of every sort, and at the same time an extreme antinomianism, a claim for the supreme authority of the moment of vision."[12]

But young Emerson, we have seen, doctrinally was deeply distrustful of any form of Antinomianism. And Professor Bercovitch has broken new ground for our understanding of the self in the American Renaissance by stressing that Emerson's "concept of representative heroism denies the tenets of antinomianism, in any meaningful sense of the term. . . . If Emerson differs from the chauvinist by his Romantic self-reliance, he differs equally from the Romantic Antinomian by his reliance on a national mission."[13] Bercovitch shows how Cotton Mather protected the Puritan dream from temporal failure by equating the inspired believer/perceiver with the "true" America, and we have seen how young Emerson used the same strategy.

Emerson's solution for declension is implicit in his complaint. He reminds his audience that America's plight cannot be blamed on external causes such as the Constitution or our "public officers." The cause of our problems, he goes on in Sermon No. CXIII, is that "every man is no better than he is." The private life of the soul and the health of the community are ineluctably wed. America's institutions are viable. But to sustain them, to keep them worthy of America's promises, our visible forms must be enlivened by the spirit of regenerate citizens; for the condition of a man's soul "in the end, determines the intercourse of men, the elections, & the laws." In drawing upon the cult of the Puritan Fathers, Emerson revitalizes the Puritan prophecy of America redeemed in time and place: He declares that "the *fear of God* in the community . . . is the salt that keeps the community clean" and is the very "foundation" of society.

IV

Throughout his ministry and more or less throughout his life, Emerson retained both his complex view of the relationship between grace and effort and his inspired vision of the corporate ramifications of the spiritual life. The challenge and the burden of his career after 1832 was, as has long been known, to find viable substitutes for unworthy institutions, to find a new personal "vocation," and continually to define the regenerate individual as representative of the ideal America. What changed during his years at Second Church, what made inevitable his resignation, was his concept of Christ and the function of sacraments in preparing souls for Christ. But Emerson's most famous sermon, "The Lord's Supper," is often misunderstood. George Santayana, one of the most astute readers of Emerson, was misleading when he wrote that Emerson "separated himself from the ancient creed of the community with a sense rather of relief than of regret."[14] On the contrary, Emerson's break with Second Church resulted from a conscientious examination of doctrine in terms that, ironically, made use of Puritan modes of thought.

According to Puritan typology, New Englanders were participants in a cosmic drama that existed in the mind of God. Secular events, properly viewed, were prefigured in the Bible. But Puritan typology went beyond the mechanical associations of symbol and allegory, granting to historical events the status of being "real" and unique, however absorbed, ultimately, into God's atemporal scheme. Thus New England, prefigured in the Old Testament, was part of the unfolding of the divine plan. New England in turn prefigured future victories over Satan; and individual New Englanders took part in an inherently valuable temporal, historical experiment.

The Bible held for Emerson eternal truths, essences to be rescued from the dead letter of symbolism in order to regain efficacy for modern man. Sermon No. XLIII opens the text of Acts 17:28: "For in him we live, & move, & have our being," Emerson declaring that contemporary religious liberals "have grown wiser than to fear the *materialism* of the Calvinists [and we] no longer interpret literally the figurative language of the Scriptures which surrounded God with clouds & darkness—& thunders." We have seen that Emerson feared that to indulge in the "mercy" of God can lead to "laxity." But he accuses the "literal" method of the "Calvinists" of delivering a dead letter to modern times: It denies nineteenth-century Christians the opportunity to perceive God face to face; it fails to move the faculties, the affections, the will; and in so doing it denies Emerson's generation its uniqueness in history. He does not advocate reading the Bible as poetry but urges us to seek the compelling spiritual truth that renders biblical figures vital and efficacious.

Emerson's evolving concept of Jesus illustrates the point. He depicts Jesus conventionally in Sermon No. V as possessing "a greatness of soul" and "a magnanimity" that are virtually unattainable by man. The true Christian is a child of "sorrow"; the best that can be said about mankind is that many people did keep vigil at the Crucifixion despite the "deep depravity" of human nature. Sermon No. V, first delivered on 24 June 1827, was given frequently; but, as we have seen, not after 27 July 1828. In the middle of Emerson's ministry, his view of Jesus changed gradually. Paradoxically, as he exalted the importance of Christlike qualities, he found the idea of superhuman mediation no longer viable. By Sermon No. LXXXIX, for example, he is proclaiming the Hebrew notion of an angry God to be "unreasonable." Innate is man's ability to achieve Christ's greatness of spirit: "[T]he *sources of happiness are always at hand.*"

Emerson is now moving toward his Transcendental belief that each person has direct access to the Over-Soul without need of mediation or church guidance. But Sermon No. XCV shows clearly how Emerson's "new views" derive from traditional Puritan concepts. In this sermon he still worries about the by-products of sin. We continue, in his view, to need regeneration, for which Christ must still somehow be the agent. But how best to appropriate the truth of Jesus? Emerson, always Pauline in matters of the Spirit, finds two distinct scriptural interpretations of the nature of Christ: The evangelists referred to his *"bodily person,"* while the "writers of the epistles" spoke of him in a spiritual sense. Emerson finds that the words of Jesus himself confirm the more truly religious dimension of the latter view: "He uses his own name for his religion as he uses the name of Moses for the law of Moses[:] 'Not I, but Moses accuseth you.' " From this Emerson concludes: "It is obvious that Christianity, or the religious truths brot by Christ to men are meant. I understand then that the expression of the text is one of the same import, that *the truth which came by Jesus Christ shall judge the world.*" He does not in this manner secularize Jesus; he tries to insure that the typological significance of Jesus will not be lost to his time. Emerson is careful to anchor himself to experience, resisting the lure of quietism or Antinomianism; he goes on in the sermon to suggest that it is *because* human nature falls so far short of Christ's perfection that each person's soul "must be judged according to its deeds." Still, to reduce Christ's divinity to a spiritual essence would seem to take great liberty with traditional typology, would seem radically contrary both to Puritanism and Unitarianism, which retained at least token respect for the "orthodox" concept of Christ as mediator. Further, to do so would seem in Puritan terms to oversimplify the spiritual life; for Thomas Hooker, "a *smoking* desire after Christ, and a longing desire after grace" had been only first steps in an arduous spiritual process.[15]

Emerson's definition of Jesus, however, holds striking parallels with the view orthodox Puritans had espoused in the 1630s. The Antinomian "Errorists" had denied the efficacy of man's role in achieving assurance of salvation, arguing that "[a] man may have all graces and poverty of spirit, and yet want Christ" (Hall 226). Such ministers as Hooker, Shepard, and Bulkeley, while they had no intention of diminishing the gap between Christ and man, disagreed. They shared the belief that one must participate in the spiritual life and that, to avoid anxiety, one must be able to measure the extent to which one possesses Christ. Peter Bulkeley went so far as to argue that justification through Christ is *not* the same thing as assurance of salvation. Believing that the Antinomian willingness to leave all to Christ ignored the needs of the heart, Bulkeley added this postscript to a letter to John Cotton: "There must be some difference betwixt Christs righteousnes, and that wch doth manifest it unto me as mine, but these 2 you seeme to confound."[16] Bulkeley knew that to put sanctification before justification would indeed constitute the Arminian heresy; but he saw no reason why evidence of salvation should not follow in terms man can discern. John Winthrop recorded the Synod's similar judgment, that Christ is indistinguishable from Christlike qualities; indeed, "he that hath righteousnesse and true holinesse, hath learned the truth, as it is in Jesus, and therefore hath Christ" (Hall 226). As Jesus (and Emerson) equated Moses with the *law* of Moses, so the Puritans identified the saving power of Christ with possession of his *attributes.*

The Puritan conviction that we must be able to gauge our progress in growing to Christ, that Christ's saving grace is not a single moment of overpowering seizure, was grounded deeply in typological habits of mind. It was a commonplace of Puritan doctrine that, as Peter Bulkeley declared, the Jewish and Christian "are but one Church." He preached that we are all "children" of Abraham if we walk "in the steps of *Abraham's* faith." In spiritual substance Passover and the Lord's Supper, baptism and circumcision, are identical. Thomas Hooker too argued that one is not excluded from a holy covenant because one does not carry its outward trappings. He quotes St. Paul: "*He is not a* Jew *that is one outwardly.*" Though circumcision is a seal that represents certain outward "prerogatives and priviledges" of the Jewish nation, one need not follow Jewish law to follow in Abraham's steps: "Abraham *is the father of the circumcision, not to them who are of the circumcision onely;* but he is the father of the circumcision, if they have faith." In the end, "*all outward priviledges, as the hearing of the Word, the partaking of the Sacraments, and the like, are not able to make a man a sound Saint of God.*" The sacraments are seals; but they are impotent until a man "not onely enjoyeth the Priviledges of the Church, but yeeldeth the obedience of faith, according to the Word of God revealed, and walketh in obedience." As non-Jews can fulfill Abraham's example, so Abraham anticipated New Testament revelation as "so fruitfull a Christian." In the unfolding of redemptive history, particular rites were unique and valid for particular times and societies; but forms lack efficacy until enlivened by the Spirit, which follows saving faith.[17]

When in Sermon No. CLXII ("The Lord's Supper") on 9 September 1832, Emerson explained his resignation from the Second Church pulpit, he did so in terms that simply carried out certain implications of Puritan typology.[18] The text of Romans 14:17 suggests to him that the Spirit, not forms, is the only requisite for salvation: "The Kingdom of God is not meat and drink; but righteousness, and peace, and joy in the Holy Ghost." He finds the necessity of the Lord's Supper unsupported by scriptural evidence on two counts. First, because Jesus "always taught by parables and symbols," we must not infer that he intended at the Last Supper "to establish an institution for perpetual observance"; Jesus was simply celebrating the traditional Passover feast. Second, because he was convinced that the value of a particular rite is relative to its spiritual efficacy, Emerson thinks it "not expedient" for Unitarians to observe a ceremony that began in a foreign culture as a symbolic "local custom"; such formalism undermines the Pauline concern with the Spirit in the nineteenth century (W 11:9, 4–5, 12, 19–20).

Later in the sermon Emerson undercuts his own scriptural explanation for his disaffection from the church in terms that are often mistaken for cavalier indifference: His critique of the Lord's Supper, he says, was done merely "for the satisfaction of others"; internal proof, he goes on, is the only compelling reason for a decision such as he has made. Characteristic of Emerson's sense of "evidence" and filtered, as we have seen, through Buckminster and Channing, this attitude is itself Puritan. Indeed, Emerson is quick to add that Paul, Jesus, and other martyrs were motivated also by hostility to "formal religion." He has admitted that "[f]orms are as essential as bodies; but to exalt particular forms," he declares, "to adhere to one form a moment after it is outgrown, is unreasonable, and it is alien to the spirit of Christ" (W 11:22, 20).[19]

Emerson's leaving the Second Church pulpit was no simple Antinomian rejection of form. Orthodox Puritans too had valued the Spirit above the letter and had sought merely to insure through forms that the Spirit might have footsteps in the world to guide personal and national destiny. Seventeenth-century Puritans would not, to be sure, have tolerated Emerson's conclusions about the validity of the Lord's Supper. But even John Winthrop allowed, when Antinomianism threatened, that the usefulness of certain rites *is* a relative matter. When the radical literalist John Wheelwright denied the efficacy of public fasting and predicted a "combustion" in church and state, Winthrop declared that his "Fast-Day Sermon" was untimely, for "every truth is not seasonable at all times." The Bible provides much evidence, Winthrop argued, that Jesus and God are aware of man's inability to perceive absolute truth; but doctrines and rituals, useful in aiding man's understanding of spiritual facts, are often expedients adapted to particular occasions: "[T]he same *Paul* would not circumcise *Titus,* though hee did *Timothy,* so the difference of persons and places, made a difference in the season of the doctrine." Hence, he concludes, Wheelwright's disruptive sermon was out of "season." To Winthrop, the sermon seemed a diatribe calculated for a particular, dangerous end (Hall 295–96).

Winthrop's reasoning reveals an ambivalence latent in Puritan typology, an inconsistent attitude toward forms which by the nineteenth century would completely alter the meaning of the New England experiment. When Peter Bulkeley declared the Jewish and Christian "are but one Church," he was thinking not of levelling denominational distinctions with a simple platonic correspondence of ideas but of the historical anticipation/fulfillment within God's eternal scheme which characterized traditional typology. But all Puritans were latent Antinomians to the extent that they considered forms subordinate to the Spirit they were meant to minister to the world. Winthrop, we have seen, was willing to judge Wheelwright's political gesture by comparison with what he deemed Paul's relativism in the use of circumcision—a sacrament Puritans esteemed as typologically equivalent to baptism itself. What in Emerson often sounds like freewheeling platonism derives from the Puritans' craving for the *spiritual substance* of sacraments that enables one truly to walk in Abraham's footsteps. He could write on 13 March 1831, for example, that Paul and Peter were inspired by the same truth: "There is one Spirit through myriad mouths"; all truth "is from God" and is indivisible (*JMN* 3:236). Emerson continued to believe, we have seen, that the Fast Day observance was not an empty memorial but an occasion for public reflection on individual and social spiritual health; to this extent he was heir to the Puritan vision of religion as a communal venture. But he also implicitly followed to its logical conclusion Winthrop's fatal ambivalence toward sacraments when he rejected the Lord's Supper itself as a mere ritual, an observance inappropriate to America in 1832.

In the seventeenth century, typology was not the tool only of Antinomian firebrands attacking formalism. Rather, orthodox Puritans could argue that Antinomian absolutism, by radically assaulting all forms and letting Christ perform all in salvation, altered the meaning of typology. Sudden seizure by Christ short-circuited one's participation in truths embodied by types that, though they transcended time, united all moments in time and provided for patterns of spiritual growth and conduct under scriptural and ecclesiastical guidance. Emerson inherited and rigorously applied authentic typological methods to revitalize for his time the spirit of Jesus. He believed, as did Hooker, Shepard, Bulkeley, and Winthrop, that one must personally *experience* the truth of which Jesus was only one, albeit a perfect, example. But for Emerson, in a day when orthodox strictures concerning original sin and the privileges of church membership were being abandoned, genuine Puritan typology led inexorably away from the last relics of orthodoxy. Christ was best appropriated for the nineteenth century not through dead sacraments but as an immediate spiritual essence.

V

Although Emerson resigned as minister of Second Church, he continued for years to occupy various pulpits as a visiting minister; he did not resign from the ministry as such. He spent the rest of his life searching for new ways to inspire and uplift a broader "congregation," to show all people that revelation is a living fact. When Emerson left Second Church, he did not soar off into a Transcendental empyrean in a lighter-than-air balloon. His ministry was a pervasive legacy in the form of a check to the more extravagant tendencies of Transcendentalism.

Emerson's thought is marked, of course, by a steady commitment to intuition and inspiration. Nineteenth-century Romanticism fed this impulse once the restraints of Puritan doctrine had fallen away. Romantic doctrine continued to speak of rebirth, but in terms that replaced God with Nature, soul with Self, grace with imagination.[20] But while Emerson celebrated the mediatory role of Nature in the divine scheme, he never gave himself over totally to a sentimental enthusiasm for Nature: "We may easily hear too much of rural influences," he cautioned; "let us be men instead of woodchucks" (*CW* 3:106).[21] Even *Nature* (1836) is not the purely Antinomian effusion that the "transparent eyeball" passage seems to suggest. Emerson is careful here to define Nature as the "NOT-ME," keeping the soul theoretically separate from the corruption of world and flesh. But he also meticulously describes the Transcendental conversion as a process of growth in which proper use of the world leads to divine power; man apprehends through his faculties the law of God in Nature.

Emerson does not reveal a thoroughgoing Antinomian frame of mind until some of the middle and late essays in which, J.A. Ward has said, he resorts to an optimism in which the conversion process "loses much of its psychological complexity," as when in "Experience" he tries "to affirm a faith independent of experience."[22] Emerson believed that the "intellect" (as mind or spirit), being "antinomian or hypernomian," is a source of both isolation and, potentially, impregnable comfort (CW 3:45). He looked in transcendence of materialism for unequivocal "grounds of assurance" for "The Transcendentalist" (CW 1:201). But the modern idealist, he knew, had not yet mastered his own vision or realized his talent. He said ambiguously that the Transcendentalist "easily incurs the charge of antinomianism" by placing himself above "every written commandment" (CW 1:204). Indeed, Emerson's measured, third-person stance in the essay is not simply a prudent rhetorical strategy to mollify an audience reluctant to endorse the new "collectors of the heavenly spark." It indicates his own hesitance to commit himself wholly to the camp of those who would in the world live on "angels' food" (CW 1:216, 206).

The urgency to reach a disembodied audience often betrays Emerson into enthusiastic pronouncements that do not deliver his whole vision. For example, he proclaims that the Over-Soul cannot be tapped by an act of will, for "visions" derive from "some alien energy"; the soul "is not a faculty, but a light" (CW 2:160, 161). And he sees in the history of religious awakening "[a] certain tendency to insanity" because of the finite mind's contemplation of the absolute, revealed above human words (CW 2:167). Despite such Antinomian utterances, however, he acknowledges the solid otherness of the world. Like the sailor described by Melville's Ishmael, in danger of toppling from the mast-head when his pantheistic daydream makes him doubt the reality of the world, Emerson occasionally has to "pinch" himself to "preserve the due decorum" necessary for social life; but he knows that "this is flat rebellion," that "Nature will not be Buddhist" (CW 3:138–39). The healthy person must "occupy" the middle ground between the life of the spirit and the flesh. To live only a sensuous life is "low and utilitarian"; to live a purely spiritual life is "too vague and indefinite for the uses of life" (CW 1:113).

It is true that Emerson's concept of the conversion process began to lose its tension. But he compensated for this loss—even as his essays dealt more often with single extremes of experience such as Prudence or Intellect—with a growing interest in "polarity." This perception that extremes are *complementary*, part of a cosmic system of checks and balances, was but another manifestation of the lessons of his ministry. He continued to believe that vision is gradually prepared, our faculties being fostered by a source beyond our comprehension; but, though truth comes "unannounced," it comes "because we had previously laid siege to the shrine." This Puritan dialectic includes the "law of undulation," which requires that you both "labor with your brains" and "forbear your activity, and see what the great Soul showeth" (*CW* 2:197). Antinomian seizure was never for Emerson a viable means of revelation. As late as 1870–72, in "Inspiration," he could still both lament that trusting wholly to vision leads to a destructive lack of "consecutiveness" and reaffirm the radical importance of insight: "I hold that ecstasy will be found normal" (*W* 8:272–73, 275). He had discovered as a minister that faith must be grounded in experience. It was the burden and the ballast of his later career that he could not completely forget this truth.

Though Emerson held instinctively to a balanced, if not complex, view of conversion, he labored to define the public implications of his new "vocation." He valued the speech of man to men above all forms of communication; but, like the Antinomians who found the influx of the Spirit independent of hearing the Word of God, he often found silence more efficacious than human utterance. He was capable, for example, of a keen analysis of political euphemism (*W* 11:259–60). Yet he came to regret his impassioned letter to President Van Buren protesting a deceitful government treaty with the Cherokee Indians, deprecating his political gesture as "this stirring in the philanthropic mud" (*W* 11:571).

However unsatisfactorily Emerson defined his own public role, he never in theory isolated the self from others. In the Divinity School Address he declares the loss of "public worship" the greatest "calamity" that can befall a nation, for "[t]hen all things go to decay" (*CW* 1:88–89). The inspired individual assumes the burden of rediscovering the spiritual base of society that the demise of Puritanism had left to erode. Emerson is as scrupulous in "Self-Reliance" as in his sermons to remind us that our "isolation must not be mechanical, but spiritual, that is, must be elevation" (*CW* 2:41). Indeed, for the Transcendentalists it is "the wish to find society for their hope and religion,—which prompts them to shun what is called society" (*CW* 1:210).

It is conventional to contrast Emerson's lofty, even frosty, ideals of society with Hawthorne's defense of the human heart, with all its imperfection. We forget that Emerson sees in "Compensation" as clearly as Hawthorne did in "Young Goodman Brown" that one who lives solely for revelations of the soul forfeits companionship, family, love. Transcendentalists seem often to make friendship and community into monstrously disembodied abstractions. But the urgent intensity with which Emerson sought to define his spiritual brotherhood derives from the orthodox Puritan habit of fastidiousness in selecting true Christians for companions. Living in a democratic age, Emerson is forced inward to people his imagined congregation with worthy nineteenth-century saints. Much was at stake. Inspired persons are inwardly compelled to share their vision. And their true nature is automatically revealed by their words and their company, for "friends are self-elected," not consciously chosen (CW 2:123).

Emerson always craved a more vigorous translation of ideals into action than he felt capable of performing. He privately confessed that his own power and vision of the nation were unstable: "Most of my values are very variable. My estimate of America, which sometimes runs very low, sometimes to ideal prophetic proportions. My estimate of my own mental means and resources is all or nothing: in happy hours, life looking infinitely rich; and sterile at others" (W 8:423 n). As Bercovitch has shown, Emerson's doctrine of the representative self would not allow him to admit uncertainty publicly. But he occasionally resorted in his anxiety and ennui to a vision of his forefathers, who, though "tormented with the fear of Sin, and the terror of the Day of Judgment," had a "bounding pulse" and knew what they were about in the world (CW 1:179, 180).

The archetypal Puritan (rarely are individuals named) joins David, Paul, Jesus, and a variety of secular representative men in Emerson's Transcendental typology. History is mere secular destiny only to the unregenerate. In the final analysis, we best carry on the Puritan mission when we appropriate the spirit of Jesus to our own lives and times. The challenge is to "be ourselves the children of the light" (CW 1:135). Indeed, Emerson's appropriation of the Puritan past is not mere sentimentality but the latest form of Puritan typology; for he insists that our sense of tradition be not hero-worship but a challenge: "Let us shame the fathers, by superior virtue in the sons" (W 12:210).

Emerson's desire to see his ideals embodied led to his desperate effort to define John Brown as the modern Puritan champion come to purge and purify the land. He even fed the myth of the hero of

Harpers Ferry by describing him, incorrectly, as a direct descendant of Peter Brown of the *Mayflower.* Generally, however, Emerson was a shrewder judge of the Puritan legacy in New England. In journal entries for 1824 he noted that the "Wild Anabaptists" had put themselves above the order of the community. But the "Puritans of 1620 had not a rash or visionary thought about them." We can learn as much, he thought, from "the wise & fortunate legislators" who established New England as from modern radicals (*JMN* 2:210, 211, 215). He condemned the "holy fury" of the "Antinomian fanatics of Cromwell's day" (*JMN* 6:147). And it was not Puritan individualism that he celebrated in his Historical Discourse but the force of the church covenant, under which all "were united by personal affection." Benevolent men like Bulkeley and Winthrop provided strong leadership and loving guidance under "the ideal social compact." This national impulse continued down to the Revolution, in which "[a] deep religious sentiment sanctified the thirst for liberty." The heroic incidents of the Battle of Concord were not "an extravagant ebullition of feeling," but a communal acting "from the simplest instincts" (*W* 11:45, 72, 75). In the rhetoric of the jeremiad, he found those principles wanting in the 1830s when Concordians doted over the pastness of the town's traditions.

As a prophet of America's unfolding mission, Emerson relished the thought that "a good principle of rebellion," "some thorn of dissent and innovation and heresy to prick the sides of conservatism," had been a Boston trademark since the days of Wheelwright and Hutchinson (*W* 12:203, 207). He always held that *enthusiasm* for purposeful action was needed to cure America's mediocrity. Paradoxically, he never trusted *enthusiasts.* In his journal he acknowledged that a predominance of good is as "unnatural" a human condition as a predominance of evil (*JMN* 1:124–25). Too often, he felt, New England reformers failed of their aims because they miscalculated man's potential for perfection; and he saw that "the fertile forms of antinomianism among the elder puritans, seemed to have their match in the plenty of the new harvest of reform" (*CW* 3:150). Although he considered many reformers oddballs, he maintained that ferment was crucial for America's health. Thus he granted the validity of the Abolitionists' singlemindedness ("They are the new Puritans, & as easily satisfied" [*JMN* 9:447]). Yet he could not bring himself to cast his lot fully with these literalist sons of the Puritans. The Puritan legacy for Emerson was an ambiguous mix of radical prototypes and orthodox restraint. A highly traditional radical, he cheered on nineteenth-century reformers from a careful distance, while directing his own energy toward uplifting the whole human condition.

Thomas Carlyle clearly put the question of cultural continuity to Emerson when he wrote on 19 July 1842: "The disease of Puritanism was *Antinomianism;*—very strange, does that still affect the *ghost* of Puritanism?" Carlyle had just met Bronson Alcott, whom he considered the modern embodiment of Antinomianism, "a kind of venerable Don Quixote" who was "all bent on saving the world by a return to acorns and the golden age."[23] Although Emerson appears not to have answered Carlyle directly, he had the same reservations about his beloved neighbor Alcott. Emerson knew, with the first-generation divines and Jonathan Edwards, that spiritual enthusiasm poses an American dilemma: To be *possessed* by visionary excitement makes one, like Alcott, "a pail of which the bottom is taken out"; but to be unduly *suspicious* of enthusiasm is to become a Whig, who is "a pail from which you cannot get off the cover" (*JMN* 9:208). Emerson challenged America to transcend both the democratic "herd" and the mercantile/political establishment. But he found the Antinomian legacy to the nineteenth century inadequate, whether it took the form of the reformer's self-righteous intensity or Alcott's fluffy idealism.

That Emerson always retained a sense of balance in spiritual matters can be attributed to the fact that he always saw himself as, in essence, a Christian, one who came to grips with the meaning of the Spirit through Puritan habits of mind. We have seen that orthodox Puritans argued that, insofar as a man possessed Christlike qualities, he may be said to have Christ. Emerson too, even while he tried in the Divinity School Address to reduce the significance of the historical church and to remove "the laws of the soul" from time and space, continued to believe that a man had to be able to measure his spiritual estate: "If a man is at heart just, then in so far is he God." This principle leads not to unbridled individualism, but to social cohesion: "Character is always known. . . . See again the perfection of the Law as it applies itself to the affections, and becomes the law of society. As we are, so we associate. The good, by affinity, seek the good; the vile, by affinity, the vile. Thus of their own volition, souls proceed into heaven, into hell" (*CW* 1:77, 78). As late as 1869 he expressed the Augustinian belief that Christianity is not historical, but essence. Yet Emerson, like the Puritans, also maintained an experiential gauge for conversion that had moral and prophetic ramifications, and that he still found compatible with belief in "the *doctrine* of Christianity" (Emerson's italics). Christian revelation could be perceived through Transcendental Nature. And Christian conversion could be reconciled to democratic Romanticism: "[T]he history of Jesus is the history of every man, written large" (W 11:486, 488, 491). Thus Emerson expressed his own inspired confidence in America's mission in terms that transcended the Jacksonian common denominator by maintaining democratic touchstones of moral and spiritual regeneration.

In most significant matters except literal church polity, Emerson's brand of Transcendentalism reconstructed the Puritan world view as it was concerned with the nature of the Spirit, human faculties and affections, moral conduct, and national mission. It was no mere rhetorical flourish that led Emerson often to measure his time against the New England past. He was not simply mollifying the old Calvinist when he wrote Aunt Mary on 21 September 1841, that "the new is only the seed of the old," that modern reform movements are "but the continuation of Puritanism though it operate inevitably the destruction of the Church in which it grew" (L 2:451). He continued to believe in the essential moral truth of Puritanism, that of "an unregenerate person . . . all his good works are sin. It is a new illustration of what I perceive to be a fact[,] that all the errors of Calvinism are exaggerations only & may generally be traced directly to some spiritual truth from which they spring" (JMN 3:225).

Emerson shared with orthodox Puritans a lifelong dedication to the spiritual life while refusing to confuse a glimpse of heaven with self-perfection. In spite of occasional indulgence in Transcendental hyperbole, he remembered the basic truths about human nature he had learned as a minister: Being finite, we need rebirth; but we must never rest assured of salvation to the point where we stop using created means to self-improvement; through our faculties we grow in spiritual awareness; and the inspired American is the keeper of the national dream. Emerson changed his mind about the role the Church plays in guiding souls to truth; but he never opted for the easy Antinomian solution to spiritual longing. In reviving the Puritan tradition for the nineteenth century, Emerson did more than devise the "latest form of infidelity." He rediscovered the dynamic synthesis of spirit and world, grace and effort, private revelation and communal destiny, which had always been the mark of Puritan integrity.

7

Preacher Out of the Pulpit

I

Elizabeth Palmer Peabody's assessment of Emerson—"always preeminently the preacher to his own generation and future ones, but as much—if not more—out of the pulpit as in it"[1]—has a ring of tooneat redefinition, of special pleading. Yet hers was not an isolated attempt to justify a career, to invent a national icon. It was Emerson, in fact, who largely established the rhetoric by which his own mystique was transmitted to posterity.

As Emerson embarked on his great Transcendentalist phase, he continued to identify with the preacher's stance, not only in the privacy of his journals but in revealing sermons preached *after* he resigned from Second Church. The very notion of eloquence, of course, implied audience, and the far-reaching republican values he associated with the ministry could not be set aside as easily as specific duties. The practice of eloquence, moreover, entailed not simply vocation but mission, calling, and "power," which Emerson aimed even more fully to realize out of the pulpit.

His growing uneasiness with the ministry emerges most dramatically in his journal in January 1832, when he declares on the 10th, "It is the best part of the man, I sometimes think, that revolts most against his being the minister. His good revolts from official goodness. . . . The difficulty is that we do not make a world of our own but fall into institutions already made & have to accomodate ourselves to them to be useful at all. & this accommodation is, I say, a loss of so much integrity & of course of so much power" (*JMN* 3:318–19). The concept of "mak[ing] a world of our own" points from the Christian Minister to the Poet. Scholars, however, have overlooked a significant qualification based on Emerson's concern for the social impact of preaching. He feels a momentary twinge of guilt: "[H]ow shall the droning world get on if all its *beaux esprits* recalcitrate upon its approved forms & accepted institutions & quit them all in order to be single minded?" A refined mission of highest "integrity" cannot be achieved in solitude; it still implies a congregation. As Emerson on 19 January continues to contemplate a vocational change, it is an enlarged concept of the Christian Minister that engages him. This new figure pushes against denominational bounds but still promises somehow to restore his own integrity and power while raising and fulfilling others. Echoing Philippians 3:14, Emerson casts his identity and aspirations in terms of an heroic Pauline faith:

> I press toward the mark of the prize of the high calling which is in Christ Jesus.
> Every man has a mark, has a high calling, to wit, his peculiar intellectual & moral constitution, what it points at, what it is becoming. Let it run, & have free course, & be glorified. (*JMN* 3:319–20).

This was the germ of Sermon No. CXLIII ("Find Your Calling," *YES* 163–69), which he delivered seven times beginning on 5 February 1832 and finally as late as 10 January 1836. All men, Emerson argues, are born with certain gifts that must not be repressed. Seldom, however, is one's "high calling" realized "in society." Giving free rein to one's soul he sees as a version of Christ's freeing us from sin. Denying the egocentric implications of self-fulfillment, he inverts it into a form of acknowledging God's will. Yet the "calling" he envisions and the voice he assumes in announcing it remain distinctly prophetic. Emerson resolved his brewing vocational unrest in 1832 not as a rejection but as an extension of his "ministry."

II

"I must feel pride in my friend's accomplishments as if they were mine,—and a property in his virtues," Emerson would write in that much-maligned essay "Friendship" (*CW* 2:115). Two eulogies preached after his departure from Second Church reveal how completely, in the process of establishing his new "vocation," Emerson *could* identify his own struggles and achievements with those of his friends, personal and professional.

Between 18 July and 9 August Emerson made only one entry in his journal: "George A. Sampson died Wednesday evening 23 July, 1834" (*JMN* 4:307). In the interim Emerson prepared the funeral sermon for this parishioner, who (though a member of the seven-man committee that had reviewed and declined Emerson's request to be relieved of the duty of administering the Lord's Supper [*Life* 160–61]) was also "the best of friends" (*L* 1:417). On 3 August 1834 he preached Sermon No. 168, the sermon that captured the attention of Elizabeth Palmer Peabody—expressing his feeling for Sampson and outlining his deeds and the representative virtues that Emerson had come to identify with character. On such an occasion, Emerson admits, "[t]he language of friends" is "partial"; only "the intensity of the emotion is a test of the greatness of our loss." As if to acknowledge that Sampson had left no finished acts of greatness, he stresses that the virtuous life consists in *becoming:* "Every thing human is in the act of unfolding." "The true hero," he declares, "is the good man. I should be ashamed," he goes on, "to express a respect for Cato & Aristides & Washington" but fail to see "the very same virtues when they appeared among my own acquaintance & in the performance of ordinary duties." Transcendentalists were fond of deflecting attacks on their respectability by reminding the orthodox of the essential hypocrisy of human nature. Clearly defending his own role as unfrocked preacher, as much as Sampson's meekness, Emerson suggests that "[t]he prophet is still without honor in his own country, & it is likely that Jesus would be popular & admired in no age that the world has seen."[2] Yet Sampson himself "was that character which we come to the house of God to consider & to seek after," "giv[ing] the lie by his clear life to the vulgar pretence that the life of a man of business is not compatible with adherence to principle."

Significant to a man for whom true eloquence was an index of true virtue, Emerson focuses on language as a sign of character. In his "commercial correspondence" Sampson prided himself on not closing with "a compliment of words that overstepped his feeling." An Idealist businessman, "[h]e saw clearly the consequences of deception. . . . loved the truth for its own sake. . . . never deceived himself or others by using words for reasons. And with the habit of such minds, sought in every conversation the simple truth with such steadiness that his words became things, & possessed the cogency of facts." In short, Sampson, though a man of commerce, was the epitome of the orator-cleric who, in a secular walk of life, embodied the virtues of eloquence Emerson had previously associated with the "power" of a profession. Both the continuity with and the departure from Emerson's ministry are captured in his envisioning such eloquence as flowing in a "common" walk of life; indeed, Sampson exerted moral "persuasion" without "speechmaking."

George Sampson was the transparent vehicle for pure spirit that Emerson had always sought—and sought to be. His very utterances were not partial and personal but representative and universal: "[W]hen he spoke upon any question of duty, his sentences had much more than the weight of an individual opinion: it was not his opinion; it was no man's opinion; it was as if truth & justice spoke through his lips." Sampson had the self-forgetfulness of those "minds which lose the desire to be thought great, in the desire to be what they were made to be." Such Christlike souls "are so great as to be meek," yet "they keep alive a habitual curiosity touching the first questions,— why they exist? whither they tend?" In Sampson, Emerson saw reflected the integration of personality, the composure in the face of a harsh and hostile world, that he had envisioned in Sermon No. V. His friend had "no surface action. Whatever he did was the act of the whole man. . . . Thus was he all principles. And but for the even balance of his own qualities, one would have been tempted to say that a man so earnest was out of place in such a selfish & superficial world."

To claim that this eulogy is nothing but a veiled self-portrait would be to reduce Emerson's psyche to a fragile set of neuroses and to deny the real love and admiration expressed. But his cherished belief that friends are "self-elected," not consciously chosen, was a hard-won insight, as well as a corollary of his conviction, expressed in "Friendship," that friends "carry out the world for me to new and noble depths, and enlarge the meaning of all my thoughts" (CW 2:115). And eulogizing his friend's character in the church he had left less than two years before, Emerson clearly took heart in a man who "cultivate[d] his own powers." Emerson must have felt his verbal construct of Sampson justifying his own new solitary status when he declared: "He never clung to any society or habit or friend, because they had been fit for him, after they had ceased to be so. He sought steadfastly growth; to arrive at truth; to do the best." Reflecting the stoic toughness that was Emerson's litmus test of genuineness and exuding the virtue of intellectual boldness and adaptability, Emerson's Sampson "was severe to himself & suspicious of remaining stationary. He had a strong relish for all speculations that had truth for their object, & his masculine understanding was not to be imposed upon. It courted frankness by its own entire sincerity."

A man dedicated to social and charitable activities, Sampson embodied the civic-mindedness crucial to a republic: "It is such men that are the cement of the state." Indeed, "his friendship was a species of religion." (Ironically, Emerson listed Sampson in his journal on 14 July 1831 as one of those friends who "goes about yet never speaks what his soul is full of" [*JMN* 3:272].) But lest Sampson's religious convictions be divided from "his character," Emerson characteristically enlists Sampson in the cause of antiformalism, stressing that "[h]is religion was indeed dear to him; but it was not a form, but a life." In terms that foreshadow the Divinity School Address, he finds that "[e]specially was the life & character of Jesus Christ grateful to him when, in the advancement of his tho'ts, he had come to contemplate him in the relation of a friend," and he demanded a religion compatible with "progress with his mind." Yet anticipating also the conciliatory spirit of the Address, Emerson hastens to add that "religious forms did engage [Sampson's] earnest attention. He was slow to change them." Thinking back to "The Lord's Supper" as well as pointing toward the Address, Emerson finds this a sign not of pique or radicalism, but of Christian meekness: Sampson "suspected himself if he found [forms] ineffectual." Such a stance would have satisfied the demand of Unitarians from Buckminster to Dewey that the congregation shoulder much of the burden of religious discrimination but not spurn form out of a spirit of mere divisiveness. Sampson "loved the substance so well as to discern between a true & a false form & to embrace every form in the arms of his charity." Emerson implicitly confers the blessing of his deceased parishioner on his own stance toward the sacrament of communion when he announces that Sampson "listened to every preacher of every sect with open heart. He forgave every thing in his preacher but insincerity. He loved those best who presented the Providence of God in the most simple & affectionate relations to man, & the words 'praise' & 'glory' he thought contributed little to the life of a prayer."

The sermon was clearly written for the occasion, in tribute to a dear friend, and Peabody, for one, was astonished by Emerson's "elaborate exposition of the character" of Sampson; "*I know that man*," she declared, "as well as I could have known him had I been his acquaintance on earth." Yet however affective Emerson's "subdued & chastened manner" (*L* 1:417, n. 42), however completely he imaginatively recreated the character of his friend, the virtues of George Adams Sampson are clearly a reflection of the values of Ralph Waldo Emerson. The sermon, in fact, seems to have forced Emerson, in coming to terms with grief, to test his own sense of self. For the next journal entry after the sermon, a meditation on Carlyle's sense of society and solitude, includes a remarkable announcement of the solitude necessary to integrity: "The true & finished man is ever alone. Men cannot satisfy him; he needs God, & his intercourse with his brother is ever condescending, & in a degree hypocritical" (*JMN* 4:308). Mortal friendship with Sampson had not been wholly satisfactory. But the distance of death freed Emerson to express the love that had been checked in life by mutual reserve. In so doing, Emerson both imaginatively fulfilled his ideal of friendship and justified his unfrocked condition.

III

Emerson's most dramatic pronouncement about the power and eloquence of the pulpit is Sermon No. 171, preached in East Lexington and in Concord on 17 July 1836—nearly four years after he resigned his Boston pulpit—in memory of the Reverend Hersey Bradford Goodwin. The sermon expresses how completely Emerson continued to define eloquence—in its full sense—with the stance of a minister.

Emerson had delivered the "Right Hand of Fellowship" on 17 February 1830 at Goodwin's ordination as assistant to Emerson's step-grandfather, the Reverend Ezra Ripley of Concord, and as late as 25 October 1835 had noted listening with pleasure to a Goodwin sermon (*JMN* 5:101). One would expect some personal comments from Emerson on the untimely death at age 30 of one with ties to his own family and ministry. Ostensibly a eulogy, the sermon is an unabashedly self-revealing celebration of the Christian minister as Waldo had distilled the figure from decades of denominational and personal struggle to define the office.

Emerson's text ("How beautiful on the mountains are the feet of him that bringeth good tidings, that publisheth salvation." Is 52:7) was appropriate enough to honor the young Goodwin's faithful character, but the sermon from the start focuses not on Goodwin but on the office of the ministry itself. Still an active supply minister, Emerson in a sense justifies, rationalizes his greater freedom, his increasingly literary vocation. More striking, however, is Emerson's continuing to define his mission clerically, indeed to regard the ministry, purely defined, as the highest, the holiest office. He declares:

> The wisdom of God has provided in the various talents of men for the greatest good of society. Men please themselves in the choice of their pursuit, & by means of the great diversity of tastes, the whole work of the world is done. Some men are fond of manual labor; others to contrive work for many hands; others to ride; others to sail; one to cast accounts; one to till land; one to speak; & one to write.

Emerson's admiration for orators and writers, so obvious in the early journals, frequently appears in the sermons in this kind of ascending order of vocations. Yet he presents the ministry here not so much as an early Romantic haven for sensitive souls as one important task within a social version of the traditional platonic concept of plenitude: Each person finds the proper level of his or her special talent, promoting the good of all within a personally fulfilling and socially beneficial "division of labor." He is deceptively modest when he offers, "Among these various offices is that of observing recording & communicating truth." Carefully avoiding reference to the ministry as a formal occupation, Emerson echoes the common Unitarian complaint that the man of truth's role "is not a coveted office." He grants that "[s]olitude & self communion are to many persons as disagreeable as a jail," implying that it is a difficult job, but that some brave soul has to do it. He is clearly not only pleading for the liberal ministry but implying that his own self-imposed vocational independence is difficult and noble. Both missions, moreover, are socially responsible, for "spiritual truth is opened to one not for his private behoof, but in trust—to be communicated to all, as it is that corn & apples do not grow for their own use. One man may see & teach truth better than another, but the truth belongs to every other as much as to him."

By asserting that access to truth is equal but perception of it is not, Emerson stakes out the unique function of the priest within a democratic culture; he asserts the need for prophets and preachers within the context of liberal religion. Bidding for his own credibility while issuing the traditional New England demand for the audience's attention and effort, he urges that the true priest's "report should be eagerly & reverently received." He argues on utilitarian grounds that "for preserving civil & social order it is as much our interest that the truth seeker & speaker, the prophet & the priest should be freed from all hindrance in their office." Given his own unmoored condition, his case for the prophetic/social significance of the true priesthood is an extraordinary piece of special pleading:

> I am very far from confining my remarks to any profession in society. I am speaking most certainly of a class, but of a natural not an artificial class. Not of men wearing certain titles and garb, & visibly exercising the offices of the church, but of the real priesthood, not made by man but by God, composed of individuals in every age of the world, in every country, in every condition & calling, who, out of love to the human soul, speak to men of its concerns.

Implicitly Goodwin was part of "the real priesthood," but Emerson's own vocational history was well known to his audience. Still, the notion of a "universal priesthood" followed naturally from the liberal-Christian view of Christ as exemplar of universal truth, and Emerson's congregations were hardly scandalized by his broad view of the ministry. Embracing Jews, Greeks, Romans, and Stoics as truth-sayers, Emerson depicts Jesus as "the instructer not of a nation but of human nature, & whose offices & works differently presented & extolled in different ages do more & more in the light of time melt into the one office of the Teacher; of all who, since, in any place, have borne witness of truth & justified the ways of God to man." Emerson thus broadens the priest's sphere of action by bestowing on him Christlike functions; but he also applies a strict test to those who venture to hold a priest's "office," literally or figurally construed.

Though Emerson habitually stresses the impersonality of pure spirit, he calls for a close personal regard of audience for Teacher. There is a certain pathos in his uncharacteristic downplaying of the power of remote truth-sayers: "Even more touching because they come more within reach of the affections, are those among our own contemporaries & acquaintance who belong to this class." Anticipating the very phraseology of Elizabeth Palmer Peabody's definition of himself as "Preacher," he stresses again that "those persons to whom this gift is committed & who are *of different calling and perhaps as often found out of the pulpit as in it* are friends whose value steadily rises in our regard with time & comes at last to be preferred to all other society" (italics mine).

Much of the remainder of the sermon stunningly anticipates Emerson's assessment of the modern pulpit in the Divinity School Address. The voice of the true priest is

> far from the voice of vanity of display of interest of tradition men who believe & therefore speak who speak that they do know. They feel & they make us feel that the Revelation is not closed & sealed but times of refreshment & words of power are evermore coming from the presence of the Lord; that neither is the age of miracles over & forever gone that the Creation is an endless miracle as new at this hour as when Adam awoke in the garden.

What would not until two years later send shock waves through Harvard was already being preached before rural Lexington and Concord congregations.

Emerson was not reluctant to trace the encrustations of materialism and formalism by which "as the church became outwardly rich it became inwardly & really poor," a crisis only partially solved when the Reformation broke "pagan idolatry." Nor was he afraid to trace contemporary versions of the same struggle. The very relationship of minister to congregation had changed overnight. "The clergy of the last generation," he explains, "were accustomed to speak & feel as if they were the shepherds of a flock; . . . over the souls [in his parish], the pastor was & would in heaven continue to be a sort of president & spiritual captain. Men were supposed to be saved or lost as one race[.] . . . But what a revolution has been completed in the hearts of men." Nominally an observation on the loss of one minister, the sermon is really about the loss of genuine pastoral relationship, a loss that is really an opportunity for new light, and it is clearly an exercise in vocational redefinition for Waldo. Today, he says, a person asks not how do I relate to my minister, but "What is *my* relation to the Supreme Being? What is *my* relation to my fellow man? What am *I* designed for? What are my duties? What is my destiny?"

That Emerson even asked these questions has, of course, enormous ramifications for the history of Romantic self-discovery (as well as the more vapid modern forms of self-examination). Specifically, it signified important changes in the concept of vocation which Emerson largely understood in the context of contemporary Unitarian concerns about the ministry. Now, he declares,

> A view more adequate to the divine nature of the soul is taken. Of course the position of the preacher is equally changed. He comes as a friend to provoke his brother to good works. He no longer dictates doctrines. He now solicits your attention to truths which engage him & therefore should engage you. He drops all shadow of a claim of authority over you.

Emerson, of course, is exaggerating both the abruptness and the degree of change in the pastoral relationship. But the change was real; Buckminster had announced it thirty years earlier. And ministers such as Orville Dewey, keenly sensing the shift, had insisted that the grounds of ministerial "authority" must be redefined. Emerson, no longer a *settled* minister, confidently proclaimed those new grounds. In "the loss of the accidental & traditional respect" that once tied flock to minister, we have really lost nothing of value, he declares, even in "a community whose love of freedom is prone to degenerate into licentiousness." For a man who feared mobocracy, welcoming the new relationship took courage:

> I am inclined to think that nothing is worth defending which rests upon a false basis; that we always gain by putting our respect to others purely on the footing of character, and that what remains of the minister's influence upon his people is more genuine & powerful than all that is taken.

Yet the conservatism that lingers in the Divinity School Address in his high regard for the Sabbath, preaching, and pure Christianity is evident in Sermon No. 171. The threatening world of Sermon No. V is not wholly dispelled for the modern minister:

> That impatience & jealousy which appears in this country against any sort of prescription is sometimes directed at him. He may even find the virulence of that ignorant love of liberty which assails every existing institution pointed at him. He may have railing & opposition from those whose pecuniary interest or whose evil habits are directly attacked by his virtuous exertions[.] But a good man is willing to wait & make his own reputation.

Here is restated the old Federalist fear of the willful mob, deaf to legitimate voices of control. Emerson's minister, now a deinstitutionalized prophet, remains a man largely unappreciated, even under attack. But the check of authority is still essential to society, and the true priest is confident of exerting moral influence—by putting off confrontation, by waiting. Significant also is that Emerson's minister, though "perhaps as often found out of the pulpit as in it," remains explicitly Christian:

> The humble disciple of Christ who in these days assumes the pastoral office, shall find that no weakness has crept upon any of the principles of Christ. They have all their omnipotence yet.

This ultimate kind of authority, one based on "lowly perfect love," Emerson never wholly relinquished. His confidence in the new priest/audience relationship is evidence of how Unitarianism prepared the way for Transcendentalist concepts of vocation, and it signifies his bold confidence in his own new direction: "I rejoice in this," he pronounces, "because it puts the minister on a perfectly natural basis. . . . [I]t permits the minister to be a man."

In an important sense, Emerson's minister has not descended into secular egalitarianism. Instead, as a knower and sayer of truth he has achieved authentic moral influence, overcoming in his independence the false "deference" that plagued the ministry for Dewey:

> If it takes away artificial respect it removes all the fences that separated the minister from the people & teaches him to use all the forces of mutual understanding & benefit which the Creator gave man to act upon his fellow.

Noting only near the end that the sermon is meant to "describe" the late Reverend Goodwin, Emerson expresses confidence that the church, by stressing genuine moral authority instead of forms, money, and false deference, is strengthened:

> The imperious spirits fond of power that in a former age would have entered the church [as a profession] find nothing there now to tempt them[.] They are now the demagogues of the bar-room & of the caucus, & the church is relieved of their turbulence.

After such an inspired picture of the modern priest and optimistic outlook for the pulpit as profession, the obligatory sketch of Goodwin's character is surprisingly bland. Emerson praises his writing and speaking skills and portrays him as a sensitive soul who would "suffer a good deal from any exhibition of hardness of heart, or of the licentious & ribald spirit which loves profanity & disorder." But this rather effete figure is depicted at the end as a transitional character. Inexorable changes are occurring and the new order will belong to stauncher "priests" like Emerson who can stand firmly in their new relationship to their peers. Goodwin is depicted as a fleeting intermediary, playing a kind of John the Baptist to Emerson and his new dispensation:

> If we are sent within the influences of a more liberal church if our lot is cast in an hour when old traditions & usages have lost some of their power & the mind has not yet attained a clear sight of a perfectly spiritual church, it is because there is a necessity for our education & redemption that such things should be. Let us give these things no careless glance. Our weal & hope are in them[.] And if a good man of lowly & loving heart, of gentle manners, & of pure life, has pleaded with us in behalf of God & the interests of our eternal nature, let us give earnest heed for he was sent to us, & the use of the talent will be asked at our hands.

This key passage epitomizes the impact traditional vocational concerns of the liberal clergy had on the shape of Emerson's Transcendental career. Emerson in July 1836 was planning publication of the manuscript that became *Nature.* Two years before the Divinity School Address, he was already declaring that the "power" of the "old" religious order was dying, though "liberal" religion had yet to reveal its full potential.[3] The implication, however, is that liberal religion has not *caused* the crisis of faith. Nor does Emerson fully shoulder responsibility for having made a personal, rational choice in leaving his own post. Currents of change are sweeping along prophets like Goodwin—and Emerson—who provide glimpses of the new order. Yet he endows the very stance of professional noncommitment with God's blessing. Despite the uncertain shape of a "perfectly spiritual church," there is no doubt that its prophets are divinely appointed; at stake is still "redemption," which more than ever demands effort by all people. Hence the Unitarian context, and the Puritan tone, of the final charge to the congregation to be not passive receivers but active participants in the new order.

On the threshold of Emerson's Transcendental "ministry," Sermon No. 171 pushes to the denominational edge certain important professional issues that had exercised Unitarians for decades. Chief among these was the source of the minister's relationship to his congregation in a world of increasing voluntarism. If Unitarian ministers often seemed excessively refined, it was because liberal theology could no longer base its "authority" on coercion and would not base it on the charismatic emotionalism of revivalism. But this sermon reveals Emerson's sense of vital continuity from his vocational concept of Priest and Prophet to that of Teacher, Scholar, and Poet.

Informing the Goodwin sermon is not simply Emerson's ongoing vocational redefinition and the formulaic sentiments of a eulogy, but also his deeper grief at the recent death (9 May) of his beloved brother Charles. Waldo had special reason to associate his brother, dead at twenty-eight, with young Goodwin and with his own ministry. For when Waldo had offered the Right Hand of Fellowship to Goodwin, he had been accompanied by "Br. Charles C. Emerson, delegate" from Second Church.[4] Emerson responded almost immediately to this latest family affliction with a kind of Wordsworthian reverie in which he hoped to recapture the sense of glory in the world that had been obscured by mourning (*JMN* 5:160). He lingered, moreover, on his characteristic themes—the inherent value of character and the self-evident nature of truth, together suggesting the consolation of compensation:

> [T]he angels will worship virtue & truth not gathered into a person but inly seen in the perspective of their own progressive being. They see the dream & the interpretation of the world in the faith that God is within them. As a spiritual truth needs no proof but is its own reason, so the Universe needs no outer cause but exists by its own perfection and the sum of it all is this, God is. (*JMN* 5:162–63)

As several critics have observed, Emerson, having been forced since childhood to cope with disease, deprivation, and death, often found his creativity *released* by grief. This facility was both an evasion, a denial, of the literalness of loss, and a willed reassurance of his own integrity. He acknowledged in the journal that "a storm of calumny will always pelt him whose view of God is highest & purest"; but this led to the heroic sentence used in "Self-Reliance": "To believe your own thought, that is Genius" (*JMN* 5:163). And on 28 May he remarked that such self-reliance is not eccentric isolation, but that reliable forces shape human endeavor: "Nothing bizarre, nothing whimsical will endure. Nature is ever interfering with Art" (*JMN* 5:164).

In this broader context, the Goodwin eulogy, like the Sampson eulogy, defines Emerson's own vocational mission while it affirms a more fundamental sense of purpose in the wake of two significant deaths. Four days after preaching the sermon, Emerson has fully regained his self-confidence, couched in both psychological and vocational terms: "Respect yourself. . . . Trust the instinct to the end. . . . Make your own Bible" (*JMN* 5:186). And on the 30th he proclaims faith in the self's relation to what he would call the Over-Soul, an utterance that is definitively Emersonian: "Man is the point wherein matter & spirit meet & marry. The Idealist says, God paints the world around your soul. The spiritualist saith, Yea, but lo! God is within you. The self of self creates the world through you, & organizations like you. The Universal Central Soul comes to the surface in my body" (*JMN* 5:187). Emerson's distinction between the Idealist and the spiritualist is a crucial reminder—to the many readers of Emerson who decline to take him at his own word—of the theological roots of Transcendentalism. His deepest faith was finally grounded not in platonic correspondences but in the indwelling Spirit that he believed animates all life.

IV

The theology, ethics, and vocational constructs of liberal religion and Transcendentalism, designed to extend the republican/Christian world view into a more democratic and fragmented time, were problematic. Redefinition of one's relation to stagnant institutions meant strategies of imaginative, fluid suspension, of noncommitment to festering realities of American life. However we finally judge this legacy to American culture, Emerson must be credited, well into old age, with the courage of living with this equivocalness.

In the late essay "The Preacher" Emerson sized up the challenge facing a new generation of ministers. The life of the spirit in America was no more substantial, the status of the clerical office no less tenuous, than they had been when he issued his most assertive Transcendentalist pronouncements in the 1830s. The terms of his complaint were unchanged.

As in the Divinity School Address, Emerson finds himself "in a moment of transition," religious institutions and "forms" having lost the power to inspire, but with nothing worthy having arisen in their place. A classic case of Romantic belatedness, "[w]e are born too late for the old and too early for the new faith" (W 10:217).

The relationship between the witness to truth and society is unchanged from that expressed in Sermon No. V or "Self-Reliance": "Of course the virtuous sentiment appears arrayed against the nominal religion, and the true men are hunted as unbelievers, and burned," until society itself partially "wakes up," only to fall into "unbelief" (220). As in his earliest sermons, Emerson regards the enemy of "faith" as abuse of reason and logic: "[A]nalysis has run to seed in unbelief" (221). But it is we who have changed; "[t]he object of adoration remains forever unhurt and identical" (222). The world is marked by constant shifting and metamorphosis. Emerson musters a long list of his religious heroes, many cited in Sermon No. XLIII, to argue that they all spoke through "real churches." Still, he will not rest in formalism: "I agree with their heart and motive; my discontent is with their limitations and surface and language" (227).

For Emerson, the mission of the "preacher," with regard to a dynamic world and intractable institutions, is unchanged since the days of his own ministry. The great need is still for authenticity: "Nothing is more rare, in any man, than an act of his own. The clergy are as like as peas. I cannot tell them apart" (229). What is needed above all is "self-possession." No less than at the Divinity School in 1838, Emerson acknowledges the tangible opportunity of the Sabbath, and the real eagerness of congregations for uplifting. Only "[l]et [the preacher] value his talent as a door into Nature. Let him see his performances only as limitations. Then, over all, let him value the sensibility that receives, that loves, that dares, that affirms" (230).

The integrity of the sermon not as artifact but as vehicle for power remains crucial. The preacher seeks "a new spirit," not because the truth changes, but because his apprehension of it must be ever-fresh if it is to be contagious. Thus Emerson's indispensable advice to a "young preacher": "When there is any difference felt between the foot-board of the pulpit and the floor of the parlor, you have not yet said that which you should say" (233). Both sound rhetorical theory and belief, he always thought, determine the proper tone: "[A]ffirmative discourse, presuming assent, will often obtain it when argument would fail"; "opinions are temporary, but convictions uniform and eternal" (234–35). Finally, Emerson appeals, as he had in his own ministry, for "flexible" use of forms, not because truth is relative, but because it is "ever present, and insists on being of this age and of this moment" (237).

"The Preacher" echoes many of Emerson's earlier convictions

about the nature of belief, the plight of the nation and the church, and the status and mission of the clergy. But if he has nothing new to say, he has refused to mellow to the extent of offering smooth advice, or deceiving himself as to his own favored place in the hearts of Americans. The challenges of the Divinity School Address unrealized, the clerical office—formal and freelance—has been routinized into a prophetic role of necessary independence, even solitude. Each generation of preachers, each sermon, enacts a ritual of renewal. The purpose of religion, whether for the lone seeker or the churchgoer, remains "to be disabused of appearances, to see realities" (237). And the gift of the preacher is "the art of subliming a private soul with inspirations from the great and public and divine Soul from which we live" (238). Emerson retained the courage to see that this insight could never be codified but, simple and essential as it was, had always to be rediscovered.

Epilogue: Saint Emerson

Emerson maintained that in resigning his pulpit he never *left* the ministry but rather was free to *fulfill* it. This vocational evasion/ commitment began as a purely personal stratagem. But it conspired with a deep-seated need of the denomination and the larger culture to enshrine Emerson as a secular Preacher to America.

The figure of Emerson as a nondenominational prophet or saint has ambiguously colored his reputation for over a hundred years, even though we have only recently begun actually to examine Emerson as *minister*. Scholarly assessments of Emerson, inevitably faced with his ethical legacy, have ranged from adulatory to scathing; more often than not, moreover, the academy's view of Emerson has stood at polar extremes from the popular image of Emerson—a symptom of deeper cultural divisions. Emerson's original role as minister was central to his becoming a national icon. And the ironies of his enshrinement are inseparable from the rich ambiguities of his moral and literary legacy.

I

A distinctive ritual was reenacted on Sunday, 21 May 1978 at First Parish, Unitarian, in Concord, Massachusetts. The Rev. Dana McLean Greeley gave the service over to a series of lay readings from

Emerson's essays and poetry, and "commentary" on "Emerson, the Man and the Minister," in commemoration of the 175th birthday of the Sage of Concord.

There was nothing remarkable in so honoring a local hero who, after William Ellery Channing, contributed (unwittingly) more than any other person to the vitality of American Unitarianism. What *was* remarkable was that none of the selections had anything *good* to say about Unitarianism. Passages about the "effulgence" of spring were strikingly appropriate to the new green lushness visible through open church windows and to the warm, fresh air, redolent of spring. But with relish approaching self-congratulation, the participants recited Emerson's most defiantly nonconformist pronouncements and his most bitingly anticlerical passages, notably the familiar critique of the "formalist" minister from the Divinity School Address.

Despite "The Lord's Supper," despite the "Address" and Andrews Norton, the Unitarian attachment to Emerson goes on unabated. In April 1982, a five-day festival of "Emerson Week Activities" in Concord and Cambridge marked the centenary of the Great Man's passing, with a blend of academic and religious celebrants conjuring up images of Greater Boston in the mid-nineteenth century, when Harvard was a bastion of Unitarianism, and liberal Christianity gave its moral stamp to education, politics, commerce, and culture. The flyer announcing the opening General Meeting in Cambridge listed a broad spectrum of luminaries: "Dr. Eugene Pickett, presiding. Participants include Woody Hayes, Elliot Richardson, Archibald Cox, David Emerson, Dana Greeley, Rhys Williams, the Harvard Band, and the Follen Church choirs"; and at the foot of the week's agenda, this expansive note: "In addition there will be Emerson Commemorative services in many UU congregations across the continent sometime during the week." Emerson today is so widely quoted and revered that, in this least dogmatic and least idolatrous of denominations, he might as well be dubbed, as a Unitarian friend has slyly quipped, "Saint Emerson."[1]

Emerson in life shocked many Unitarians, and he spurned his own congregation's offer to compromise on the issue of administering the sacrament of communion. But the denomination went to work immediately upon his death to *reclaim* him as one of their own, curiously fulfilling Emerson's prophetic journal entry written three months before he resigned his pastorate: "I have sometimes thought that in order to be a good minister it was necessary to leave the ministry. The profession is antiquated. In an altered age, we worship in the dead forms of our forefathers. Were not a Socratic paganism

better than an effete superannuated Christianity?" (*JMN* 4:27). Paradoxically, Emerson's rising "official" status among Unitarians can
be charted in the *Christian Examiner*, which, having condemned the
Divinity School Address as "utterly distasteful" in 1838, by 1861
would "gratefully rejoice" in "his prophetic mission."[2]

One of Emerson's successors at Second Church, E. A. Horton,
eulogized him as "our best, our greatest American." In terms suggesting nostalgia for the Federalist figure of the minister as moral guide,
he praised him as "our noblest expression, pure and simple, of a
Christian Republic."[3] Indeed, Horton declared, "I look upon Mr.
Emerson as a preacher, throughout his life." "His prose productions,"
Horton went on, "are beautiful, analogical and striking sermons,
on the grandeur of character, the nobility of duty, the loftiness of
sincerity, the everlastingness of truth, the sources of true power, the
over-soul, spiritual laws, and heroism" (6–7).

Horton acknowledged that Emerson's faith in "instincts" ran afoul
of "Christian customs and doctrines" (8). But in a remarkable analogy
revealing not only the extent to which Unitarians had forgiven Emerson but also that they had come to conflate *Emerson's* writings with
Holy Scripture, he argued: "It is unfair to test the Bible by a few
texts: so this man cannot be understood by disjointed extracts" (9).
"If some passages shock us, or others mystify us, the best solution,"
Horton recommended, "is to go to the heart of his thought. There
you find reverence, purity, morality, high aim, unselfishness, love,
candor, truthfulness, worship, Godlikeness" (10–11). Horton here
shows that the legacy of the Higher Criticism was not simply to
challenge the authority of the Bible; applied to "secular" scripture,
it could *invigorate* rational religion by emphasizing *essence*, while
obscuring the doctrinal supports of revealed religion in a cloud of
relativist comparison.

Horton admitted that he, of course, could not be a Transcendentalist and still "preach in a Christian pulpit" (11; neither, for that
matter, could Emerson), but taking his lead from Emerson's essay
"Character," Horton decreed that "Emerson was always greater than
his utterances" (14). Emerson, then, is redefined by Horton not only
as a preacher and a seer but as a kind of immortal patron saint as
well: "He was an active, practical force; and will continue to be. . . .
If the true object of a sermon is to communicate life, Emerson's
essays are sermons. . . . If the best work done for religion by the pulpit
is to so present ideal virtues that humanity shall long to incarnate
them in character, then Emerson has outstripped us all" (19–20).

Curiously, Horton concludes his eulogy by recalling his audience—in un-Emersonian terms—to the need for revealed Christianity: Christ, whose "name is Immanuel, *God with us*," is the essential reminder of "the deeper truths of self-sacrifice and immortality" (21). Even here, however, Horton completes the process of Emerson's rehabilitation through redefinition: "Sifted by time's unfailing tests, the errors of his utterance shall be winnowed away, and the truth he faithfully sought to tell his fellow-men, shall be preserved" (22).[4] Emerson emerges from Horton's apology as a truer minister, Unitarian, and Christian than he would have been had he dutifully continued to tend his Second Church flock.

Cyrus Bartol observed the posthumous sanctification of his old friend with irony: "Half a century ago, cast out as one having the devil which the old Pharisees found in Jesus, he is now welcomed as a seer—in Scripture phrase, 'man of God,' truly divine—on all hands."[5] Though Bartol held a higher view of the Lord's Supper than Emerson did and was willing to compromise what reservations he had, he too regarded Emerson as a "saint" whose poems celebrated "the unbroken unity" (6). Emerson the lecturer and writer was still essentially the preacher: "He had good right to preach the essays which were sermons, ethical to the end, heirlooms of seven generations of priests. What industry is shown in his style,—not a river or a fire like that of Milton, Byron, or Webster, but a collection and condensation of wisdom, illustration, and wealth of allusion, a cabinet of gems!" (11).

Yet Bartol too betrays the classic Unitarian strategy of redefining Emerson back into the fold. He sentimentalizes Emerson's funeral in "the old sanctuary, which he never abandoned or took his name from, but clung in manhood to, with his child's Christian faith" (14). And he declares Emerson "more Christian than the Christians in presenting their Master as not differing from other children of God save in degrees of wisdom and goodness, not distinct in kind" (15). For Bartol, Emerson is (in a fresher if more grandiose version of the "preacher-out-of-the-pulpit" cliché) "the unfrocked priest of the human mind" (19).

Frederic H. Hedge joined the chorus in his "Memorial Address," declaring Emerson "once for a few years a preacher in the technical, ecclesiastical sense. . . . always a preacher in the higher, universal sense,—a prophet,—the greatest, I think, this country or this age has known."[6] Hedge specifically acknowledges the "debt" which the American Unitarian Association owed Emerson in "the cause of spiritual emancipation" (212). Singled out are Emerson's "triumphant optimism" and his quotability: "No moral teacher has been so instructive to his generation" (214, 215). Hedge went on to offer the most explicit assessment of Emerson's reputation and continuing appeal among the Unitarians:

> If forty years ago one had ventured to commend him to this Association, he would have pronounced his own doom of ecclesiastical ostracism. Forty years ago he was a heretic, a blasphemer, a pest and peril to Church and State. To-day he is acknowledged a prophet, and those who reviled him are ready to garnish his sepulchre. . . .
>
> As a preacher born and nurtured in our communion, he belongs to us; and I have to say of him that, as a preacher, he was one of the few in all the ages who in the realm of spirit have spoken with authority,—authority in the high sense in which the supreme Teacher from whom our Christendom dates was said to speak 'as one having authority, and not as the scribes.' . . . His is the authority of an original, independent witness. (216–17)

Completing the process of canonizing Emerson as saint and of declaring his *utterances* canonical, Hedge finds "Absolute sincerity" (217) the hallmark of Emerson's authority: "To be, not seem, is the lesson of his life" (218).

The Unitarian rehabilitation of Emerson was but a forerunner of his enshrinement by the larger Genteel Tradition as, in H. L. Kleinfield's phrase, the first American "apostle of light."[7] This very sanctification was a key factor in Emerson's popular and critical decline in the middle decades of the twentieth century, for the values of the Genteel Tradition have seemed monstrously aloof, polite, elite, and superficial to generations that have endured World Wars and the Great Depression. Indeed, in the waning years of the nineteenth century, in an age when "restless radicalism [was] invading much of American life,"[8] Emerson as Sage of Concord offered a reassuring ethical tone hinting at cultural stability and continuity, and a comforting religiosity without doctrinal complications. Even Matthew Arnold had sensed this appeal in Emerson, denying that he was "a great poet," "a great writer," or "a great philosophy-maker" but declaring him the "friend and aider of those who would live in the spirit."[9]

Emerson's immense inspirational appeal for his younger contemporaries is evidenced by the spate of reverential biographies and the reminiscences and conversations collected by his many disciples.

Charles J. Woodbury wryly noted that some of the faithful "believe that the ghost of Transcendentalism will rise again, and are even waiting to see the stone rolled away from its sepulchre."[10] The true spirit of Emerson's followers, Woodbury argued, should be to regard "his Transcendentalism . . . as a fragment, existing less as a religious idiosyncracy, much less a passing fashion, than as a lifting and permanent force in general religious culture" (114). Occasionally playing the doubting Thomas to a master whose cosmic optimism could seem insufferable and who did not, at any rate, *want* disciples, Woodbury evokes the pseudo-religious aura that clung to Emerson's memory.

II

The actual content of the Emersonian Gospel has been notoriously more difficult to assess than what he has in the main seemed to *represent* to his followers. Emerson's uplifting tone is apparent to all. *What* he has to say has met with no such consensus. Andrews Norton's attack on the atheistic implications of Transcendentalism is well enough known. But some more sympathetic to "the newness" were also worried about where Emerson was heading in the late 1830s. Elizabeth Palmer Peabody recalled showing William Ellery Channing a passage in his own "Likeness to God" that seemed to anticipate Transcendentalism. Channing acknowledged the connection, but he drew a clear distinction:

> "The danger that besets our Transcendentalists is that they sometimes mistake their individualities for the Transcendent. What is common to men and revealed by Jesus transcends every single individuality, and is the spiritual object and food of all individuals."
> I asked, "Don't you think Mr. Emerson recognizes this?"
> "Yes," he replied, "in the poems of the 'Problem' and of the 'Sphinx' I think he does. But many of his professed followers *do not*, and fall into a kind of *ego-theism*, of which a true understanding of Jesus Christ is the only cure, as I more and more believe."[11]

Modern readers less charitable to Emerson than Channing have laid at his feet blame for all manner of perversions of the ego, from capitalistic boosterism, to fascist will to power, to the more vapid manifestations of self-absorption evident in the "Me Generation."

Assessment of Emerson's legacy has been tied implicitly to the legacy of liberal religion, which Tom Wolfe in our own day finds bankrupt: "[I]t is precisely the most rational, intellectual, secularized, modernized, updated, relevant religions—all the brave, forward-looking Ethical Culture, Unitarian, and Swedenborgian movements of only yesterday—that are finished, gasping, breathing their last."[12] Nearly a hundred years ago O. B. Frothingham was already charging Unitarianism with failure as a major force in American life. In rejecting Calvinism, he argued, Unitarianism lost the masses, "more especially as no equally absorbing ideas were substituted for them." Emerson (who was acutely aware of this very dilemma), he granted, at least had the consistency and courage, in leaving scriptural revelation behind, to stand "squarely upon the spiritual laws as disclosed to the soul." But the denomination was content with "half-way measures" that were "neither brave nor thorough."[13] Others have thought *Emerson* neither brave nor thorough. For David Leverenz, Emerson's essays, with elitism masquerading as democratic inclusiveness, "inaugurate the tradition of alienated liberalism that is still the dominant ideology in American literary criticism."[14]

Theodore Parker, however, was one of many within the denomination who felt "roused" by the Divinity School Address, inspired to carry on his own work.[15] And while Emerson is to some a great equivocator and to others a radical challenger of fundamental theological tenets of the Unitarian establishment, he also helped transmit the *spirit* of liberal religion beyond its own denominational bounds. Key Emersonian convictions with distinctly Unitarian roots became staples of a national secular scripture as his disciples completed the process of his canonization. The centennial of his birth elicited countless tributes to Emerson as Preacher to America. George Willis Cooke pronounced him "the greatest of modern ethical teachers"; "[h]e is, in fact, a great religious teacher. . . . He is preached in all churches, but many who have found truth in him will not belong to any company of worshipers. . . . He has helped many everywhere to find in religion something real, vital, and natural; something that is in harmony with the facts of life and the daily experiences of men."[16]

For Senator George F. Hoar, "The purpose of Emerson, like that of Milton, is to justify the ways of God to man, and they do not need to be clothed in a veil." Hoar could recommend Emerson's version of divine light with none of the old stigma of Calvinism: "He affirms that inspiration and the process of revelation did not end with the

Apostles and the Scriptures. It is going on to-day, and all the time, to him that hath ears to hear."[17] Yet Hoar's praise is colored by the obfuscation characteristic of so many paeans to Emerson, the sort of high-sounding yet fuzzy effusion that prompted Yvor Winters' famous, reactionary charge that "Emerson at the core is a fraud and a sentimentalist."[18] For Hoar continues that Emerson "has made the best statement in all secular literature of the doctrine of immortality. He shows us that the world and the human soul are not only unreasonable, but inexplicable, without it. Yet he makes no absolute affirmation, except that we shall be immortal if that be best." Though Emerson may not have had answers to the ultimate questions of human destiny that have motivated Western religions, it was enough for Hoar that "[h]e sees no God of force or of disdain looking down on mankind as on a race of groveling swine or chattering apes" (9). A religion of poetry and ethics self-conscious about its identity, American Unitarianism continues to reestablish the grounds of its opposition to Calvinism over 150 years after Channing made the point.

Thomas Wentworth Higginson offered the quintessential praise of Emerson from a disciple undaunted by the Master's lack of "formal method": "He holds us by his detached sentences; if we take those to heart, each reader perhaps carrying away a different sentence, it is all we ask."[19] The image of Emerson as holy Teacher and Preacher-out-of-the-pulpit had become such an American article of faith that knowing what he said (or meant) was not requisite to paying homage or subscribing to his secular scripture. Emerson had become invested with the holy mystery, impenetrability, and veneration of the very Scripture he had sought to bring alive for the nineteenth century.

Malcolm Cowley's claim that "hardly anyone read Emerson" in the 1920s says more about the taste of a generation of alienated artists and intellectuals than about the wider culture.[20] Invocation of Emerson as a non-doctrinaire religious teacher reached its apex in uplifting collections like Newton Dillaway's eccentric *The Gospel of Emerson* (1939), "conceived as inspirational, and not as a technical anthology." Dillaway quivered before the Transcendental mysteries, himself assuming the role of Emerson's oracle: "This volume may be seen as a digest of Emerson's gospel of the Real. It is not easy to detect this gospel, for it is hidden in a hundred essays, letters, poems, notes; and in many entries of the journals. After years of study and thought, and consultation with other students of Emerson, the gospel herein presented has gradually emerged from some twenty-five volumes of the seer's writings"(!). This oddly genteel exercise in religiosity was offered as "something that would really open up the inner life of the sensitive reader."[21]

The tougher-minded Edgar Lee Masters admitted the difficulty of "verifying" that "Emerson, of all Americans, has been the most inspiring and formative influence in American life."[22] Yet Masters reminds us that beyond the polite, pseudo-religious, vapid invocations of the Emerson oracle, Emerson really has spoken to a longing in the national psyche, an appeal modern criticism has proved singularly inept at explaining. Masters conveys the impact of Emerson on an Illinois youth craving assurance that "we had possibilities . . . that we were potential geniuses, ready to expand wings and fly if we laid our hands upon the springs of courage that were within us and within the human breast everywhere." Masters' recollection of his own groping for identity and heroic purpose evokes the voice of Emerson in the early journals and sermons. Particularly suggestive of the continuing legacy of America's preacher-out-of-the-pulpit is the fact that Masters "had never joined a church or experienced conversion" (2). In fact, Masters' condemnation of "the local preaching and proselyting" as a repressive force ("how they interfered with rational enjoyments, with mental advancement, with intelligent investigation and conviction") echoes Emerson's reaction against an allegedly repressive Calvinist tradition (3).

Masters' Emerson, however, is not merely a projection of his own repressed Midwestern imagination. He sees the Janus-faced legacy of Emersonianism embodied in two of his classmates who embraced what they perceived to be his message: One "went from Emerson into the quackery of mental healing, into the belief that everything is possible through the assertion of the will, the genius of the mind" (3); "[t]he other girl became a very sensible and enterprising teacher and traveller. Her life was blessed by Emerson" (4).

Invoking Emerson as spiritual guide has been an ambiguous American venture. His words to some have been heady, dangerous stuff, to some reinforcement of all manner of egocentric self-indulgence, to others a source of stoic wisdom and courage, to still others justification for Manifest Destiny. But in all cases he has continued, paradoxically, to speak both to sensitive young souls eager to transcend stale convention, and to those seeking reassurance in a world of terror and uncertainty. The open-ended richness and ironies of Emerson's legacy have been the object of more than academic scrutiny. A *Time* magazine essay during the recent centennial of Emerson's death noted: "He gave America a metaphysics: he sought to join the nation's intellect to its power. Emerson sanctified America's ambitions

.... He was the wonder-rabbi of Concord, Mass., our bishop, the mystic of our possibilities."[23]

For over 100 years Emerson has seemed, to use his phrase, the "representative man" in American letters. He has been an inspiration to every kind of reformer and social critic, and at the same time, the favorite author of Henry Ford and of football genius and amateur military historian Woody Hayes. Emerson has been a presence our theologians, philosophers, writers, and scholars have felt compelled to honor or revile. A Romantic humbug, selecting what he could use in religion and discarding what was inconvenient, or a nineteenth-century St. Paul, asserting authentic spirituality—our sense of Emerson has been an index of the nation's self-image.

Emerson seems to speak to an American anxiety over not only personal empowerment, but also national and even cosmic purpose. The obfuscation that has enveloped his installation as a secular saint speaks to our desire for transcendence, and to our uncertainty of success in carrying out his demanding agenda. Emerson's undeniable appeal to disparate constituencies may seem paradoxical. But the tradition of the liberal ministry *encouraged* "representativeness" in the preacher and in his message. Throughout the "stages" we are accustomed to seeing in Emerson's career runs a steady dialectic embracing inspiration and constraint, individual and society, virtue and action, expression and audience—the self-defined sphere of concern for the post-Revolutionary liberal clergy. The more Emerson celebrated the "idiosyncratic," the more he found it "general & infinite" (*JMN* 3:199). It is no wonder that, however radical certain of Emerson's pronouncements may sound, almost all readers find themselves reflected in his prose. Our continuing to look for answers in Emerson—for reassurance, consolation, inspiration—bespeaks the dilution of mainline theology in our culture—and its persistence. Despite our changing expectations of him, Emerson is still our "representative man."

One can imagine Emerson recoiling from his own canonization and being shocked by some of the causes in which his "uplifting" aphorisms have been invoked. Yet the sundry attempts to codify his "gospel" might have elicited a wry smile. For his cardinal principle that the experience of the divine is personal, that moral growth and discovery is continual, *invited* "creative insecurity"[24] as a ground for being human. And though he believed individuals responsible for their own salvation, he never lost sight of the communal aspect of our nature.

Emerson's ministerial encounter with eloquence had been anything but repressive. It afforded him a socially viable "calling" that could be adapted to new vocational needs; a "vantage ground," as Emerson called it, that enabled him, in finding his voice, to uplift others even as he overcame his own timidity and self-doubt; and a growing sense that "eloquence" was not, at its best, a contrivance to be taken up for self-aggrandizement but an essential emanation of virtue, character, and expression, a means of restoring the fragile synthesis of republican ideals that comprised his inherited world view.

That Emerson continued to regard institutions, including churches, as the lengthened shadows of inspired heroes accounts for a genuine note of conciliation even in the notorious Divinity School Address. For despite the radical implications of his assertion that "the need was never greater of new revelation than now" (*CW* 1:84), "faith makes its own forms." The church, whatever its present corruptions, originally sprang from such faith. Do not be concerned to destroy the old, Emerson proclaims to a class of new ministers; "[r]ather let the breath of new life be breathed by you through the forms already existing" (*CW* 1:92).

Emerson was not ready to dispense with the great moral contributions of Christianity: the Sabbath and "the institution of preaching,—the speech of man to men,—essentially the most flexible of all organs, of all forms" (*CW* 1:92). Flexibility of doctrine for Emerson meant not laxness but room for all people in all times personally to experience the divine, which alone created moral law. Flexibility of preaching meant that the sermon must tap vital resources of inspiration and not regard Scripture slavishly; it was also coming to mean that to convey new truth continually, the very form of the sermon could melt into lecture, essay, verse. Elizabeth Palmer Peabody understood this when she summed up Emerson as "always the preacher of the eternal life, entirely emancipated from the 'letter which killeth,' and minister of the Spirit which maketh alive."[25]

Notes

Introduction

1. "Emerson as Preacher," *The Genius and Character of Emerson*, ed. F. B. Sanborn (Boston: Houghton Mifflin, 1898), 146.

2. Peabody, "Emerson as Preacher," 154.

3. "History and Biography in Emerson's Unpublished Sermons (A Report of Progress and of Research Possibilities)," *Proceedings of the American Antiquarian Society* 66, pt. 2 (October 1956): 103–18; partially reprinted in *Emerson Society Quarterly* no. 12 (Third Quarter 1958): 2–9.

4. Besides the twenty-five sermons published in *YES*, these include "The Lord's Supper" (*W* 11:1–25), first printed in Octavius Brooks Frothingham, *Transcendentalism in New England: A History* (New York: Putnam's, 1876), 363–80; and *Printed Copy of Sermon Preached by Ralph Waldo Emerson on the Death of George Adams Sampson 1834* (n.p.: privately printed, 1903). A related discourse, "Right Hand of Fellowship," was published in James Kendall, *A Sermon, Delivered at the Ordination of Hersey Bradford Goodwin, as Colleague Pastor with Ezra Ripley, D.D. . . . Feb. 17, 1830* (Concord: Gazette Office, 1830), 29–31; reprinted in *Uncollected Writings* (New York: Lamb, 1912), 11–14.

5. Sealts, review of *Ralph Waldo Emerson: A Descriptive Bibliography*, by Joel Myerson, *The Papers of the Bibliographical Society of America* 77 (First Quarter 1983): 88–89.

6. The major studies are Conrad Wright, *The Beginnings of Unitarianism in America* (Boston: Starr King, 1955), and *The Liberal Christians: Essays on American Unitarian History* (Boston: Beacon, 1970); William R. Hutchison, *The Transcendentalist Ministers: Church Reform in the New England Renaissance* (New Haven: Yale Univ. Press, 1959); and Daniel Walker Howe, *The Unitarian Conscience: Harvard Moral Philosophy, 1805–1861* (Cambridge: Harvard Univ. Press, 1970).

7. Joel Porte, *Representative Man: Ralph Waldo Emerson in His Time* (New York: Oxford Univ. Press, 1979); Gay Wilson Allen, *Waldo Emerson: A Biography* (New York: Viking, 1981). Lawrence Buell has shown how Unitarian moral and aesthetic concerns helped shape the American Renaissance, in *Literary Transcendentalism: Style and Vision in the American Renaissance* (Ithaca: Cornell Univ. Press, 1973).

8. Yukio Irie, *Emerson and Quakerism* (Tokyo: Kenkyusha, 1967).

9. Sue Kelsey Tester, "Ralph Waldo Emerson's Sermons: A Critical Introduction" (Ph.D. dissertation, Boston Univ., 1978).

10. William B. Barton, Jr., *A Calendar To The Complete Edition Of the Sermons of Ralph Waldo Emerson* (Memphis: Bee Books, 1977).

11. Robinson, *Apostle of Culture: Emerson as Preacher and Lecturer* (Philadelphia: Univ. of Pennsylvania Press, 1982); Whicher, *Freedom and Fate: An Inner Life of Ralph Waldo Emerson* (Philadelphia: Univ. of Pennsylvania Press, 1953).

12. I borrow this phrase from the title of an MLA session chaired by Robert Milder in New York on 29 December 1986.

13. His youthful poems on heroic themes are a case in point. See Albert J. von Frank, "Emerson's Boyhood and Collegiate Verse: Unpublished and New Texts Edited from Manuscript," *Studies in the American Renaissance 1983*, ed. Joel Myerson (Charlottesville: Univ. Press of Virginia, 1983), 1–56, esp. 34–35.

14. Lewis P. Simpson, ed., *The Federalist Literary Mind: Selections from the 'Monthly Anthology and Boston Review', 1803–1811* (Baton Rouge: Louisiana State Univ. Press, 1962), 6.

15. John R. Howe, Jr., "Republican Thought and the Political Violence of the 1790s," *American Quarterly* 19 (Summer 1967): 147–65. Donald M. Scott discusses the implications of Federalist thought for the ministry, in *From Office to Profession: The New England Ministry 1750–1850* (Philadelphia: Univ. of Pennsylvania Press, 1978), esp. chap. 2. On the age's anxiety concerning the vulnerability of republicanism, see also Nathan O. Hatch, *The Sacred Cause of Liberty: Republican Thought and the Millennium in Revolutionary New England* (New Haven: Yale Univ. Press, 1977), 104–5. Gary B. Nash has argued that the French Revolution, while never actually viewed in the United States as a direct, tangible threat, came to serve as a rhetorical straw man through which a variety of perceived *internal* dangers could be attacked. See Nash, "The American Clergy and the French Revolution," *William and Mary Quarterly*, 3rd Series, 22 (July 1965): 392–412.

For a concise assessment of the theme of republican insecurity in the literature of the period, see William L. Hedges, "The Old World Yet: Writers and Writing in Post-Revolutionary America," *Early American Literature* 16 (Spring 1981): 3–18.

16. *Piety and Arms: A Sermon, Preached at the Request of the Ancient and Honourable Artillery Company* (Boston: Manning & Loring, 1799), 9.

17. *An Historical Sketch of the First Church in Boston* (Boston: Munroe & Francis, 1812), 190, 189. This, of course, was the mixed legacy of the Great Awakening. As much as liberals like William Emerson feared revivalism, Evangelicals distrusted classical "Ciceronian eloquence" as ineffectual show, believing that only the *converted* had the power to preach the gospel. See Dennis Barone, "James Logan and Gilbert Tennent: Enlightened Classicist Versus Awakened Evangelist," *Early American Literature* 21 (Fall 1986): 109.

18. *The Federalist Literary Mind*, 165–67.

19. *A Sermon, Preached at the Ordination of the Rev. Robinson Smiley* (Windsor, Vt.: Nahum Mower, 1801), 9, 13–17.

20. *A Sermon, Delivered March 2, 1803, at the Ordination of the Rev. Thomas Beede* (Amherst, N.H.: Joseph Cushing, 1803), 24.

21. Buckminster, *A Sermon, Delivered at the Interment of the Reverend William Emerson* (Boston: Joseph T. Buckingham, 1811), 7–9.

22. William B. Sprague, *Annals of the American Pulpit* (New York: Robert Carter & Brothers, 1865), 8:241–46.

Chapter 1

1. In the 1820s Emerson emphasizes moral growth by learning from and participating in history. Often during this period, however, as Emerson seeks to define heroism and his own personality, he depicts the viciousness of tyrants and mobs who threaten the existence of the saint and the rebel. Gustaaf Van Cromphout shows that in the 1830s Emerson's "hero" is, in the "positive" sense, "antithetical" to society and thus discovers/makes history; in the 1840s, as hero and society become more compatible, "Emerson's Representative Men do not share his earlier heroes' independence from history." See "Emerson and the Dialectics of History," *PMLA* 91 (January 1976): 55, 57–58.

2. Lewis P. Simpson presents the development of Emerson's thought against a backdrop of "poverty, illness, and death" and of "agonizing doubts about his personality," in "Emerson's Early Thought: Institutionalism and Alienation," *The Man of Letters in New England and the South* (Baton Rouge: Louisiana State Univ. Press, 1973), 63–64. Joel Porte has interpreted Emerson's search to become a "great man" in Eriksonian terms in *Representative Man*.

3. The classic essay is Henry Nash Smith, "Emerson's Problem of Vocation: A Note on 'The American Scholar,' " *New England Quarterly* 12 (March 1939): 52–67.

4. Emerson's lifelong reluctance to give up completely on Christianity can be traced to the fact that, as David Robinson points out, "[h]e had largely identified Christianity with morality in his early years." *Apostle of Culture*, 78.

5. *Literary Transcendentalism*, chap. 4.

6. In view of Emerson's preoccupations with the threatening "mob" and his failure to win renown, Richard Lebeaux's observations on the young Thoreau apply in some degree to young Emerson's vision of militant Christianity: "Thoreau's 'military nature' may partly be attributed to his need to keep at a distance those many people by whom he felt threatened"; "military imagery gave Thoreau an opportunity to express hostility and aggressiveness, and to feel that he was 'manly' " (*Young Man Thoreau* [Amherst: Univ. of Massachusetts Press, 1977], 122).

7. Emerson's southern journey constituted a kind of Eriksonian "moratorium," an interval that permitted delay of further preaching duties and a chance to reflect on the tangle of personal, theological, and vocational issues that fill the early journals. Richard Lebeaux argues that the postponement of commitment to a variety of American institutions and values was particularly appealing to the Transcendentalists. For the "moratorium" afforded Thoreau by the two-years' stay at Walden Pond, see *Young Man Thoreau*. See also Lebeaux's "Emerson's Young Adulthood: From Patienthood to Patiencehood," *ESQ: A Journal of the American Renaissance* 25 (Fourth Quarter 1979): 203–10.

8. Emerson's method of composing Sermon No. V yields added glimpses of autobio-

graphical and theological significance. The editors of vol. 3 of *JMN* observe that "although Emerson wrote down many an idea for a sermon in his journals, as time went on he wrote the sermons independently," and that the sermons are "different versions of his journals—structured, more formal, prepared for a live audience, but still the embodiment of what he was thinking from day to day" (ix). Sermon No. V includes two long journal entries and a short one composed over a seven-month period; the longer passages were carefully revised and significantly expanded when adapted to the sermon. The remaining two-thirds of the sermon was written just before it was first delivered. The composition suggests, then, a fusion of relatively spontaneous journal entries and substantial "independent" material in the final product.

9. Emerson's condescending criticism of middle-class values of improvement, progress, and materialism, while it ostensibly yearns for a kind of Calvinist moral toughness, suggests by its generality the kind of vague sentimentalism Ann Douglas shows evolved in the nineteenth century in a ministry bereft of real power and needing to redefine its sphere of authority. See *The Feminization of American Culture* (New York: Alfred A. Knopf, 1977).

10. *Literary Transcendentalism*, 109.

11. *William Ellery Channing: Selected Writings*, ed. David Robinson (New York: Paulist Press, 1985), 135.

12. Because Emerson had "committed" himself to a respectable career, one cannot strictly term the period of his ministry a "moratorium." But it is wrong to view the period of Emerson's ministry as a time of self-repression. While Emerson never rested easy with his vocation, Unitarian theology was flexible enough that he never had to commit himself fully to firm doctrinal positions; it is significant that before he opted for the freedom of the European trip in December 1832, he forced the issue of the Lord's Supper on a congregation willing to compromise to avoid contention (*Life* 160–61).

13. Channing's Jesus also "looked forward to the accomplishment of his design"; "this calm, unshaken anticipation of distant and unbounded triumphs, are remarkable traits, throwing a tender and solemn grandeur over our Lord, and wholly inexplicable by human principles, or by the circumstances in which he was placed" (*Selected Writings* 136).

14. Joel Porte rightly calls attention to the "severity" of expression in this journal entry, a severity "perhaps surprising" to the reader acquainted only with the great essays (*Representative Man*, 169). Sermon No. V, however, is ultimately less important as a revelation of Emerson's gloomy private assessment of human nature than for the triumphant depiction of Jesus, with whose final victory Emerson clearly identifies.

15. David Porter comments on the importance of personae in Emerson's sermons and later, in *Emerson and Literary Change* (Cambridge: Harvard Univ. Press, 1978), 189–205.

16. Arthur C. McGiffert, Jr., edits Sermon No. LXXVI, "The Authority of Jesus," in *YES* (90–98), and cites a variety of references to Jesus in other Emerson sermons (233–35).

17. *Representative Man*, 76.

18. David Robinson fully traces the ways in which Emerson absorbed Jesus into broader patterns of "moral inspiration" and "self-culture," in *Apostle of Culture*, 22–25, 55–60.

19. Carol Johnston discusses the address as a jeremiad in "The Underlying Structure of the Divinity School Address: Emerson as Jeremiah," *Studies in the American Renaissance 1980*, ed. Joel Myerson (Boston: Twayne, 1980), 41–49.

Chapter 2

1. Bailey, "The Effect of Character on Ministerial Usefulness," *Christian Examiner* 2 (May and June 1825): 161–62. The *Christian Examiner* is frequently cited in this study as a benchmark for Unitarian views on issues that concerned Emerson. O. B. Frothingham observed that many leading Unitarian clergymen contributed to the periodical, "often, and at length, giving their best work to it, and elaborating for it their ripest ideas. The *Examiner* was, on the whole, a perfect representative of the body—broad, free, elastic, undogmatical, unecclesiastical, literary." *Boston Unitarianism, 1820–1850: A Study of the Life and Work of Nathaniel Langdon Frothingham* (New York: G. P. Putnam's Sons, 1890), 206.

2. J. William T. Youngs, Jr., *God's Messengers: Religious Leadership in Colonial New England, 1700–1750* (Baltimore: The Johns Hopkins Univ. Press, 1976), 138.

3. Daniel H. Calhoun, *Professional Lives in America: Structure and Aspiration, 1750–1850* (Cambridge: Harvard Univ. Press, 1965), 102, 107. See also James A. Henretta, *The Evolution of American Society, 1700–1815: An Interdisciplinary Analysis* (Lexington, Mass.: D. C. Heath, 1973), 210–12.

4. Scott, *From Office to Profession*, 34.

5. Timothy Dwight, *Travels in New England and New York*, ed. Barbara Miller Solomon, 4 vols. (Cambridge: Harvard Univ. Press, 1969), 4:295.

6. On the literary cultivation valued by liberal ministers, and its contribution to New England's literary renaissance, see Buell, *Literary Transcendentalism*, esp. chap. 1.

7. Dwight, *Travels*, 4:226.

8. Buckminster, *A Sermon, Delivered at the Interment of the Reverend William Emerson*, 16, 17. For an excellent overview of Buckminster's career and his extraordinary appeal, see Lawrence Buell, "Joseph Stevens Buckminster: The Making of a New England Saint," *The Canadian Review of American Studies* 10 (Spring 1979): 1–29.

9. Buell, *Literary Transcendentalism*, 46–51.

10. In the months following Emerson's resignation from the Second Church pulpit, the *Christian Examiner* featured various schemes for securing the financial health of the churches. The editors professed not to fear proposals to repeal the Third Article of the Massachusetts Bill of Rights (permitting state support of churches). But one writer complained that the "subscription" method would compromise the minister's "independence" by making him "seek the favor of man, rather than that of God"; the "pew-tax," already used in Boston with negative results, would drive away all but the well-to-do. For this writer, the fairest method was "a legal provision for supporting [the church] at the public expense." It would be "peculiarly inexpedient at the present time" to repeal the Third Article. Though believing sectarianism to be passing away, the writer insisted—invoking post-Revolutionary categories of thought—that the necessary fight against "infidelity," skepticism, and atheism ought to be seen as a *political* issue. "Defence of the Third Article," *Christian Examiner* 13 (January 1833): 355–58.

11. "Charge, by Rev. John Lathrop, D.D.," in *A Sermon, Delivered at the Ordination of the Reverend Nathaniel Langdon Frothingham, A.M. Pastor of First Church, Boston*, by Joseph McKean, LL.D. (Boston: Munroe, Francis & Parker, 1815), 30–33. Lathrop (1740–1816) was a former Calvinist and ardent Revolutionary patriot who had softened but not wholly abandoned such doctrines as the divinity of Christ and

the atonement, and believed in a literal future punishment of the unregenerate. But his emphasis on moral and spiritual truth over doctrine made him sympathetic to the liberals. On Lathrop see Sprague, *Annals of the American Pulpit*, 8:68–72.

12. Quincy, *Figures of The Past From the Leaves of Old Journals* (Boston: Roberts Brothers, 1883), 303–4.

13. Conway, *Autobiography, Memories and Experiences*, 2 vols. (Boston: Houghton Mifflin, 1904), 2:49.

14. Dewey, "On Clerical Duties; and Particularly on Some Misapprehensions of Their Importance," *Christian Examiner* 5 (March and April 1828): 103. Dewey invited Waldo to preach in his New Bedford pulpit not only before Emerson's ordination and during his ministry but also after he left Second Church. They were always cordial, Dewey having shared his books with Emerson during the latter's formative years. When Dewey accepted a pastorate in New York in 1833 he hoped in vain that his untethered friend would succeed him in New Bedford.

15. Richard Mather and William Tompson, for example, wrote impatiently to their brethren in England: "[I]f you harden your hearts, and refuse to hearken to the gracious call of the Lord, your damnation is just, your bloud will be upon your own heads: you have been warned and warned again and again, by many worthy Ministers and messengers of God." *An Heart-Melting Exhortation* (London: Printed by A. M. for I. Rothwell, 1650), 28–29.

16. Buckminster, "Sermon XIV," *Sermons by the late Rev. J. S. Buckminster. With a Memoir of His Life and Character* (Boston: John Eliot, 1814), 232–34. Emerson borrowed this work from the Boston Library Society on at least three occasions, as early as 23 April 1818, and he encountered it later as part of "Dr. Channing's Course of Study for Students in Divinity." See *JMN*, 3:354–55.

17. Ware, "The Connection between the Duties of the Pulpit and the Pastoral Office," *The Works of Henry Ware, Jr., D.D.*, 4 vols. (Boston: James Munroe and Company, 1846–47), 2:178, 186–87.

18. See Robinson, *Apostle of Culture*, esp. 30–35.

19. Boston *Daily Evening Transcript*, 18 September 1830, p. 1, col. 2.

20. Boston *Daily Evening Transcript*, 1 October 1830, p. 2, col. 1.

21. Dewey, "Dignity of the Clerical Office," *Christian Examiner* 12 (July 1832): 351, 350.

22. Channing, *The Works of William E. Channing, D.D.*, Twelfth Complete Edition (Boston: Crosby, Nichols, and Company, 1853), 3:258.

23. This strategy of reappropriating the moral dangers of olden times for a too-familiar secular age became a staple of Transcendentalist rhetoric. Thus, for example, could Thoreau invest his own experience with the bolder hues of the colonial period: "We have need to be as sturdy pioneers still as Myles Standish or Church. We are to follow on another trail, perhaps, but one as convenient for ambushes, and with not so much as a moccasin print to guide us. What if the Indians are exterminated? Do not savages as grim defile down into the clearing to-day?" See Perry Miller, *Consciousness in Concord* (Boston: Houghton Mifflin, 1958), 145.

Chapter 3

1. Porte, *Emerson and Thoreau: Transcendentalists in Conflict* (Middletown, Conn.: Wesleyan Univ. Press, 1966), 53; Santayana, "The Genteel Tradition," *Se-*

lected Critical Writings of George Santayana, ed. Norman Henfrey, 2 vols. (Cambridge, England: Cambridge Univ. Press, 1968), 2:95; Matthiessen, *American Renaissance: Art and Expression in the Age of Emerson and Whitman* (New York: Oxford Univ. Press, 1941), 112.

2. In his journal for 10 April 1642, for example, Thomas Shepard wrote: "At a sacrament, in preparation the day before thereunto, I did consider (1) Is there a God and a Christ? And somewhat of them both I saw, but yet saw need of living by faith upon God to reveal himself more evidently to me. (2) Is this God in Christ mine or no? For I knew it was my duty so to examine myself as to bring my thoughts unto an issue one way or other. And so I saw on the one side there were those things made me doubt most of my sonship." *God's Plot: The Paradoxes of Puritan Piety Being the Autobiography & Journal of Thomas Shepard*, ed. Michael McGiffert (Amherst: Univ. of Massachusetts Press, 1972), 169–70.

3. Wright, *The Beginnings of Unitarianism in America*, 158–59.

4. Reid, *Christian Apologetics* (Grand Rapids, Mich.: William B. Eerdmans Publishing, 1970), 154–56.

5. *Christian Apologetics*, 156–57.

6. Letter to Dr. Morse, 24 April 1799. Eliza Buckminster Lee, *Memoirs of Rev. Joseph Buckminster, D.D., and of His Son, Rev. Joseph Stevens Buckminster* (Boston: Wm. Crosby and H. P. Nichols, 1849), 322–23.

7. Quoted in H. Shelton Smith, *Changing Conceptions of Original Sin: A Study in American Theology Since 1750* (New York: Charles Scribner's Sons, 1955), 75–76.

8. *The Liberal Christian*, vol. 1, no. 4 (14 March 1823): 27.

9. Green, review of Lant Carpenter, *A Harmony of the Gospels*, *Christian Examiner* 10 (July 1831): 361–62.

10. See Howe, *Unitarian Conscience*, chaps. 3 and 4, and Barbara Packer, "Origin and Authority: Emerson and the Higher Criticism," *Reconstructing American Literary History*, ed. Sacvan Bercovitch (Cambridge: Harvard Univ. Press, 1986), 67–92. Karen Kalinevitch demonstrates Emerson's familiarity with European Higher Critics such as Eichhorn, Gieseler, and Schleiermacher, and provides edited texts, in "Turning from the Orthodox: Emerson's Gospel Lectures," *Studies in the American Renaissance 1986*, ed. Joel Myerson (Charlottesville: Univ. Press of Virginia, 1986), 69–112.

11. On Transcendentalist implications of the concept of evidence, see Michael J. Colacurcio, "A Better Mode of Evidence—The Transcendental Problem of Faith and Spirit," *Themes, Tones and Motifs in the American Renaissance*, ed. Reginald Lansing Cook (Hartford: Transcendental Books, 1969), 12–22.

12. *Literary Transcendentalism*, 34, 36. The Unitarian desire for internal, spiritual evidence could lead to strange shows of willed vacuousness and obscurantism, and posturings of genteel world-weariness. An unidentified reviewer, finding Sampson Reed's *Observations on the Growth of the Mind* garbled, parodied this gullibility: "There is throughout a high tone of moral and religious feeling, amounting almost to enthusiasm, which we like. Even when we cannot entirely go along with it, or fully understand it, we like it. It is refreshing to a mind, wearied out by intercourse with a world like this, to find that we can dream at least of a better state of things." *Christian Examiner* 3 (September and October 1826): 418.

13. Howe, *Unitarian Conscience*, 84.

14. Buckminster, *Sermons*, 22–23.

15. Eliot, review of Gulian C. Verplanck, *Essays on the Nature and Uses of the Various Evidences of Revealed Religion*, *Christian Examiner* 2 (March and April 1825): 128.

16. Channing, *Selected Writings*, 124, 128, 129, 143. Ironically, Channing was later accused by Orville Dewey of giving fuel to the enemies of Unitarianism by stressing *reason* in "Christianity a Rational Religion." Dewey stressed that "revelation is founded on human nature," a belief he felt Channing certainly shared but was not careful enough to emphasize. Review of "Dr. Channing's *Writings*," *Christian Examiner* 14 (March 1833): 73–74.

17. The immediate occasion of Ware's criticism was probably Emerson's Sermon No. XXVIII. Preaching on 15 March, Emerson had charged that the minister "has very low & humble views of this office who satisfies his conscience with uttering the commonplaces of religion for twenty or thirty minutes, reciting a lazy miscellany of quotations from Scripture & then dismisses his unfed unedified audience, hugging himself that he has not spoken an offensive syllable, & that he has come off so cheaply from his Sabbath work." In his letter to Ware he had continued: "All I meant . . . was to say that my views of a preacher's duties were very high & he sh'd be ashamed of so shabby a discharge of them as who has not witnessed in numberless written & printed sermons that are nothing but a patch-work of unchosen texts."

18. In his journal two years before he first delivered Sermon No. XLIII, Emerson recorded seeing such an experiment (*JMN* 3:93).

19. *Apostle of Culture*, 77.

20. Coleridge, in *Aids to Reflection* (1825), had already dismissed the evidential school of Paley as an ineffective response to Hume: "I more than fear the prevailing taste for books of Natural Theology, Physico-Theology, Demonstrations of God from Nature, Evidences of Christianity, and the like. EVIDENCES OF CHRISTIANITY: I am weary of the word. Make a man feel his WANT of it, and you can safely trust to its own Evidence—remembering only the express declaration of Christ Himself: No man cometh to Me unless the Father leadeth him." Quoted in Avery Dulles, *A History of Apologetics* (New York: Corpus, 1971), 169.

Even the *Christian Examiner* gave Paley mixed reviews. Convers Francis admitted that Paley lacked the eloquence of Buckminster but thought him still the best guide to the Christian evidences (review of *Sermons on Various Subjects*, 5 [March and April 1828]: 127). Samuel Edmund Sewall praised Paley's unostentatious style and recommended his *Natural Theology* as a means "to relieve the doubts" of youth; but Sewall raised an increasingly heard complaint, that *Moral Philosophy* "rests moral obligation on utility," which "encourage[s] a very dangerous casuistry, especially in immature minds" (review of *Natural Theology*, 6 [July 1829]: 392–93). George Ripley claimed to rate Paley "as highly as any one," but decried his moral emphasis on "expediency" and "self-interest" ("Degerando on Self-education," 9 [September 1830]: 73). Indeed, by 1832 James Walker, in welcoming Latham Wainewright's *A Vindication of Dr. Paley's Theory of Morals*, lamented that "[i]t has been so much the fashion, of late years, to decry Paley's doctrine of expediency" that colleges were finding it difficult to justify using Paley as a text (13 [November 1832]: 187).

21. *Apostle of Culture*, 62.

22. *Apostle of Culture*, 44.

23. A rather conventional definition of Emmanuel appears in *The Liberal Christian* on 5 July 1823: "THE NAME EMMANUEL. Matt. 1.23. This name, as it occurs Isai. vii.14. is given to a child, born soon after the prediction of his birth was delivered, because he was a sign that God would be with his people to save them from their enemies who invaded their country, verse 16. As given to Jesus, it can only prove that through him God is with men, as by him he revealed his truth and communicated the riches of his grace" (1, no. 11:83).

Emerson apparently borrowed his variation ("this life within life, this literal Emmanuel *God within us*") from a letter or journal entry for 17 December 1827 (see *J* 2:225).

24. *Christian Examiner* 10 (March 1831): 30–32.

25. Ware granted the "unspeakable value" of the internal evidences but argued that to claim "for them an exclusive authority, to the detriment of the evidence of facts, and to the contempt of the original history" is to rest "on no basis more solid than the reveries or reasonings of the self-confiding mind." "The Divine Government.— Miracles," *Works* 3:62.

26. Emerson's remark is not an isolated piece of daydreaming. Cf. W. B. O. Peabody: "Feeling that we are immortal, we shall not set our hearts on perishing things, to be answerable when we leave them. Feeling that we are immortal, we shall not look on death as a passing away from life, nor as the beginning of any new existence." "Retribution," *Christian Examiner* 8 (July 1830): 395. Unitarians clung to this Christian promise, avoiding morbidity by stressing the need for moral action as the best preparation. See [Anon.], "Erroneous Views of Death," *Christian Examiner* 2 (May and June 1825): 178–85; and Orville Dewey, "Erroneous Views of Death," *Christian Examiner* 9 (November 1830): 165.

27. *Freedom and Fate*, 11–12.

28. Ware, "The Difficulties of the Bible," *Works* 3:365, 368–69.

29. William Emerson, *A Sermon, Preached at the Ordination of the Rev. Robinson Smiley*, 9; Delbanco, *William Ellery Channing: An Essay on the Liberal Spirit in America* (Cambridge: Harvard Univ. Press, 1981), 114.

30. Norton, *The Evidences of the Genuineness of the Gospels* (1837–44), Abridged Edition (Boston: American Unitarian Association, 1871), 335. The reference is to 1 Corinthians 2:14, the text of Emerson's Sermon No. CXXI.

31. *Evidences*, 413.

32. Walker, review of Charles P. M'Ilvaine, *The Evidences of Christianity in their External Division*, *Christian Examiner* 14 (May 1833): 195, 198.

33. Dewey, *Autobiography and Letters of Orville Dewey, D.D.*, ed. Mary E. Dewey (Boston: Roberts Brothers, 1883), 61–62. See also Dewey's "On the Nature, and Proper Evidences of a Revelation," *Christian Examiner* 26 (May 1839): 222–46.

34. Allen, *Our Liberal Movement in Theology* (Boston: Roberts Brothers, 1882), 67.

35. Peabody, *Reminiscences of Rev. Wm. Ellery Channing, D.D.* (Boston: Roberts Brothers, 1880), 375, 376–77. On the controversial question of whether Channing was a Transcendentalist, David P. Edgell argues that Channing inclined in that direction as preferable to "the traditional evidences of Christianity." *William Ellery Channing: An Intellectual Portrait* (Boston: Beacon Press, 1955), 69.

36. *Christian Examiner* 25 (November 1838): 268.

Chapter 4

1. For background, see Jerry Wayne Brown, *The Rise of Biblical Criticism in America, 1800–1870: The New England Scholars* (Middletown, Conn.: Wesleyan Univ. Press, 1969). Julie Ellison observes that Waldo "never had much taste for Biblical scholarship," and in her fine discussion of "The Lord's Supper" she shows that he used it "eclectically" (*Emerson's Romantic Style* [Princeton, N.J.: Princeton Univ.

Press, 1984], 43, 62). Karen Kalinevitch reveals, however, that he was certainly familiar with, and capable of, sustained biblical criticism ("Turning from the Orthodox").

2. Gura's *The Wisdom of Words: Language, Theology, and Literature in the New England Renaissance* (Middletown, Conn.: Wesleyan Univ. Press, 1981) is the best study of Unitarian theories of language and their implications for the American Renaissance.

3. Liebman, "Emerson's Transformation in the 1820's," *American Literature* 40 (May 1968): 133–54, and "The Development of Emerson's Theory of Rhetoric, 1821–1836," *American Literature* 41 (May 1969): 178–206; Gura, *Wisdom of Words*, 104; Ellison, *Emerson's Romantic Style*, 4, 50–51.

4. Emerson, of course, came to locate types not in Scripture but in nature, as metaphors and symbols of spiritual truths. See Charles Feidelson, Jr., *Symbolism and American Literature* (Chicago: Univ. of Chicago Press, 1953).

5. William Ellery Channing went so far as to argue "that our chief hopes of an improved literature, rest on our hopes of an improved religion," and he blamed Calvinism for our lack of progress in this regard: "It wraps the Divine nature and human nature in impenetrable gloom. It overlays Christianity with technical, arbitrary dogmas" ("National Literature," *Christian Examiner* 7 [January 1830]: 291).

6. Hopkins, *A Treatise on the Millennium* (Boston: Printed by Isaiah Thomas and Ebenezer T. Andrews, 1793), 11, 13.

7. Buckminster, "Sermon XIV," *Sermons*, 239–40.

8. Here and elsewhere, Emerson echoes the sentiments W. B. O. Peabody was expressing in the *Christian Examiner* in the same month Emerson first preached this sermon. "Strong and highly colored figures," Peabody complained, "are taken from the Old Testament, and applied to the revelations of Christianity, with which they have no concern." David, for example, speaks in language representing "the savage character of the age in which it was spoken." Moreover, the "misery" Calvinists converted into doctrine "is a natural and inseparable consequence of sin, not a judgment sent directly down by the Almighty." To believe so is to shirk our obligation to grow in "character" ("Injudicious Use of the Old Testament," *Christian Examiner* 9 [September 1830]: 63, 64, 67). For an earlier discussion of scriptural figural language, see Warren Burton, "The New Creation of the Gospel," *Christian Examiner* 1 (July and August 1824): 257–62.

9. See Robert Lee Stuart, "Jonathan Edwards at Enfield: 'And Oh the Cheerfulness and Pleasantness. . .' " *American Literature* 48 (March 1976): 46–59.

10. "National Literature," 269.

11. Emerson was not the first to regard the sacraments not as supernaturally fixed forms but as strictly mediatory. Indeed, Orville Dewey, who later regretted Emerson's public "reason" for resigning his pulpit, declared that "the rite of the Lord's supper is a language; it is a symbolical language, and nothing else. It is simply and only a means of conveying certain ideas to the mind, and of awakening correspondent emotions in the heart. . . . [T]hese symbols are a showing forth, an emblematic communication of these facts" ("The Rite of the Lord's Supper a Symbolical Language," *Christian Examiner* 5 [May and June 1828]: 204). See also Dan Vogel, "Orville Dewey on Emerson's 'The Lord's Supper,' " *ESQ* 31 (Second Quarter 1963): 40–42.

12. Packer, *Emerson's Fall: A New Interpretation of the Major Essays* (New York: Continuum, 1982), 1. Feidelson believed that "Emerson could never feel the potential disunity of thought, word, and object as a tragic dilemma; this was Melville's discovery" (*Symbolism and American Literature* 160). But Joseph G. Kronick argues that Emerson found that "language takes us away from, rather than toward, truth," the

Nature/language gap in *Nature* being a surprisingly short step from the nihilism of Melville's *Pierre* (*American Poetics of History: From Emerson to the Moderns* [Baton Rouge: Louisiana State Univ. Press, 1984], 25). Similarly, Evan Carton views language in *Nature* not only as "the mediator" between nature and spirit but also as "the original mark of that division" (*The Rhetoric of American Romance: Dialectic and Identity in Emerson, Dickinson, Poe, and Hawthorne* [Baltimore: The Johns Hopkins Univ. Press, 1985], esp. 25–36, 78–82).

13. See Gura, *Wisdom of Words,* 85.

14. Emerson thought Buckminster singularly eloquent in addressing the mourner (*JMN* 3:194).

15. "Difficulties in Parishes," *Christian Examiner* 9 (September 1830): 1–20.

16. "Stuart and Whitman," *Christian Examiner* 10 (March 1831): 124, 128–29.

17. "Religion in France," *Christian Examiner* 10 (July 1831): 291.

18. "The Way of Truth and Union," *Christian Examiner* 10 (May 1831): 263, 270.

19. "Religious Controversy," *Christian Examiner* 6 (May 1829): 241, 243, 249. Even the forthright Greenwood was not above the common Unitarian ploy of following a subtle polemic with a disavowal of disputatious spirit. He concluded one lively argument thus: "We have spoken in defence and apology alone. We have attacked the sincerity and piety of no sect or denomination of Christians" ("Misapprehensions of Unitarianism," *Christian Examiner* 8 [May 1830]: 146).

20. "On Reading the Scriptures," *Christian Examiner* 12 (May 1832): 141, 160. Elsewhere Dewey was emphatic that language was central to the Calvinist/Unitarian dispute over the Bible: "Let no one say, 'The question is not about words.' Indeed it *is* about words. It is about the vehicle of communication, about style, about the manner of writing. The mode of communication is the point in debate; and this includes phraseology, figures, metaphors, illustrations, allegories, arguments" ("Nature and Extent of Inspiration," *Christian Examiner* 8 [July 1830]: 390).

21. Moncure D. Conway quotes from an Emerson letter written in 1838: "Truth has already ceased to be itself if polemically said" (*Autobiography* 1:173).

22. *American Renaissance,* 115.

23. John Winthrop recorded these Antinomian "Errors": "There is a testimony of the Spirit, and voyce unto the Soule, meerely immediate, without any respect unto, or concurrence with the word"; "No Minister can teach one that is anoynted by the Spirit of Christ, more then hee knowes already" (*The Antinomian Controversy, 1636–1638: A Documentary History,* ed. David D. Hall [Middletown, Conn.: Wesleyan Univ. Press, 1968], 230, 233). Alfred Habegger has argued that the degree to which Puritan divines stressed preparation for salvation determined the degree of efficacy they placed on their sermons (see "Preparing the Soul for Christ: The Contrasting Sermon Forms of John Cotton and Thomas Hooker," *American Literature* 41 [1969]: 342–54). Following this line of thought with particular sensitivity to questions of audience, Teresa Toulouse discusses formal concerns of Emerson, as well as Cotton, Colman, and Channing, in *The Art of Prophesying: New England Sermons and the Shaping of Belief* (Athens: Univ. of Georgia Press, 1987). She does not, however, note three of my studies that bear directly on her concern with Antinomian and Unitarian aesthetic contexts of Emerson's sermons.

24. "Milton," *North American Review* 47 (July 1838): 64. Emerson's essay joins a long tradition of *NAR* articles stressing the importance and uniqueness of eloquence and character in a democracy, a vision connecting Emerson to the republican values of an earlier generation. His teacher Edward Tyrrel Channing declared "the eloquence, which suited the wild rabble of the early democracies [unsuited to] these colder days

of good sense" and worried about the disruptive influence of "mere declaimers" (Review of "Ogilvie's Philosophical Essays," *NAR* 4 [March 1817]: 381, 384). Emerson's early idol Edward Everett thought the rise of "parliamentary eloquence" coincident with "the march of free principles" in England; he thought our "congressional eloquence" disreputable and argued that we should learn from our likeness to Rome about the significance of "the art of communication" to the "representative system" ("Speeches of Henry Clay," *NAR* 25 [October 1827]: 428, 430, 451, 447). Emerson's kinsman Orville Dewey thought public speaking the cement of social order. He disdained "dulness," but thinking it a mistake to wait for inspiration before an audience, he recommended Cicero, Quinctilian, and Hugh Blair as rhetorical models ("Principles of Elocution," *NAR* 29 [July 1829]: 38–67).

25. "The Christian Minister a Defender of the Gospel," *Works* 4:268–70. For Ware, this kind of "argument" included "the inexhaustible premises of nature, the affluent fountains of human affection, the character of God, the history of his providence, the declarations of his word, the promises of immortality, the destinies of the intelligent soul. These, and such as these, are sources of arguments for the pulpit, within the comprehension of all, and interesting to the affections of all."

26. Emerson's notion of impersonality, despite its obvious Romantic implications, owes much to Unitarian theories of rhetoric. Even the rather stodgy Edward T. Channing told his Harvard undergraduates that the preacher must have "free exercise of his natural powers and feelings; for with him, as with every other orator, eloquence must come from our common nature" ("Eloquence of the Pulpit.—The Preacher's Resources," *Lectures Read to the Seniors in Harvard College*, ed. Dorothy I. Anderson and Waldo W. Braden [Carbondale: Southern Illinois Univ. Press, 1968], 146).

27. "Emerson's Foreground," *Emerson Centenary Essays*, ed. Joel Myerson (Carbondale: Southern Illinois Univ. Press, 1982), 41–64.

28. Buell, "Reading Emerson for the Structures: The Coherence of the Essays," *Quarterly Journal of Speech* 58 (February 1972): 58–69. Barbara Packer describes his style: "The ambiguities, lacunae, paradoxes, and understatements with which Emerson is so generous turn the sentences of his essays into charged terminals that the reader must take the risk of connecting" (*Emerson's Fall* 6).

Chapter 5

1. Ralph L. Rusk believed that Emerson "abandon[ed] his lonely tower" for the social realm only after achieving "acceptance and success" with his earlier writings (*Life* 387). Joel Porte gave fullest expression to the old stereotype that Emerson's ideals had to await Thoreau to be put into "action," suggesting that Emerson's role as mystic was a "fantasy" that clashed with the necessity of living in the real world (*Emerson and Thoreau* 41). And Emerson's support of John Brown has been diagnosed as either an act of sudden courage or the desperate gesture of an aloof visionary for whom patriotic bloodshed was fine imagery masking real carnage. One of the most devastating critiques of Emersonian idealism in this regard is Stephen Donadio, "Emerson, Christian Identity, and the Dissolution of the Social Order," in *Art, Politics, and Will: Essays in Honor of Lionel Trilling,* ed. Quentin Anderson, Stephen Donadio, and Stephen Marcus (New York: Basic Books, 1977), 99–123.

2. *The Puritan Dilemma: The Story of John Winthrop* (Boston: Little, Brown, 1958).

3. *Religion in America* (New York: Charles Scribner's Sons, 1965), 161.

4. See Len Gougeon, "Abolition, the Emersons, and 1837," *New England Quarterly* 54 (1981): 345–64; and "Emerson and Abolition: The Silent Years, 1837–1844," *American Literature* 54 (December 1982): 560–75.

5. "The Politics of Emerson's Man-Making Words," *PMLA* 101 (January 1986): 38–56.

6. *Beginnings of Unitarianism*, 249.

7. *Boston Unitarianism*, 251.

8. *Federalist Literary Mind*, 49.

9. Ronald P. Formisano, *The Transformation of Political Culture: Massachusetts Parties, 1790s–1840s* (New York: Oxford Univ. Press, 1983), 96, 60–61, 97.

Marvin Meyers denies that the rise of Jackson heralded essentially a class struggle, suggesting that the "anti-Bank crusade" was rooted in a populist concept of republican simplicity, and noting the irony of "the Jacksonian struggle to reconcile again the simple yeoman values with the free pursuit of economic interest, just as the two were splitting hopelessly apart." *The Jacksonian Persuasion: Politics & Belief* (Stanford: Stanford Univ. Press, 1960), 12, 15. George Dangerfield stresses that political parties were hardly coalesced by the 1828 election. The voters, he argues, were offered "a choice between stereotypes, such as Aristocracy and Democracy," with neither side addressing such issues of real national concern as "free education, abolition of imprisonment for debt, a more equitable militia system, a mechanics' lien law, and, in general, . . . equality of opportunity in every sense of the term." The immediate legacy of the election of 1828 was "a Jeffersonian world in decay." *The Awakening of American Nationalism, 1815–1828* (New York: Harper & Row, 1965), 289, 290, 298–99.

10. Channing, "The Union," *Christian Examiner* 6 (May 1829): 147, 169.

11. Joseph Ellis argues that Emerson, in inheriting the Federalists' alienated impulse to withdraw from the crass corruptions of democracy, "successfully cultivated an intentional obliviousness of the social dimension of human existence and counseled others to do likewise. He was the supreme individualist." *After the Revolution: Profiles of Early American Culture* (New York: W. W. Norton, 1979), 222. On the continuity from the *Monthly Anthology* to Transcendentalism, see Lewis P. Simpson, *The Federalist Literary Mind*, 47, and *The Man of Letters*, 68–71. John F. Berens regards the providential rhetoric of Waldo Emerson's day as *Republican*, arguing that Federalist rhetoric had been discredited after the War of 1812, which the party had opposed, and that the party itself was effectively discredited after the Hartford Convention. *Providence & Patriotism in Early America, 1640–1815* (Charlottesville: Univ. Press of Virginia, 1978), 163–66.

12. William H. Pease and Jane H. Pease, *The Web of Progress: Private Values and Public Styles in Boston and Charleston, 1828–1843* (New York: Oxford Univ. Press, 1985), 11–12, 23.

13. For a case study of the previous generation's reconciling of money, culture, and virtue, see Lewis P. Simpson, "The Tudor Brothers: Boston Ice and Boston Letters," in *The Man of Letters*, 32–61. The Tudors, writes Simpson, reassured a Boston fearful of Jacobinism that "commerce makes mankind an intellectual and spiritual community" (54).

14. Ware, "The Duties of Young Men in Respect to the Dangers of the Country," *Works* 2:208–9.

15. "The Duties of Young Men," *Works* 2:214, 215, 218.

16. *Web of Progress*, 82.

17. *Web of Progress*, 108, 222.

18. *Web of Progress,* 137. Emerson's Second Church was only moderately influential in Boston politics. Between 1828 and 1836, of the 91 members of the Boston City Council with known church affiliation, "more than half were Unitarian, but only 11 worshipped at Second Church." *Web of Progress,* 291, n. 24.

Still, Emerson's very entry into study for the ministry was largely inspired, according to Mary Cayton, by a desire to inculcate virtues fostered by the private individual in opposition to a dangerous, "perverse" democracy. In positing "conscience" as the wise alternative to "popular opinion," "Emerson thought he was building on the principles of his Federalist childhood." " 'Sympathy's Electric Chain' and the American Democracy: Emerson's First Vocational Crisis," *New England Quarterly* 55 (March 1982): 23.

19. Noting Emerson's responsiveness to economic conditions, Michael T. Gilmore observes that Emerson's early "ideal of self-reliance from the agrarian or Jeffersonian past" became most "antimarket" during the depression of 1837–1843. "Emerson's own tendencies toward Idealism," Gilmore shows, "were strengthened by the Crash of 1837," though in his later, more affluent years he would *celebrate* wealth. *American Romanticism and the Marketplace* (Chicago: Univ. of Chicago Press, 1985), 19, 24.

We have seen that, during his ministry, Emerson was not, like the Jacksonians, endorsing a Jeffersonian yeoman ideal. He had made fundamental accommodations to the commercial order of Boston, while preaching republican virtues as a basis of civic order.

20. Like the Puritans, Emerson insisted that we learn to love the world with "weaned affections." He accepted the principle, however, that "property" and "Commerce" are essential to satisfy our "animal wants" (Sermon No. 169). The Puritan background of Emerson's concept of works is discussed in the next chapter. For a related study, see my "Thoreau and the Puritan Ethic," *New England Journal of Business & Economics* 2 (Fall 1975): 33–42.

21. *American Renaissance,* 4. The Peases quote a sentiment remarkably like Emerson's—dating from the early days of his preaching—by Nathan Appleton, who wrote to the Rev. Ezra Stiles Gannett that "there was 'no purer morality' than that of 'the counting room.' " Letter of 24 January 1828, quoted in *Web of Progress,* 219–20.

22. Ware, *Works* 2:182, 350.

23. "Religious Feeling," *Christian Examiner* 2 (March and April 1825): 94.

24. "The Orator and His Times," *Lectures,* 5, 7, 10.

25. Edward T. Channing believed in "the necessity of a wise and eloquent clergy in an improved age, and growing out of its improvement." The goal of preaching was not collective action (the realm of politics), "[y]et the interest is common to all, of equal moment to all," and the themes of the preacher pervade all corners of the auditors' lives. Though a religious service is a collective event, much preaching is devoted to "that most personal concern, the religious preparation of the heart," said Channing. "But we wish the preacher to be kindled by the presence of numbers like any other orator," he went on, "because there is a power in eloquence thus inspired which is sure to go to the heart." "Eloquence and the Pulpit.—Reasons for Preaching," *Lectures,* 126, 128, 130, 131–32.

26. Peabody, "The Nature and Powers of the Christian Church," *Christian Examiner* 12 (March 1832): 136.

27. *A Discourse, Delivered in Harvard, July 4, 1794 . . .* (Boston: Printed at the Apollo Press by Joseph Belknap, 1794); *Piety and Arms* (Boston: Manning & Loring, 1799).

28. See Nathan O. Hatch, *The Sacred Cause of Liberty.*

29. Sacvan Bercovitch, *The American Jeremiad* (Madison: Univ. of Wisconsin Press, 1978). See especially chap. 5.

30. E. T. Channing, "Eloquence of the Pulpit.—The Preacher and His Audience," *Lectures*, 135.

31. W. H. Channing, *Memoir of William Ellery Channing*, 9th ed., 3 vols. (Boston: American Unitarian Association, 1868), 2:3–4.

32. The Peases observe a consensual strain in Boston political rhetoric, which is mirrored in the Unitarian pulpit: "Boston politics . . . were, especially on economic issues, pragmatic. The Revolution was venerated, but revolutionary rhetoric was not. . . . Economics should not be politicized. . . . And politics should remain subservient to the community's economic well-being." Although lay power was eclipsing that of the ministry, Unitarian liberalism "encouraged innovative responses to new economic forces without at the same time threatening social or political stability." *Web of Progress*, 82, 137.

33. Emerson's prophetic stance in Sermon No. LXX was anticipated by J. S. Buckminster, who in 1809 wrote that the man of letters hoping to usher in New England's "Augustan age" must avoid the temptation to yield to "factions" or to seek "after popular favour," and must not be lured by "the minutiae of local politicks." At the same time, Buckminster called for the interests of statesmen and men of letters to be merged. For there is an "opposite temptation," he warned, for the intellectual to withdraw "in disgust" from active life. One must resist "the natural tendency of a life of retirement and contemplation to generate the notion of innocence and moral security . . . [for] in the eye of reason and of Christianity, simple unprofitableness is always a crime." Simpson, *Federalist Literary Mind*, 97, 99, 101.

34. On the American colonists' use of the classics and their understanding of republicanism, see Bernard Bailyn, *The Ideological Origins of the American Revolution* (Cambridge: Harvard Univ. Press, 1967), esp. 22–26, 281–84.

35. See Robert A. Ferguson, *Law and Letters in American Culture* (Cambridge: Harvard Univ. Press, 1984).

36. Samuel Edmund Sewall, "Indian Controversy," *Christian Examiner* 9 (September 1830): 107–60.

37. *The American Jeremiad*, esp. chaps. 5 and 6. Leonard Neufeldt traces the legacy of "Revolutionary republicanism" to Thoreau but observes that, within broad cultural consensus, "A language that on the surface appeared to reflect common assumptions and behavior, in reality could be used to report a wide variety of convictions." "Henry David Thoreau's Political Economy," *New England Quarterly* 57 (September 1984): 360. Emerson shared Thoreau's essential vision of national mission and individual rights, but by inclination, education, and profession favored the conservative version of republicanism.

38. *The American Jeremiad*, 159, 179.

Chapter 6

1. See Perry Miller's influential "From Edwards to Emerson," *New England Quarterly* 13 (December 1940): 589–617; rpt. in *Errand into the Wilderness* (New York: Harper & Row, 1956), 184–203. Miller was not the first to identify the strain of Protestant extremism in Emerson. Emerson's early biographer James Elliot Cabot saw that Transcendentalism belonged to the New England tradition of "various outbursts

of religious enthusiasm overflowing the boundaries of accredited doctrine," in *A Memoir of Ralph Waldo Emerson*, 2 vols. (Boston: Houghton Mifflin, 1887), 1:253. Vernon L. Parrington believed that Transcendentalism heralded the release of "mystical aspirations" that Puritanism had "repressed," in *Main Currents in American Thought*, 3 vols. (New York: Harcourt, Brace, 1930), 2:379.

2. See, for example, John Lydenberg's review of Edward Wagenknecht's *Ralph Waldo Emerson: Portrait of a Balanced Soul* and Jeffrey L. Duncan's *The Power and Form of Emerson's Thought*, in *American Literature* 47 (March 1975): 121–23.

3. Larzer Ziff, "The Literary Consequences of Puritanism," *ELH* 30 (September 1963): 293.

4. Orthodox Puritans had a higher toleration of spiritual anxiety than had Anne Hutchinson and her followers; indeed, the Synod of 1636–38 declared "sweete doubts" to be a part of preparation for grace. *The Antinomian Controversy*, 224.

5. Emerson's belief that the mind yearns instinctively for the Spirit resembles that of his ancestor Bulkeley: "Similitude breeds content. The soul is a spirit, and desires spirituall things." *The Gospel-Covenant; or the Covenant of Grace Opened*, 2nd ed. (London: Printed by Matthew Simmons, 1651), 195.

6. John Winthrop recorded the first "Error" of the Antinomians: "In the conversion of a sinner, which is saving and gracious, the faculties of the soule, and workings thereof, in things partaining to God, are destroyed and made to cease." The Synod proclaimed that Scripture "speaketh of the faculties of the soule, (as the understanding and the will) not as destroyed in conversion, but as changed, *Luk.* 24.45" (Hall 219).

7. Compare Emerson's "The Father is in me—I am the Father. Yet the Father is greater than I" (Sermon No. 165) with Thomas Hooker's "The childe holds the father, because the father holds him. So we hold God, because he holds us" (*The Soules Ingrafting into Christ* [London: Printed by J. H. for Andrew Crooke, 1637], 3). Cf. also John, chap. 14, and Philippians 3:9–12.

8. *The Sincere Convert* (London: Printed by Thomas Paine, for Matthew Symmons, 1640), 258.

9. Sermon No. LXXXI opens the text of Matthew 7:20—"By their fruits, ye shall know them"—a text popular with Puritans because it declares visible signs to be indexes of regeneration.

10. Hooker, *A Survey of the Summe of Church-Discipline* (London: Printed by A. M. for John Bellamy, 1648), part I, 188; "The Soules union with Christ," in *The Soules Exaltation* (London: Printed by John Haviland, for Andrew Crooke, 1638), 53. Ames, *The Marrow of Theology*, trans. from the Latin by John D. Eusden (Boston: Pilgrim Press, 1968), 302.

11. *The Puritan Origins of the American Self* (New Haven: Yale Univ. Press, 1975), 115, 125.

12. *The Imperial Self: An Essay in American Literary and Cultural History* (New York: Alfred A. Knopf, 1971), 24, 46, 54.

13. *Puritan Origins*, 175.

14. *Selected Critical Writings of George Santayana*, 1:126.

15. *The Soules Vocation or Effectuall Calling to Christ* (London: Printed by John Haviland, for Andrew Crooke, 1638), 201.

16. Bulkeley to Cotton, Department of Rare Books and Manuscripts, Boston Public Library. Quotation is by courtesy of the Trustees of the Boston Public Library.

17. Bulkeley, *The Gospel-Covenant*, 131–34; Hooker, "The Activitie of Faith: or, Abraham's Imitators," in *The Saints Dignitie, and Dutie* (London: Printed by G. D. for Francis Eglesfield, 1651), 158, 157, 163.

18. Ursula Brumm has pointed out that Emerson's rejection of Unitarianism was based upon "his reading the Bible in the radically literal manner of the Puritans." *American Thought and Religious Typology*, trans. John Hoaglund (New Brunswick, N.J.: Rutgers Univ. Press, 1970), 6.

19. Lawrence Buell notes that "one of Unitarianism's chief weapons against Orthodoxy was a strategy of redefinition by appealing to essence." *Literary Transcendentalism*, 114.

Karl Keller has traced Emerson's evolving metaphysics through what he sees as a "melting" of Christian typology into Transcendental ideas by the use of "conceit" and "metaphor." "From Christianity to Transcendentalism: A Note on Emerson's Use of the Conceit," *American Literature* 39 (March 1967): 94–98.

20. M. H. Abrams treats primarily the British and continental aspects of Romanticism's appropriation and transformation of Christian metaphysics in *Natural Supernaturalism: Tradition and Revolution in Romantic Literature* (New York: W. W. Norton, 1971).

21. Randall Stewart accuses Emerson of a Romantic "Nature-worship" that confuses itself with "God-worship": "The basic theological error here is the confusion of the Creator with the Thing Created." *American Literature & Christian Doctrine* (Baton Rouge: Louisiana State Univ. Press, 1958), 44–45.

However, Joe Lee Davis, in distinguishing between "Enthusiastic" and "Mystical" sensibilities, implicitly shed different light on Emerson's attitude toward nature. Enthusiasts, Davis observed, inclined toward "a kind of emotional Deism, a pantheism so crudely stamped with the pathetic fallacy that it would have made a Ruskin weep," while Mystics (with whom he associates "the orthodox Puritans") looked at nature more rationally. Although scholars do not now generally term the Puritan mind "mystical," Davis's distinction is useful: Emerson, despite his famous enthusiastic pronouncements, was clearly aware of the danger of nature-worship and, in this sense, "orthodox" in his uses of nature. Davis, "Mystical Versus Enthusiastic Sensibility," *Journal of the History of Ideas* 4 (June 1943): 301–19.

22. Ward, "Emerson and 'The Educated Will': Notes on the Process of Conversion," *ELH* 34 (1967): 506, 511. Lawrence Buell also has noted that in the later essays, as Emerson's tone becomes more personal and cozy, his concept of the poet changes from one of active imagination to "a mere medium (though a glorious one)." *Literary Transcendentalism*, 290.

23. *The Correspondence of Emerson and Carlyle*, ed. Joseph Slater (New York: Columbia Univ. Press, 1964), 326–27.

Chapter 7

1. Peabody, "Emerson as Preacher," 146.

2. A year and a day after the execution of John Brown, Thoreau argued with Walcott and Staples whether or not Brown had been right. When the two others said Brown should not have risked his life, Thoreau asked whether "Christ did not foresee that he would be crucified if he preached such doctrines as he did. . . . Of course, they as good as said that, if Christ *had* foreseen that he would be crucified, he would have 'backed out.' Such are the principles and the logic of the mass of men." *The Writings of Henry David Thoreau*, ed. Bradford Torrey (Boston: Houghton Mifflin, 1906), 20:291–92.

3. Cf. his lament in the Divinity School Address: "The Puritans in England and America, found in the Christ of the Catholic Church, and in the dogmas inherited from Rome, scope for their austere piety, and their longings for civil freedom. But their creed is passing away, and none arises in its room" (*CW* 1:88).

4. Charles had become a member of Second Church on 26 July 1829, four and a half months after Waldo's ordination. See Second Church Records, vol. 9, Massachusetts Historical Society.

Sanford E. Marovitz emphasizes Charles's importance as personal and intellectual "confidant" to Waldo, in "Emerson's Shakespeare: From Scorn to Apotheosis," *Emerson Centenary Essays*, 130–32. For a less complimentary view of Charles, see John McAleer, *Ralph Waldo Emerson: Days of Encounter* (Boston: Little, Brown, 1984), 222–27.

Epilogue

1. Clifford Dillhunt, of Madison, Wis.

2. Edward E. Chielens, ed., *American Literary Magazines: The Eighteenth and Nineteenth Centuries* (Westport, Conn.: Greenwood Press, 1986), 104–5.

3. Edward Augustus Horton, *Ralph Waldo Emerson: His services as minister of the Second Church, and his qualities as a Religious Teacher...* (Boston: Beacon Press, [1882?]), 5.

4. Emerson himself, of course, frequently distilled the essence of truth from his own "representative men"—but to rescue them from, not for, orthodoxy. Thus he predicted the imminent popularity of Swedenborg: "He needs only to be regarded as a poet instead of a sectarian & low religious dogmatist to be read & admired for his verities" (*JMN* 5:177).

5. Cyrus A. Bartol, *Ralph Waldo Emerson, A Discourse in West Church* (Boston: A. Williams & Co., 1882), 4.

6. Frederic H. Hedge, "Memorial Address" (30 May 1882), in Joseph Henry Allen, *Our Liberal Movement in Theology*, 211–12.

7. H. L. Kleinfield, "The Structure of Emerson's Death," in *Ralph Waldo Emerson: A Profile*, ed. Carl Bode (New York: Hill and Wang, 1968), 199.

8. Kleinfield, 198.

9. See Merton M. Sealts, Jr., "Emerson as Teacher," *Emerson Centenary Essays*, ed. Joel Myerson, 180–81.

10. Woodbury, *Talks with Emerson* (New York: Horizon Press, 1970), 113.

11. Peabody, *Reminiscences of Rev. Wm. Ellery Channing*, 364–65.

12. Wolfe, from *Mauve Gloves & Madmen, Clutter & Vine* (Farrar, Straus and Giroux, 1976), in *The Modern Age*, ed. Leonard Lief and James F. Light, 4th ed. (New York: Holt, Rinehart and Winston, 1981), 431.

13. Frothingham, *Boston Unitarianism*, 242–43.

14. Leverenz, "The Politics of Emerson's Man-Making Words," 53.

15. John Weiss, *Life and Correspondence of Theodore Parker*, 2 vols. (New York: D. Appleton & Company, 1864), 1:113.

16. Cooke, rpt. "From the New England Magazine, May, 1903," in *The Emerson Centennial, May 25, 1903: Extracts from a few of the Many Tributes...* (n.p., n.d.), 3, 4.

17. Hoar, rpt. "From the address at Concord, Mass., May 25, 1903," in *The Emerson Centennial*, 8.

18. Winters, *In Defense of Reason* (New York: The Swallow Press, 1947), 279. More recently, Ormond Seavey has labeled Emerson "a slippery character," in "Emerson as Itinerant," *Emerson and His Legacy: Essays in Honor of Quentin Anderson*, ed. Stephen Donadio, Stephen Railton, and Ormond Seavey (Carbondale: Southern Illinois Univ. Press, 1986), 17.

19. Higginson, rpt. "From the Outlook, May 23, 1903," in *The Emerson Centennial*, 7.

20. Cowley, *Exile's Return* (New York: Viking Press, 1934; Viking Compass Edition, 1956), 227.

21. Dillaway, *The Gospel of Emerson* (Reading, Mass.: Newton Dillaway Books, 1939), ix.

22. Masters, *The Living Thoughts of Emerson* (London: Cassell and Company, 1947), 1.

23. Lance Morrow, "The Bishop of Our Possibilities," *Time*, 10 May 1982, 124.

24. The phrase is Peter A. Bertocci's. *Religion as Creative Insecurity* (New York: Association Press, 1958).

25. Peabody, "Emerson as Preacher," 154.

Bibliography

I. Sources

Ames, William. *The Marrow of Theology.* Trans. from the Latin by John D. Eusden. Boston: Pilgrim Press, 1968.

Bailey, Winthrop. "The Effect of Character on Ministerial Usefulness." *Christian Examiner* 2 (May and June 1825): 161–68.

Boston *Daily Evening Transcript,* 1830.

Buckminster, Joseph Stevens. *A Sermon, Delivered at the Interment of the Reverend William Emerson.* Boston: Joseph T. Buckingham, 1811.

————. *Sermons by the late Rev. J. S. Buckminster. With a Memoir of His Life and Character.* Boston: John Eliot, 1814.

Bulkeley, Peter. *The Gospel-Covenant; or the Covenant of Grace Opened.* 2nd ed. London: Printed by Matthew Simmons, 1651.

————. Manuscript correspondence with John Cotton. Department of Rare Books and Manuscripts, Boston Public Library.

Burton, Warren. "The New Creation of the Gospel." *Christian Examiner* 1 (July and August 1824): 257–62.

Channing, Edward T. *Lectures Read to the Seniors in Harvard College.* Edited by Dorothy I. Anderson and Waldo W. Braden. Carbondale: Southern Illinois Univ. Press, 1968.

————. Review of "Ogilvie's Philosophical Essays." *North American Review* 4 (March 1817): 378–408.

Channing, William Ellery. "National Literature." *Christian Examiner* 7 (January 1830): 269–95.

————. "The Union." *Christian Examiner* 6 (May 1829): 146–69.

————. *William Ellery Channing: Selected Writings.* Edited by David Robinson. New York: Paulist Press, 1985.

————. *The Works of William E. Channing, D.D.* Twelfth Complete Edition. Boston: Crosby, Nichols, and Company, 1853.

"Defence of the Third Article." *Christian Examiner* 13 (January 1833): 351–63.

Dewey, Orville. *Autobiography and Letters of Orville Dewey, D.D.* Edited by Mary E. Dewey. Boston: Roberts Brothers, 1883.

————. "Belief and Unbelief." *Christian Examiner* 7 (January 1830): 345–65.

————. "On Clerical Duties; and Particularly on Some Misapprehensions of Their Importance." *Christian Examiner* 5 (March and April 1828): 101–12.

————. "Dignity of the Clerical Office." *Christian Examiner* 12 (July 1832): 349–75.

————. "Erroneous Views of Death." *Christian Examiner* 9 (November 1830): 161–82.

————. "Nature and Extent of Inspiration." *Christian Examiner* 8 (July 1830): 362–91.

————. "On the Nature, and Proper Evidences of a Revelation." *Christian Examiner* 26 (May 1839): 222–46.

————. "Principles of Elocution." *North American Review* 29 (July 1829): 38–67.

————. "On Reading the Scriptures." *Christian Examiner* 12 (May 1832): 141–62.

————. Review of "Dr. Channing's *Writings*." *Christian Examiner* 14 (March 1833): 54–84.

————. "The Rite of the Lord's Supper a Symbolical Language." *Christian Examiner* 5 (May and June 1828): 203–8.

Dwight, Timothy. *Travels in New England and New York.* Edited by Barbara Miller Solomon. 4 vols. Cambridge: Harvard Univ. Press, 1969.

Eliot, Samuel Atkins. Review of Gulian C. Verplanck, *Essays on the Nature and Uses of the Various Evidences of Revealed Religion. Christian Examiner* 2 (March and April 1825): 127–34.

Emerson, Ralph Waldo. *The Collected Works of Ralph Waldo Emerson.* Edited by Alfred R. Ferguson et al. 4 vols. to date. Cambridge: Harvard Univ. Press, 1971–

————. *The Complete Works of Ralph Waldo Emerson.* Edited by Edward Waldo Emerson. 12 vols. Centenary Edition. Boston: Houghton Mifflin, 1903–4.

————. *The Correspondence of Emerson and Carlyle.* Edited by Joseph Slater. New York: Columbia Univ. Press, 1964.

————. *The Early Lectures of Ralph Waldo Emerson.* Edited by Stephen E. Whicher, Robert E. Spiller, and Wallace E. Williams. 3 vols. Cambridge: Harvard Univ. Press, 1959–71.

————. *The Journals and Miscellaneous Notebooks of Ralph Waldo Emerson.* Edited by William H. Gilman et al. 16 vols. Cambridge: Harvard Univ. Press, 1960–82.

————. *Journals of Ralph Waldo Emerson.* Edited by Edward Waldo Emerson and Waldo Emerson Forbes. 10 vols. Boston: Houghton Mifflin, 1909–14.

————. *The Letters of Ralph Waldo Emerson.* Edited by Ralph L. Rusk. 6 vols. New York: Columbia Univ. Press, 1939.

————. Manuscript sermons. The Houghton Library, Harvard Univ.

————. "Milton." *North American Review* 47 (July 1838): 56–73.

————. Review of *A Collection of Psalms and Hymns for Christian Worship. Christian Examiner* 10 (March 1831): 30–34.

————. *Young Emerson Speaks: Unpublished Discourses on Many Subjects.* Edited by Arthur C. McGiffert, Jr. Boston: Houghton Mifflin, 1938.

Emerson, William. *A Discourse, Delivered in Harvard, July 4, 1794. . . .* Boston: Printed at the Apollo Press by Joseph Belknap, 1794.

———. *An Historical Sketch of the First Church in Boston.* Boston: Munroe & Francis, 1812.

———. *Piety and Arms: A Sermon, Preached at the Request of the Ancient and Honourable Artillery Company.* Boston: Manning & Loring, 1799.

———. *A Sermon, Delivered March 2, 1803, at the Ordination of the Rev. Thomas Beede.* Amherst, N.H.: Joseph Cushing, 1803.

———. *A Sermon, Preached at the Ordination of the Rev. Robinson Smiley.* Windsor, Vt.: Nahum Mower, 1801.

"Erroneous Views of Death." *Christian Examiner* 2 (May and June 1825): 178–85.

Everett, Edward. "Speeches of Henry Clay." *North American Review* 25 (October 1827): 425–51.

Francis, Convers. Review of William Paley, *Sermons on Various Subjects. Christian Examiner* 5 (March and April 1828): 113–34.

Green, James Diman. Review of Lant Carpenter, *A Harmony of the Gospels. Christian Examiner* 10 (July 1831): 358–84.

Greenwood, F. W. P. "Misapprehensions of Unitarianism." *Christian Examiner* 8 (May 1830): 133–46.

———. "Religious Controversy." *Christian Examiner* 6 (May 1829): 241–52.

Hall, David D., ed. *The Antinomian Controversy, 1636–1638: A Documentary History.* Middletown, Conn.: Wesleyan Univ. Press, 1968.

Hooker, Thomas. *The Saints Dignitie, and Dutie.* London: Printed by G. D. for Francis Eglesfield, 1651.

———. *The Soules Exaltation.* London: Printed by John Haviland, for Andrew Crooke, 1638.

———. *The Soules Ingrafting into Christ.* London: Printed by J. H. for Andrew Crooke, 1637.

———. *The Soules Vocation or Effectuall Calling to Christ.* London: Printed by John Haviland, for Andrew Crooke, 1638.

———. *A Survey of the Summe of Church-Discipline.* London: Printed by A. M. for John Bellamy, 1648.

Hopkins, Samuel. *A Treatise on the Millennium.* Boston: Printed by Isaiah Thomas and Ebenezer T. Andrews, 1793.

Lathrop, John. "Charge, by Rev. John Lathrop, D.D.," in *A Sermon, Delivered at the Ordination of the Reverend Nathanael Langdon Frothingham, A.M. Pastor of First Church, Boston,* by Joseph McKean, LL.D. Boston: Munroe, Francis & Parker, 1815.

The Liberal Christian, 1823–24 (Brooklyn, Conn.).

Mather, Richard, and William Tompson. *An Heart-Melting Exhortation.* London: Printed by A. M. for I. Rothwell, 1650.

Norton, Andrews. *The Evidences of the Genuineness of the Gospels* (1837–44). Abridged edition. Boston: American Unitarian Association, 1871.

Peabody, W. B. O. "Injudicious Use of the Old Testament." *Christian Examiner* 9 (September 1830): 58–70.

———. "The Nature and Powers of the Christian Church." *Christian Examiner* 12 (March 1832): 125–40.

———. "Retribution." *Christian Examiner* 8 (July 1830): 392–402.

———. "The Way of Truth and Union." *Christian Examiner* 10 (May 1831): 262–72.

"Perversion of Scripture Language." *Christian Examiner* 2 (March and April 1825): 98–103.

"Religious Feeling." *Christian Examiner* 2 (March and April 1825): 94–98.

Review of Sampson Reed, *Observations on the Growth of the Mind*. *Christian Examiner* 3 (September and October 1826): 418–26.

Reviews of R. W. Emerson's Divinity School Address and of Henry Ware, Jr.'s *The Personality of the Deity*. *Christian Examiner* 25 (November 1838): 266–68.

Ripley, George. "Degerando on Self-education." *Christian Examiner* 9 (September 1830): 70–107.

———. "Religion in France." *Christian Examiner* 10 (July 1831): 273–96.

Second Church Records. Massachusetts Historical Society.

Sewall, Samuel Edmund. "Indian Controversy." *Christian Examiner* 9 (September 1830): 107–60.

———. Review of William Paley, *Natural Theology*. *Christian Examiner* 6 (July 1829): 389–93.

Shepard, Thomas. *God's Plot: The Paradoxes of Puritan Piety Being the Autobiography & Journal of Thomas Shepard*. Edited by Michael McGiffert. Amherst: Univ. of Massachusetts Press, 1972.

———. *The Sincere Convert*. London: Printed by Thomas Paine, for Matthew Symmons, 1640.

Simpson, Lewis P., ed. *The Federalist Literary Mind: Selections from the 'Monthly Anthology and Boston Review', 1803–1811*. Baton Rouge: Louisiana State Univ. Press, 1962.

Thoreau, Henry David. *The Writings of Henry David Thoreau*. Edited by Bradford Torrey. 20 vols. Boston: Houghton Mifflin, 1906.

Walker, James. "Difficulties in Parishes." *Christian Examiner* 9 (September 1830): 1–20.

———. Review of Charles P. M'Ilvaine, *The Evidences of Christianity in their External Division*. *Christian Examiner* 14 (May 1833): 181–99.

———. "Stuart and Whitman." *Christian Examiner* 10 (March 1831): 87–129.

———. "Wainewright's *Vindication of Paley*." *Christian Examiner* 13 (November 1832): 187–99.

Ware, Henry, Jr. *The Works of Henry Ware, Jr., D.D.* 4 vols. Boston: James Munroe and Company, 1846–47.

II. Secondary Works

Abrams, M. H. *Natural Supernaturalism: Tradition and Revolution in Romantic Literature*. New York: W. W. Norton, 1971.

Allen, Gay Wilson. *Waldo Emerson: A Biography*. New York: Viking, 1981.

Allen, Joseph Henry. *Our Liberal Movement in Theology*. Boston: Roberts Brothers, 1882.

Anderson, Quentin. *The Imperial Self: An Essay in American Literary and Cultural History*. New York: Alfred A. Knopf, 1971.

Bailyn, Bernard. *The Ideological Origins of the American Revolution*. Cambridge: Harvard Univ. Press, 1967.

Barone, Dennis. "James Logan and Gilbert Tennent: Enlightened Classicist Versus Awakened Evangelist." *Early American Literature* 21 (Fall 1986): 103–17.

Bartol, Cyrus A. *Ralph Waldo Emerson, A Discourse in West Church.* Boston: A. Williams & Co., 1882.

Barton, William B., Jr. *A Calendar To The Complete Edition Of the Sermons of Ralph Waldo Emerson.* Memphis: Bee Books, 1977.

Baumgartner, A. M. " 'The Lyceum is My Pulpit': Homiletics in Emerson's Early Lectures." *American Literature* 34 (January 1963): 477–86.

Bercovitch, Sacvan. *The American Jeremiad.* Madison: Univ. of Wisconsin Press, 1978.

———. *The Puritan Origins of the American Self.* New Haven: Yale Univ. Press, 1975.

Berens, John F. *Providence & Patriotism in Early America, 1640–1815.* Charlottesville: Univ. Press of Virginia, 1978.

Bertocci, Peter A. *Religion as Creative Insecurity.* New York: Association Press, 1958.

Bishop, Jonathan. *Emerson on the Soul.* Cambridge: Harvard Univ. Press, 1964.

Brown, Jerry Wayne. *The Rise of Biblical Criticism in America, 1800–1870: The New England Scholars.* Middletown, Conn.: Wesleyan Univ. Press, 1969.

Brumm, Ursula. *American Thought and Religious Typology.* Trans. John Hoaglund. New Brunswick, N.J.: Rutgers Univ. Press, 1970.

Buell, Lawrence. "Joseph Stevens Buckminster: The Making of a New England Saint." *The Canadian Review of American Studies* 10 (Spring 1979): 1–29.

———. *Literary Transcendentalism: Style and Vision in the American Renaissance.* Ithaca: Cornell Univ. Press, 1973.

———. "Reading Emerson for the Structures: The Coherence of the Essays." *Quarterly Journal of Speech* 58 (February 1972): 58–69.

Burkholder, Robert E. "Emerson, Kneeland, and the Divinity School Address." *American Literature* 58 (March 1986): 1–14.

Cabot, James Elliot. *A Memoir of Ralph Waldo Emerson,* 2 vols. Boston: Houghton Mifflin, 1887.

Calhoun, Daniel H. *Professional Lives in America: Structure and Aspiration, 1750–1850.* Cambridge: Harvard Univ. Press, 1965.

Cameron, Kenneth Walter. "History and Biography in Emerson's Unpublished Sermons (A Report of Progress and of Research Possibilities)." *Proceedings of the American Antiquarian Society* 66, pt. 2 (October 1956): 103–18; partially reprinted in *Emerson Society Quarterly* no. 12 (Third Quarter 1958): 2–9.

———. *Ralph Waldo Emerson's Reading: A Corrected Edition.* Hartford: Transcendental Books, 1962.

———. *Research Keys to the American Renaissance.* Hartford: Transcendental Books [c. 1967]; includes William Cushing, "Index to the *Christian Examiner*" (1879), 3–82, and "Index to the *North American Review*" (1878), 83–160.

Carton, Evan. *The Rhetoric of American Romance: Dialectic and Identity in Emerson, Dickinson, Poe, and Hawthorne.* Baltimore: The Johns Hopkins Univ. Press, 1985.

Cayton, Mary. " 'Sympathy's Electric Chain' and the American Democracy: Emerson's First Vocational Crisis." *New England Quarterly* 55 (March 1982): 3–24.

Channing, William Henry. *Memoir of William Ellery Channing.* 9th ed. 3 vols. Boston: American Unitarian Association, 1868.

Chielens, Edward E., ed. *American Literary Magazines: The Eighteenth and Nineteenth Centuries.* Westport, Conn.: Greenwood Press, 1986.

Clark, Harry Hayden. "Conservative and Mediatory Emphases in Emerson's Thought." In *Transcendentalism and Its Legacy*. Edited by Myron Simon and Thornton H. Parsons. Ann Arbor: Univ. of Michigan Press, 1967. Pp. 25–62.

Colacurcio, Michael J. "A Better Mode of Evidence—The Transcendental Problem of Faith and Spirit." In *Themes, Tones and Motifs in the American Renaissance*. Edited by Reginald Lansing Cook. Hartford: Transcendental Books, 1969. Pp. 12–22.

Conway, Moncure Daniel. *Autobiography, Memories and Experiences*, 2 vols. Boston: Houghton Mifflin, 1904.

Cowley, Malcolm. *Exile's Return*. New York: Viking Press, 1934. Viking Compass Edition, 1956.

Dangerfield, George. *The Awakening of American Nationalism, 1815–1828*. New York: Harper & Row, 1965.

Davis, Joe Lee. "Mystical Versus Enthusiastic Sensibility." *Journal of the History of Ideas* 4 (June 1943): 301–19.

Delbanco, Andrew. *William Ellery Channing: An Essay on the Liberal Spirit in America*. Cambridge: Harvard Univ. Press, 1981.

Dillaway, Newton. *The Gospel of Emerson*. Reading, Mass.: Newton Dillaway Books, 1939.

Donadio, Stephen. "Emerson, Christian Identity, and the Dissolution of the Social Order." In *Art, Politics, and Will: Essays in Honor of Lionel Trilling*. Edited by Quentin Anderson, Stephen Donadio, and Stephen Marcus. New York: Basic Books, 1977. Pp. 99–123.

Douglas, Ann. *The Feminization of American Culture*. New York: Alfred A. Knopf, 1977.

Dulles, Avery. *A History of Apologetics*. New York: Corpus, 1971.

Edgell, David P. *William Ellery Channing: An Intellectual Portrait*. Boston: Beacon Press, 1955.

Ellis, Joseph J. *After the Revolution: Profiles of Early American Culture*. New York: W. W. Norton, 1979.

Ellison, Julie. *Emerson's Romantic Style*. Princeton, N.J.: Princeton Univ. Press, 1984.

The Emerson Centennial, May 25, 1903: Extracts from a few of the Many Tributes . . . (n.p., n.d.).

Faust, Clarence H. "The Background of the Unitarian Opposition to Transcendentalism." *Modern Philology* 35 (February 1938): 297–324.

Feidelson, Charles, Jr. *Symbolism and American Literature*. Chicago: Univ. of Chicago Press, 1953.

Fénèlon, François de Salignac de la Motte. *Fenelon's 'Dialogues on Eloquence.'* Trans. Wilbur Samuel Howell. Princeton, N.J.: Princeton Univ. Press, 1951.

Ferguson, Robert A. *Law and Letters in American Culture*. Cambridge: Harvard Univ. Press, 1984.

Formisano, Ronald P. *The Transformation of Political Culture: Massachusetts Parties, 1790s–1840s*. New York: Oxford Univ. Press, 1983.

Frothingham, Octavius Brooks. *Boston Unitarianism, 1820–1850: A Study of the Life and Work of Nathaniel Langdon Frothingham*. New York: G. P. Putnam's Sons, 1890.

———. *Transcendentalism in New England: A History*. New York: Putnam's, 1876.

Gilmore, Michael T. *American Romanticism and the Marketplace*. Chicago: Univ. of Chicago Press, 1985.

Goen, C. C. *Revivalism and Separatism in New England, 1740–1800: Strict Congrega-*

tionalists and Separate Baptists in the Great Awakening. New Haven: Yale Univ. Press, 1962.

Gohdes, Clarence. "Some Remarks on Emerson's *Divinity School Address.*" *American Literature* 1 (March 1929): 27–31.

Gougeon, Len. "Abolition, the Emersons, and 1837." *New England Quarterly* 54 (1981): 345–64.

———. "Emerson and Abolition: The Silent Years, 1837–1844." *American Literature* 54 (December 1982): 560–75.

Gura, Philip F. *The Wisdom of Words: Language, Theology, and Literature in the New England Renaissance.* Middletown, Conn.: Wesleyan Univ. Press, 1981.

Habegger, Alfred. "Preparing the Soul for Christ: The Contrasting Sermon Forms of John Cotton and Thomas Hooker." *American Literature* 41 (1969): 342–54.

Hatch, Nathan O. *The Sacred Cause of Liberty: Republican Thought and the Millennium in Revolutionary New England.* New Haven: Yale Univ. Press, 1977.

Hedges, William L. "The Old World Yet: Writers and Writing in Post-Revolutionary America." *Early American Literature* 16 (Spring 1981): 3–18.

Henretta, James A. *The Evolution of American Society, 1700-1815: An Interdisciplinary Analysis.* Lexington, Mass.: D. C. Heath, 1973.

Horton, Edward Augustus. *Ralph Waldo Emerson: His services as minister of the Second Church, and his qualities as a Religious Teacher. A Discourse Preached in the Second Church, Boston, Sunday, April 30, 1882.* Boston: Beacon Press [1882?].

Howe, Daniel Walker. *The Unitarian Conscience: Harvard Moral Philosophy, 1805–1861.* Cambridge: Harvard Univ. Press, 1970.

Howe, John R., Jr. "Republican Thought and the Political Violence of the 1790s." *American Quarterly* 19 (Summer 1967): 147–65.

Hudson, Winthrop S. *Religion in America.* New York: Charles Scribner's Sons, 1965.

Hutchison, William R. *The Transcendentalist Ministers: Church Reform in the New England Renaissance.* New Haven: Yale Univ. Press, 1959.

Irie, Yukio. *Emerson and Quakerism.* Tokyo: Kenkyusha, 1967.

Johnston, Carol. "The Underlying Structure of the Divinity School Address: Emerson as Jeremiah." *Studies in the American Renaissance 1980.* Edited by Joel Myerson. Boston: Twayne, 1980. Pp. 41–49.

Kalinevitch, Karen. "Turning from the Orthodox: Emerson's Gospel Lectures." *Studies in the American Renaissance 1986.* Edited by Joel Myerson. Charlottesville: Univ. Press of Virginia, 1986. Pp. 69–112.

Keller, Karl. "From Christianity to Transcendentalism: A Note on Emerson's Use of the Conceit." *American Literature* 39 (March 1967): 94–98.

Kleinfield, H. L. "The Structure of Emerson's Death." *Bulletin of the New York Public Library* 65 (January 1961): 47–64; rpt. in *Ralph Waldo Emerson: A Profile.* Edited by Carl Bode. New York: Hill and Wang, 1968. Pp. 175–99.

Kronick, Joseph G. *American Poetics of History: From Emerson to the Moderns.* Baton Rouge: Louisiana State Univ. Press, 1984.

Lebeaux, Richard. "Emerson's Young Adulthood: From Patienthood to Patiencehood." *ESQ: A Journal of the American Renaissance* 25 (Fourth Quarter 1979): 203–10.

———. *Young Man Thoreau.* Amherst: Univ. of Massachusetts Press, 1977.

Lee, Eliza Buckminster. *Memoirs of Rev. Joseph Buckminster, D.D., and of His Son, Rev. Joseph Stevens Buckminster.* Boston: Wm. Crosby and H. P. Nichols, 1849.

Lee, Roland. "Emerson through Kierkegaard: Toward a Definition of Emerson's Theory of Communication." *ELH* 24 (September 1957): 229–48.

Leverenz, David. "The Politics of Emerson's Man-Making Words." *PMLA* 101 (January 1986): 38–56.

Liebman, Sheldon W. "The Development of Emerson's Theory of Rhetoric, 1821–1836." *American Literature* 41 (May 1969): 178–206.

———. "Emerson's Transformation in the 1820's." *American Literature* 40 (May 1968): 133–54.

Loving, Jerome. "Emerson's Foreground." *Emerson Centenary Essays.* Edited by Joel Myerson. Carbondale: Southern Illinois Univ. Press, 1982. Pp. 41–64.

Lydenberg, John. Review of *Ralph Waldo Emerson: Portrait of a Balanced Soul,* by Edward Wagenknecht, and *The Power and Form of Emerson's Thought,* by Jeffrey L. Duncan. *American Literature* 47 (March 1975): 121–23.

McAleer, John. *Ralph Waldo Emerson: Days of Encounter.* Boston: Little, Brown, 1984.

Marovitz, Sanford E. "Emerson's Shakespeare: From Scorn to Apotheosis." *Emerson Centenary Essays.* Edited by Joel Myerson. Carbondale: Southern Illinois Univ. Press, 1982. Pp. 122–55.

Masters, Edgar Lee. *The Living Thoughts of Emerson.* London: Cassell and Company, 1947.

Matthiessen, F. O. *American Renaissance: Art and Expression in the Age of Emerson and Whitman.* New York: Oxford Univ. Press, 1941.

Meyers, Marvin. *The Jacksonian Persuasion: Politics & Belief.* Stanford: Stanford Univ. Press, 1960.

Miller, Perry. *Consciousness in Concord.* Boston: Houghton Mifflin, 1958.

———. "From Edwards to Emerson." *New England Quarterly* 13 (December 1940): 589–617; rpt. in *Errand into the Wilderness.* New York: Harper & Row, 1956. Pp. 184–203.

———. *The Life of the Mind in America from the Revolution to the Civil War.* New York: Harcourt, Brace & World, 1965.

Morgan, Edmund S. *The Puritan Dilemma: The Story of John Winthrop.* Boston: Little, Brown, 1958.

Morrow, Lance. "The Bishop of Our Possibilities." *Time.* 10 May 1982, p. 124.

Mott, Wesley T. "Emerson and Thoreau as Heirs to the Tradition of New England Puritanism." Ph.D. dissertation, Boston Univ., 1975.

———. "Thoreau and the Puritan Ethic." *New England Journal of Business & Economics* 2 (Fall 1975): 33–42.

Nash, Gary B. "The American Clergy and the French Revolution." *William and Mary Quarterly* 3rd Series, 22 (July 1965): 392–412.

Neufeldt, Leonard. " 'The Fields of My Fathers' and Emerson's Literary Vocation." *American Transcendental Quarterly* no. 31 (Summer 1976): 3–9.

———. "Henry David Thoreau's Political Economy." *New England Quarterly* 57 (September 1984): 359–83.

———. *The House of Emerson.* Lincoln: Univ. of Nebraska Press, 1982.

Packer, Barbara L. *Emerson's Fall: A New Interpretation of the Major Essays.* New York: Continuum, 1982.

———. "Origin and Authority: Emerson and the Higher Criticism." *Reconstructing American Literary History.* Edited by Sacvan Bercovitch. Cambridge: Harvard Univ. Press, 1986. Pp. 67–92.

Parrington, Vernon L. *Main Currents in American Thought.* 3 vols. New York: Harcourt, Brace and Company, 1930.

Peabody, Elizabeth Palmer. "Emerson as Preacher." *The Genius and Character of Emerson.* Edited by F. B. Sanborn. Boston: Houghton Mifflin, 1898. Pp. 146–72.

———. *Reminiscences of Rev. Wm. Ellery Channing, D.D.* Boston: Roberts Brothers, 1880.

Pease, William H., and Jane H. Pease. *The Web of Progress: Private Values and Public Styles in Boston and Charleston, 1828–1843.* New York: Oxford Univ. Press, 1985.

Pettit, Norman. *The Heart Prepared: Grace and Conversion in Puritan Spiritual Life.* New Haven: Yale Univ. Press, 1966.

Pommer, Henry F. "The Contents and Basis of Emerson's Belief in Compensation." *PMLA* 77 (June 1962): 248–53.

Porte, Joel. *Emerson and Thoreau: Transcendentalists in Conflict.* Middletown, Conn.: Wesleyan Univ. Press, 1966.

———. *Representative Man: Ralph Waldo Emerson in His Time.* New York: Oxford Univ. Press, 1979.

Porter, David. *Emerson and Literary Change.* Cambridge: Harvard Univ. Press, 1978.

Quincy, Josiah. *Figures of The Past From the Leaves of Old Journals.* Boston: Roberts Brothers, 1883.

Railton, Stephen. "Seeing and Saying: The Dialectic of Emerson's Eloquence." In *Emerson and His Legacy: Essays in Honor of Quentin Anderson.* Edited by Stephen Donadio, Stephen Railton, and Ormond Seavey. Carbondale: Southern Illinois Univ. Press, 1986. Pp. 48–65.

Reid, J. K. S. *Christian Apologetics.* Grand Rapids, Mich.: William B. Eerdmans Publishing Company, 1970.

Reynolds, David S. "From Doctrine to Narrative: The Rise of Pulpit Storytelling in America." *American Quarterly* 32 (Winter 1980): 479–98.

Richardson, Robert D., Jr. *Myth and Literature in the American Renaissance.* Bloomington: Indiana Univ. Press, 1978.

Roberson, Susan L. "The Private Voice behind the Public Text: Two Emerson Sermons." *ESQ: A Journal of the American Renaissance* 32 (Third Quarter 1986): 173–82.

Robinson, David. *Apostle of Culture: Emerson as Preacher and Lecturer.* Philadelphia: Univ. of Pennsylvania Press, 1982.

Rusk, Ralph L. *The Life of Ralph Waldo Emerson.* New York: Charles Scribner's Sons, 1949.

Santayana, George. *Selected Critical Writings of George Santayana.* 2 vols. Ed. Norman Henfrey. Cambridge, England: Cambridge Univ. Press, 1968.

Scott, Donald M. *From Office to Profession: The New England Ministry 1750–1850.* Philadelphia: Univ. of Pennsylvania Press, 1978.

Sealts, Merton M., Jr. "Emerson as Teacher." *Emerson Centenary Essays.* Edited by Joel Myerson. Carbondale: Southern Illinois Univ. Press, 1982. Pp. 180–90.

———. "Emerson on the Scholar, 1833–1837." *PMLA* 85 (March 1970): 185–95.

———. "Mulberry Leaves and Satin: Emerson's Theory of the Creative Process." *Studies in the American Renaissance 1985.* Edited by Joel Myerson. Charlottesville: Univ. Press of Virginia, 1985. Pp. 79–94.

————. Review of *Ralph Waldo Emerson: A Descriptive Bibliography*, by Joel Myerson. *The Papers of the Bibliographical Society of America* 77 (First Quarter 1983): 87–89.

Seavey, Ormond. "Emerson as Itinerant." In *Emerson and His Legacy: Essays in Honor of Quentin Anderson*. Edited by Stephen Donadio, Stephen Railton, and Ormond Seavey. Carbondale: Southern Illinois Univ. Press, 1986. Pp. 1–22.

Simpson, Lewis P. *The Man of Letters in New England and the South: Essays on the History of the Literary Vocation in America*. Baton Rouge: Louisiana State Univ. Press, 1973.

Sloan, John H. " 'The Miraculous Uplifting': Emerson's Relationship with His Audience." *Quarterly Journal of Speech* 52 (February 1966): 10–15.

Smith, H. Shelton. *Changing Conceptions of Original Sin: A Study in American Theology Since 1750*. New York: Charles Scribner's Sons, 1955.

Smith, Henry Nash. "Emerson's Problem of Vocation: A Note on 'The American Scholar.' " *New England Quarterly* 12 (March 1939): 52–67.

Sprague, William B. *Annals of the American Pulpit*. New York: Robert Carter & Brothers, 1865.

Stewart, Randall. *American Literature & Christian Doctrine*. Baton Rouge: Louisiana State Univ. Press, 1958.

Stuart, Robert Lee. "Jonathan Edwards at Enfield: 'And Oh the Cheerfulness and Pleasantness . . .' " *American Literature* 48 (March 1976): 46–59.

Tester, Sue Kelsey. "Ralph Waldo Emerson's Sermons: A Critical Introduction." Ph.D. dissertation, Boston Univ., 1978.

Thundyil, Zacharias. "Emerson and the Problem of Evil: Paradox and Solution." *Harvard Theological Review* 62 (January 1969): 51–61.

Toulouse, Teresa. *The Art of Prophesying: New England Sermons and the Shaping of Belief*. Athens: Univ. of Georgia Press, 1987.

Van Cromphout, Gustaaf. "Emerson and the Dialectics of History." *PMLA* 91 (January 1976): 54–65.

Vogel, Dan. "Orville Dewey on Emerson's 'The Lord's Supper.' " *ESQ* 31 (Second Quarter 1963): 40–42.

von Frank, Albert J. "Emerson's Boyhood and Collegiate Verse: Unpublished and New Texts Edited from Manuscript." *Studies in the American Renaissance 1983*. Edited by Joel Myerson. Charlottesville: Univ. Press of Virginia, 1983. Pp. 1–56.

Ward, J. A. "Emerson and 'The Educated Will': Notes on the Process of Conversion." *ELH* 34 (1967): 495–517.

Weiss, John. *Life and Correspondence of Theodore Parker*. 2 vols. New York: D. Appleton & Company, 1864.

Whicher, Stephen E. *Freedom and Fate: An Inner Life of Ralph Waldo Emerson*. Philadelphia: Univ. of Pennsylvania Press, 1953.

Winters, Yvor. *In Defense of Reason*. New York: The Swallow Press, 1947.

Wolfe, Tom. From *Mauve Gloves & Madmen, Clutter & Vine* (Farrar, Straus and Giroux, 1976). In *The Modern Age*. Edited by Leonard Lief and James F. Light. 4th ed. New York: Holt, Rinehart and Winston, 1981.

Woodbury, Charles J. *Talks with Emerson*. New York: Horizon Press, 1970.

Wright, Conrad. *The Beginnings of Unitarianism in America*. Boston: Starr King, 1955.

————. *The Liberal Christians: Essays on American Unitarian History.* Boston: Beacon, 1970.

Youngs, J. William T., Jr. *God's Messengers: Religious Leadership in Colonial New England, 1700–1750.* Baltimore: The Johns Hopkins Univ. Press, 1976.

Ziff, Larzer. "The Literary Consequences of Puritanism." *ELH* 30 (September 1963): 293–305.

Index